FINANCIAL ACCOUNTING AS A SECOND LANGUAGE

FINANCIAL ACCOUNTING AS A SECOND LANGUAGE

DAVID P. WEINER

School of Business and Management
University of San Francisco

WILEY

JOHN WILEY & SONS, INC.

ASSOCIATE PUBLISHER	Christopher DeJohn
PRODUCTION SERVICES MANAGER	Dorothy Sinclair
PRODUCTION EDITOR	Janet Foxman
SENIOR MARKETING MANAGER	Julia Flohr
CREATIVE DIRECTOR	Harry Nolan
DESIGNER	Jim O'Shea
EDITORIAL ASSISTANT	Katie Fraser
MEDIA EDITOR	Allison Morris
ASSISTANT MARKETING MANAGER	Carly DeCandia
MARKETING ASSISTANT	Alana Filipovich
PRODUCTION SERVICES	Kelly Ricci/Aptara®, Inc.

This book was set in 10/12 Times Roman by Aptara®, Inc. and printed and bound by Courier/Westford. The cover was printed by Courier/Stoughton.

This book is printed on acid-free paper. ∞

To order books or for customer service, please call 1-800-CALL WILEY (225-5945).

Library of Congress Cataloging-in-Publication Data
Weiner, David P., 1942–
   Financial accounting as a second language / David P. Weiner.
     p. cm.
   ISBN 978-0-470-04388-2 (pbk. : acid-free paper)
1. Accounting.   I. Title.

   HF5636.W45 2009
   657—dc22   2008014510

Printed in the United States of America

10 9 8 7 6 5 4 3 2 1

*To my wife Beth, our two sons
Grant and Ian, and to Gisell
who watches the baby so daddy
can work on the book.*

ABOUT THE AUTHOR

Professor Weiner has been teaching accounting at the University of San Francisco since 1970. He has also taught (part time and summers) at San Francisco State University, the University of California at Berkeley (Evening MBA Program), and the University of California at Santa Barbara. He was the seminar manager and principal instructor for the Miller/Conviser-Duffy CPA Review Course in San Francisco. He has taught literally thousands of students how to earn high grades in accounting and how to pass the CPA exam.

Professor Weiner has a BA from Harpur College at Binghamton University, an MBA from Cornell University, and a PhD from the University of Michigan, where he was a William Paton Fellow. He earned his CPA certification in New York State and has had audit experience with Touche, Ross & Co. (New York City), Arthur Young (San Francisco), and Arthur Andersen (San Francisco).

Dr. Weiner is a recipient of an Arthur Andersen Dissertation Fellowship, and the St. Ignatius Faculty Service Award at the University of San Francisco. He is the founding faculty advisor of the Epsilon Iota chapter of Beta Alpha Psi, the national accounting fraternity.

Dr. Weiner, his wife Beth, and their two sons Grant and Ian live in Redwood City, California.

PREFACE

You are about to begin an exhilarating and fantastic journey. You are about to enter the world of business communications. *Financial Accounting as a Second Language* covers core concepts of financial accounting. You may think of these concepts as the language of accounting. In fact, accounting is often referred to as the language of business.

Accounting is all about collecting, analyzing, and communicating financial information. Much of the communication of financial information is done through formal financial statements. You will learn a great deal about financial statements; how the numbers are accumulated, summarized, and formatted into an income statement, a balance sheet, and a statement of cash flows. You will learn the basic rules of accounting, which are collectively referred to as generally accepted accounting principles (GAAP).

This book is designed to do three things:

1. Introduce the language of accounting
2. Explain the core concepts of accounting
3. Instruct how to apply these core concepts to solve accounting problems

Financial Accounting as a Second Language is loaded with study skills and strategies. These are techniques that I have developed over a forty-year teaching career. These techniques will help you learn the core concepts of accounting and achieve high grades on exams. I have spent a number of years teaching students how to study accounting and how to take accounting exams. I want to pass these tips and techniques on to you. I spend a good deal of time on basic problem solving, as well as techniques that can be used to solve specific accounting problems.

My objective is to cover only the basics and to present these core concepts of accounting in an easy-to-understand manner, with lots of illustrations and examples, so you can see exactly how it is done.

After some introductory material, each chapter presents a number of basic accounting concepts. Illustrative journal entries are presented to show how various business transactions are recorded, and a series of demonstration problems are presented in a step-by-step manner to show exactly how to apply the core accounting concepts that you have learned.

The exams that you take in an accounting course will probably include multiple-choice questions. This allows your instructor to cover a great many different topics on a single exam. To help you review what you have learned, each chapter contains Practice Multiple Choice Questions (and answers). Doing these practice questions will help you prepare for exams. To make these practice questions as informative as possible, I explain why the "right answer" is the correct one, and why each of the "wrong answers" are incorrect.

The book includes a brief outline at the beginning of each chapter to let you know exactly where we are going in that chapter. It bears repeating that accounting is the language of business, so a great deal of terminology is introduced and explained in the body of the chapters, and again in an extensive glossary at the back of the book. Also included at the end of each chapter is a section of Review Questions (and answers) to make sure that you understand the material and that you have a firm grasp of the basic fundamental concepts.

Throughout each chapter are a series of **Exam Tips** to help advance your knowledge of accounting to get the highest grades possible. Because a good deal of what you do in college involves studying and taking exams, Appendix A is devoted entirely to study skills. I think you will find a great deal of useful information in this appendix. I cover such topics as doing homework, preparing for exams, taking exams, and more.

Chapter 1 introduces basic financial statements, as well as some essential accounting principles. Chapter 2 covers the complete accounting cycle, from engaging in transactions to preparing a set of financial statements. Chapters 3 through 7 cover accounting for specific business transactions. In Chapter 8 you will learn how to prepare the statement of cash flows. Everything covered in the first eight chapters is brought together in Chapter 9. Here you will review the financial statements and learn how to analyze and interpret a set of statements. Appendix B includes a very simple explanation of the time value of money—future value and present value. An extensive glossary is included at the end of the book, which includes all of the accounting terminology that was covered in the various chapters. You can get a fairly complete understanding of an accounting term or concept from the entry in the glossary.

ACKNOWLEDGMENTS

I would like to thank a number of individuals who helped me as I worked on this project: Mark Bonadeo, Chris DeJohn, and Katie Fraser at John Wiley, Brian Baker at WriteWith Inc., and Kelly Ricci at Aptara. Special thanks to Beth Demesa, my secretary, who was able to read my handwriting and convert it to electronic text. I would also like to recognize the encouragement and support from the faculty, staff, and most of all the students of the McLaren School of Business, University of San Francisco, especially the members of Beta Alpha Psi.

David P. Weiner
Redwood City, California

CONTENTS

CHAPTER 1

BASIC FINANCIAL ACCOUNTING CONCEPTS

LEARNING OBJECTIVES

After studying this chapter, you will understand

- the accounting equation
- the seven different types of accounts
- the objectives of financial reporting
- generally accepted accounting principles (GAAP) and
- the three primary financial statements

HERE IS where we are going in our study of basic accounting concepts. We begin by introducing the accounting equation. This fundamental accounting concept sets forth the relationship between the business entity and the two groups that have an interest in the business: the creditors and the owners. The accounting equation is simply this:

$$\text{Assets} = \text{Liabilities} + \text{Owners' Equity}.$$

Everything we do in accounting is based on this equation. The **assets** represent the resources of the business. Two groups have a claim on these resources: the creditors of the business and the owners of the business. The creditors' claims are referred to as liabilities. **Liabilities** are the measure of cash, goods, and/or services that are owed to others as a result of past transactions or events. The remaining resources represent the owners' claims or **owners' equity**. The owners' equity is sometimes referred to as the net worth of the business. If you take all the company's resources and subtract the liabilities, the balance is the net worth.

Accounting is all about financial information. Most of this is contained in the company's accounts; therefore, you need to know what an account is, how many different types of accounts there are, and what information is contained in each account. The account is the basic storage unit used in accounting. All the information regarding the transactions of the business is recorded in the accounts. In chapter 2 we will cover accounts in detail—what they are, how they are used, and how we enter information into them. The information contained in these accounts is the information that will be reported in the firm's financial statements. There are three principal

1

financial statements: the income statement, the balance sheet, and the statement of cash flows. The **income statement** reports the results of operations for a specified period—how much income the business earned during the period. The **balance sheet** shows the financial position of the business as of a specific date—the amount of resources the company has, how much it owes to others, and the owners' equity. The **statement of cash flows** does what you might expect; it shows all the inflows and outflows of cash, divided into the three categories of activities: operating, investing, and financing. The basic elements of these three statements are explored in this chapter.

Finally, 10 basic concepts of accounting are introduced. These concepts, which include assumptions, principles, and modifying conventions, are important because they tell the accountant how to measure and report the financial information that goes into the financial statements.

To assist accountants in the preparation of the financial statements and to help the user understand these statements, a set of objectives, or rules, of financial reporting have been developed. We will review these objectives, and explore their impact on financial reporting.

The rules of accounting are referred to as **generally accepted accounting principles**, or **GAAP**. This book's main focus is on GAAP.

ACCOUNTING AS THE LANGUAGE OF BUSINESS

Accounting is a system designed to accumulate, organize, and communicate financial information. In many ways, accounting is simply the language of business. All accounting is based on the following simple equation:

$$\text{Assets} = \text{Liabilities} + \text{Owners' Equity.}$$

As all languages do, accounting has a unique vocabulary. Here are some basic definitions:

Assets are resources that the company owns and/or controls that will provide benefits in the future.

Liabilities are obligations of the firm to provide cash, products, or services to others according to the terms of a past transaction or event.

Owners' equity is the owners' interest in the company.

Another way to look at the owners' equity is to rearrange the accounting equation:

$$\text{If Assets} = \text{Liabilities} + \text{Owners' Equity,}$$

then

$$\text{Owners' Equity} = \text{Assets} - \text{Liabilities.}$$

Owners' equity is sometimes referred to as the net worth of the company. (Assets equal the total worth of the business; if we subtract from the assets the amount of money owed to others (the liabilities), we arrive at the net worth of the business.)

In the business world, owner's equity consists of two parts:

Paid in capital is the money that the owners have invested in the business.

Retained earnings are calculated as a running total of all the income the company has earned, less the amount of earnings distributed to the owners as a dividend.

The basic building block of accounting is the **account**; it is the basic storage unit in accounting. The accountant keeps track of all the various business transactions of the entity in the accounts. There are seven different types of accounts—three permanent or real accounts, and four temporary accounts.

We have already seen the three types of permanent accounts in the accounting equation. They are

1. Assets,

2. Liabilities, and

3. Owners' equity.

Permanent accounts, or real accounts, are concerned with items that reflect an amount of money as of a specific date. A permanent account is an account that always has a balance. For example, cash is an asset account. It represents money in a checking account in a bank as of a specific date. If you go to sleep on December 31 with $5,000 in the bank; when you wake up on January 1 of the following year, you will still have $5,000 in your account. As we shall see, the permanent accounts are the ones that appear on the balance sheet.

The four temporary accounts are defined as follows:

Revenues represent an increase in the net assets of the business that results from selling a product or a service.

Expenses are the costs of doing business. When we subtract expenses from revenues (accountants call this matching revenue and expenses), we determine the income of the business. Some of the expenses of the business, referred to as **product costs**, are directly related to the products that the company sells. Other expenses, called **period costs**, are associated with a specific period of time. Rent is a good example of a period cost.

Gains are increases in net assets that occur when the company sells an item that it is not in the business of selling for more than the original cost of the item.

Losses can occur in two ways:
By selling something that the entity is not in the business of selling for less than the entity paid for the item, or
As a result of a natural disaster, such as an earthquake, fire, or flood.

Temporary accounts reflect an amount of money for a transaction or activity that took place over a period of time. For example, all the sales for the period reflect revenue for a particular month or year. Cost of goods sold and telephone expenses are temporary accounts because they represent an expense for a specific period. At the end of each period, all the temporary accounts are closed; consequently, when the next period begins, all the temporary accounts will have a zero balance.

The following description may help you understand these terms: Permanent accounts represent **stocks** measured and recorded as an amount of money on a particular date. On the other hand, temporary accounts represent **flows**—amounts that are asociated with transactions that took place over a period of time. Cash in the bank is a stock—an amount on a specific date. The interest that was earned by having the money in the bank for the month is a flow; it represents the interest income that was earned over a period of time.

Key Takeaway: The balance sheet, which shows the financial position of the firm on a specific date, is made up of the three permanent accounts:

1. Assets,
2. Liabilities, and
3. Owners' equity.

The income statement, which shows the results of operations for a period of time, is made up of the four temporary accounts:

1. Revenues,
2. Expenses,
3. Gains, and
4. Losses.

OBJECTIVES OF FINANCIAL REPORTING

The organization that is responsible for establishing accounting rules in the United States is the FASB, the Financial Accounting Standards Board. When the board was established in 1973, one of its first projects was to set forth the objectives of financial reporting. These objectives help accountants measure and report the **transactions** of the business entity. According to the FASB, the primary objectives of financial reporting are:

To provide information

that is useful in investment and credit decisions;

that is useful in assessing future cash flows; and

that is useful in assessing the company's resources, claims to these resources, and changes in them.

The two basic qualitative characteristics that make accounting information useful are

1. **relevance**, and
2. **reliability**.

We refer to the rules of accounting as GAAP, generally accepted accounting principles. These rules were established by Luca Pacioli in 1495. In some instances, accounting rules were modified to be able to account for new types of transactions. In other instances, formal rules were established by various rule-making or standards-setting bodies. In the United States, there have been three quasi-official rule-making bodies: the Committee on Accounting Procedure, which issued 51 bulletins; the Accounting Principles Board, which issued 31 opinions; and the FASB (the current rule-making body), which has issued more than 150 standards.

BASIC ACCOUNTING CONCEPTS

Before we look at the three primary types of financial statements, we will focus on a number of basic concepts that guide accountants as they do accounting work. These concepts are often referred to in accounting textbooks and it would be wise for you to spend time learning about them. They will help you as you study the subject of accounting and as you do accounting work.

In this section, we will briefly cover 10 accounting concepts that are critical in understanding what accountants do and why they do it. Several of these concepts are essentially assumptions and others are more like principles; but all of them are important (see fig. 1-1).

Economic Entity

Accounting is performed for an entity. It may be a sole proprietorship, a partnership, or a corporation; the form of ownership does not matter. The key point is that we account for the entity separately and apart from the owners of the entity.

1. Economic Entity
2. Going Concern
3. Stable Monetary Unit
4. Accounting Periods
5. Historical Cost
6. Revenue Recognition
7. Matching
8. Full Disclosure
9. Materiality
10. Conservatism

FIGURE 1-1 Basic Accounting Concepts

Going Concern

Accountants make the assumption that the entity we are accounting for is not about to go bankrupt, but will continue to exist and stay in business for the foreseeable future. This assumption is important, because it helps to explain why we usually list assets on the balance sheet at their cost. If the company were about to go out of business, it would be sensible to list the assets at liquidation prices, that is, what the company could get for them if it sold them tomorrow. But since we expect or assume that the company will continue indefinitely, historical cost is a better way to value assets. We can allocate the cost of the company's assets to the periods during which the company will benefit from using them; doing so will permit us to match revenues and expenses.

Stable Monetary Unit

We do accounting work by using the U.S. dollar as the measuring unit. Unlike the inch, mile, or quart, the value of the dollar is constantly changing in terms of its purchasing power. You may have heard people say, "the dollar isn't worth what it used to be" and that is true. The fluctuations in the purchasing power of the dollar (or inflation) are real. That's the bad news. The good news is that from year to year, the dollar is relatively stable, so we can assume that the dollar is a stable measuring unit, knowing that the slight eroding of its purchasing power does not adversely affect our accounting.

Accounting Periods

We make the assumption that the life of the business entity is indefinite, and that we can divide this indefinite life into smaller periods of months and years.

Historical Cost

This principle is a critical element of accounting. Why do we continue to measure assets at their cost, when current market values seem more relevant? Historical cost is a very objective measure, and objectivity is an important attribute in accounting. We can determine exactly how much was paid to acquire an asset by simply looking at the purchase documents or the cancelled check. Also, since we assume that we are accounting for a going concern, how much money the company could realize by selling its assets is not really relevant because the company is not planning on selling them.

It should also be pointed out that the FASB is currently working on requiring more disclosure of current market values. Accountants are apparently willing to give up some objectivity in order to gain more relevance. Thus, we may see more disclosure of current market value and less of an emphasis on historical cost in the future.

Revenue Recognition

This is a very important principle. We have determined that revenue is earned when a sale takes place. This principle seems to be somewhat self-evident because a sale is recorded when a buyer and a seller enter into a purchase/sale transaction. If you walk into Macy's and purchase a shirt for $75, it seems pretty clear that Macy's made a sale and they should record $75 of sales revenue.

However, in today's complex business world, it is often ambiguous as to precisely when the revenue should be recognized. Therefore we need a very clear and unambiguous rule that tells us when a company should recognize revenue. The basic rule is that revenue should be recognized when it is realized or realizable (the company has received cash or a valid receivable) and it is earned (a service has been performed, or a product delivered to the buyer). As you study financial accounting, pay particular attention to this rule.

Matching

This is the basic principle that drives the preparation of the income statement. First, we determine the entity's revenue by applying the revenue recognition principle. Then we match against this revenue the expenses that were incurred to generate that revenue.

Full Disclosure

Accountants interpret this concept to mean that any information which would be of interest to the readers of the financial statements should be disclosed in some manner— either on the face of a statement, parenthetically, or in a note to the financial statements. If some information would "make a difference" to a reader, it should be disclosed.

Materiality

Materiality, is a concept that helps accountants determine when we must apply a specific accounting principle, or when we can simply ignore the rule and treat the matter in a more expeditious manner. For example, when a business buys something that will be of benefit during several periods, it is treated as an asset and amortized (written off) over each period that will show a benefit from its use. Thus, when we buy a computer or an office printer, we **capitalize** the expenditure (create an asset) and then we **depreciate** the asset (spread the cost of the asset) over its useful life.

Let us say that General Motors purchases a hammer for $25. Furthermore, the company thinks that the hammer will be used for 5 years. Does it make sense for a multi-billion dollar company like General Motors to create a $25 asset and go to the trouble of recording $5 (25 ÷ 5) of depreciation expense each year for five years? Probably not. Why? Because $25 is insignificant or immaterial to a company the size of General Motors. Calling the $25 an expense on the day it was purchased would not really make a difference; it is simply not material. Many companies have a policy that any expenditure under $10,000, or even $50,000, should simply be expensed (recorded as an expense for the period) instead of being categorized as an asset and amortized or depreciated over its useful life.

Conservatism

This might be the most misunderstood of all the accounting concepts. Accountants apply conservatism in the following manner. Suppose there is an issue regarding a certain transaction or event and there are two or more ways to account for the transaction. Suppose that each approach has merit, but no approach is any more "correct" or "appropriate" than another. In a case like this one, conservatism tells the accountant to select the approach that is least likely to overstate income or overstate assets.

Note that conservatism functions to reduce the risk of overstatement. It is employed **only** when there are several equally compelling choices; it breaks the tie. However, the accountant's role is not to make things look "as bad as possible." The accountant's role is to make things look "as they really are"—to present the most accurate and objective information available. We apply conservatism only as a last resort to select an accounting approach where there is no clear, simple correct answer.

THE BASIC FINANCIAL STATEMENTS

As pointed out earlier, accounting involves the communication of financial information. One of the major ways that this information is communicated is through the basic financial statements.

The three primary financial statements are

1. The **income statement**,
2. The **balance sheet**, or **statement of financial position**, and
3. The **statement of cash flows**.

In addition, most companies prepare a statement of owner's equity.

The Income Statement

The income statement reports the results of operations for a specific period, most typically a month, a quarter, or a year. The income statement includes revenues, expenses, gains, and losses. These are the four temporary accounts. There are two different formats for preparing an income statement: a **single-step** statement (see fig.1-2) and a **multiple-step** statement (see fig.1-3). Both approaches will produce the identical net income. The differences primarily involve appearances and what types of subtotals are calculated.

Cost of goods sold is usually the first expense listed on the income statement. It represents exactly what the words imply, namely the cost to the company of each of the units of merchandise sold during the period.

If a company has sales of $10,000 for a period, does that mean the company has a profit of $10,000? No, we calculate net income by subtracting from the revenue all the expenses associated with generating that revenue.

A true single-step income statement would not show income tax on a **separate line**, after all the operating expenses, Income tax expense would be listed **with** the other expenses. However, the custom or tradition prevails of showing income tax expense separately, rather than lumping it in with all the other expenses.

With the subtotals, the multiple-step income statement provides more meaningful information than the single-step income statement. For example, if we were trying

Company Name Income Statement for year ending 12/31/2008	
Sales Revenue	$200,000
Interest Revenue	25,000
Total Revenue	225,000
Less Expenses:	
Cost of Goods Sold	120,000
Selling Expense	10,000
Administrative Expense	20,000
Interest Expense	10,000
Loss on Discontinued Operations	< 5,000>
Extraordinary Item (flood loss)	< 10,000>
Less Total Expenses	175,000
Income Before Taxes	50,000
Less Income Tax Expenses	<15,000>
Net Income	$ 35,000

FIGURE 1-2 A Single-Step Income Statement

to predict next year's income, we would probably look at one of the subtotals, such as this year's income from operations or income from continuing operations, instead of this year's net income. This is because some of the "other revenue and gains" and "other expenses and losses" many not occur again.

The **income from operations** represents how much the company earned from its regular, year-after-year operations and does not include unusual, one-shot items.

Company Name Income Statement for the year ending 12/31/2008	
Sales Revenue	$200,000
Less Cost of Goods Sold	<120,000>
Gross Margin or Gross Profit	80,000
Less Operating Expenses:	
Selling Expense	10,000
Administrative Expense	20,000
Total Operating Expenses	<30,000>
Income from Operations	50,000
Other Revenue and Gains:	
Interest Revenue	25,000
Other Expenses and Losses:	
Interest Expense	<10,000>
Income from Continuing Operations, before taxes	65,000
Income Tax Expense	<15,000>
Income from Continuing Operations	50,000
Loss on Discontinued Operations	<5,000>
Extraordinary Items (flood loss)	<10,000>
Net Income	$ 35,000

FIGURE 1-3 A Multiple-Step Income Statement

The income statement also includes **earnings per share** data. Earnings per share is exactly what the term implies: the earnings or net income of the business divided by the number of shares of common stock. The numerator is net income minus preferred dividends, also called "net income available to the common shareholders," or simply "net to common." The denominator is the weighted average number of shares of common stock outstanding during the period. In addition to the earnings per share based on net income, the following line items on the income statement must also be shown on a per share basis:

- **Income from continuing operations** (income from the basic, everyday, routine business transactions),
- **Discontinued operations** (income, gain, or loss from a major segment of the business that was eliminated during the year), and
- **Extraordinary items** (special gains and losses that are both unusual in nature and occur infrequently).

Furthermore, the reader of the financial statements must be alerted to potential **dilution** of the earnings per share. Dilution would occur if individual stockholders who own securities that are not common stock now, but could be converted into common stock, decide to convert (or exercise, in the case of stock options). Just as you dilute a drink by putting water in the glass, the earnings per share can be diluted if more shares of stock are issued, because the net income will be divided by more shares of stock. Therefore, companies with a complex capital structure (common stock plus other **potentially dilutive securities**) are required to make a dual presentation of earnings per share. (A potentially dilutive security is a security that is not common stock now, but can be converted into shares of common stock at the option of the owner of the securities.) Companies with a complex capital structure must show two sets of per share data on the face of the income statement:

> **Basic earnings per share** are based on the actual net income and the actual number of shares outstanding.

> **Diluted earnings per share** are based on what earnings would be **if** all the individual stockholders decided to convert all their securities and options into additional shares of common stock. (This is simply a "what if" calculation).

The Balance Sheet

The balance sheet shows the financial position of the company **on a specific date**. This date is the last day of the period covered by the income statement. The balance sheet is based on the following accounting equation:

$$\text{Assets} = \text{Liabilities} + \text{Owners' Equity}$$

The balance sheet is a listing of all the assets, liabilities, and owners' equity of the company. Assets are the resources that the company owns or controls that will provide future benefits. Liabilities are money, goods, or services owed to others.

Owners' equity is the owners' interest in the company. Another term for owners' equity is net worth.

The assets are presented on the balance sheet in four categories:

1. Current assets
2. Long-term investments
3. Property, plant, and equipment
4. Intangible assets

The current asset category is the only category in which the items are always listed in the same order—from most **liquid** to least liquid. Liquidity refers to amounts that are cash or that can be quickly converted into cash. Cash is simply the most liquid asset. There are generally five types of current assets, always shown in this order:

1. Cash
2. Marketable securities
3. Accounts receivable
4. Inventory
5. Prepaid expenses

Cash is what you think it is—currency on hand and money in the bank. **Marketable securities** are short-term investments in other companies' stocks and bonds. It is interesting to note that these securities are shown on the balance sheet at current market value, and changes in the market value from period to period are included in computing net income. **(Note: This is an exception to the rule that requires assets to be shown at some variant of historical cost.)** We usually record assets and liabilities at historical cost. However, the FASB is moving in the direction of requiring or allowing more fair market value on the balance sheet.

Accounts receivable represent the money owed to the company by its customers who purchased products or services, and instead of paying cash, they charged their purchases. We refer to these transactions as "sales on account."

Inventory represents the merchandise on hand that the company is in the business of selling. This merchandise may be purchased from another company (Macy's or Nordstrom buy their merchandise from suppliers) or it may be manufactured by the company (Ford and General Motors make their cars). Merchandising companies (those that buy products and resell them) usually have a single inventory account. Manufacturing companies usually have three separate inventory accounts:

1. Raw Materials
2. Work in Process
3. Finished Goods

The final current asset is **prepaid expenses**. Prepaid expenses are expenses that have been paid in advance. The amount in a prepaid expense account will never become cash. But the fact that we have paid this particular expense in advance means that we will not have to come up with cash to pay for this expense, it has already been paid.

The **long-term investments** category includes stocks and bonds of other companies that the company plans to hold for the long term. In many cases, the company may own 80% or even 100% of the stock. (If it owns 100% of the stock, we refer to the investment as a wholly owned subsidiary.)

The **property, plant, and equipment** category includes land, buildings, equipment, vehicles, computers, and so forth. Remember that assets are things that are **owned** or **controlled** by the business that will provide future benefits. Most assets are owned by the company; in some cases, the assets may be leased instead of owned. In either case, they are listed as assets.

With the exception of land, all the assets in this category are shown net of accumulated depreciation (i.e., we show the assets at historical cost, and we then subtract all of the depreciation that has been recorded from the date of purchase to the current date). Depreciation is the allocation of the cost of an asset over its useful life. Each year, we determine that some amount of the asset's cost has been "used up," and thus that amount becomes an expense for the period. The accumulated depreciation account accumulates all the depreciation taken on a particular asset, year by year. The cost of the asset minus the accumulated depreciation is shown on the balance sheet. We refer to the cost of the asset minus the accumulated depreciation as the **book value** or the **undepreciated cost** of the asset. There are several different methods used to calculate depreciation. We will cover much more about plant assets and depreciation in chapter 5.

The final asset category is **intangible assets**. Sometimes assets are the product of an individual's intellect; we refer to these assets as **intellectual property**. The most common intangible assets are patents, copyrights, trademarks, trade names, and franchises. These assets are shown on the balance sheet at historical cost net of amortization, which is similar to depreciation. (Actually, the word amortization means the gradual writing off of an item over time; depreciation is a form of amortization.)

There is one other intangible asset—it is called **goodwill**. Goodwill can arise in two different ways. It can be generated internally over time through advertising, providing excellent customer service, earning a reputation for fair dealing, and so forth. For example, Nordstrom seems to have developed a lot of goodwill of this type, simply by providing outstanding service to its customers. This type of goodwill, which is certainly real and does exist, **is not** recorded in the company accounts and is **not** listed as an asset on the balance sheet.

The other type of goodwill is referred to as purchased goodwill. This arises when one company buys another entire company and pays more for the company than the current value of all the individual assets. Why would a company pay $200 million to buy a company whose net assets are worth only $150 million? There must be something else of value in the company being purchased. This "something else" is purchased goodwill, or simply goodwill.

In past years, goodwill that was recorded as part of a purchase transaction was then written off as an annual expense (amortized) over a useful life not to exceed 40 years. That rule was recently changed. Now, goodwill is recorded on a purchase and not amortized at all; it just remains on the balance sheet. However, goodwill is now subject to **impairment**. This means that periodically the accountant checks to see if the value of the goodwill has declined below its cost. If this happens, we say that the goodwill has become **impaired**; it is written down to a lower value and a loss on impairment is recorded.

On the right-hand side of the balance sheet, the company lists its liabilities and owners' equity. The liabilities are presented in two categories: current and noncurrent. The current liabilities represent money owed to other entities that must be paid within one year. Typical current liabilities include accounts payable, salaries payable, taxes payable, and so on.

The noncurrent or long-term liabilities include bank loans, bonds, and long-term lease obligations.

Owners' equity represents the owners' interest in the business. On the balance sheet, owners' equity consists of two elements: paid in capital and retained earnings. Paid in capital represents the amount that the owners contributed to the company to become owners. In the case of a corporation, the owners purchased shares of stock in the company and became owners or stockholders. Corporations issue stock infrequently, thus paid in capital on the balance sheet rarely changes from year to year.

The other component of owners' equity—**retained earnings**—does change each year. Retained earnings represents the running total of all the company's earnings since the first day that the company opened for business, less any earnings paid out to the owners in the form of a **dividend**. Dividends are distributions of the profits to the owners of a business. Corporations often create a simple statement to show the changes in retained earnings:

Retained Earnings (beginning balance)	$500,000
Net Income	300,000
Total	800,000
Less Dividends	<200,000>
Retained Earnings (ending balance)	$600,000

The retained earnings of a business consist of exactly what the words indicate—all of the income of the company that has **not** been paid to the owners—therefore, it is the earnings that have been "kept in" or retained in the business. Figure 1-4 illustrates a classified balance sheet.

Did you notice that this company has two different types of stock—**common stock** and **preferred stock**? Common stock is the basic type of stock that is issued by every corporation. Preferred stock is a special kind of stock that contains one or more preferences. We will cover common stock and preferred stock in chapter 7.

Figure 1-5 is the actual balance sheet of Best Buy Co., Inc. that was included in the company's 2007 annual report, submitted to the SEC (Security and Exchange Commission), as part of its 10K filing. Note that it includes virtually all of the items that we have just covered.

Grant Incorporated
Balance Sheet as of 12/31/2007

Assets
Current Assets:

Cash	$7,000
Market Securities	10,000
Accounts Receivable	21,000
Inventory	50,000
Prepaid Expenses	2,000
Total Current Assets	90,000

Long-term Investments:

Investment in Bonds	100,000
Investment in Stock	50,000
Land Held for Future Use	10,000
Bond Sinking Fund	5,000
Total Long-term Investments	165,000

Property, Plant, and Equipment:

Land	50,000
Building	100,000
Less Accumulated Depreciation	< 20,000>
	80,000
Equipment	75,000
Less Accumulated Depreciation	< 25,000>
	50,000
Total Property, Plant, and Equipment	180,000

Intangible Assets:

Patents	5,000
Copyrights	3,000
Goodwill	12,000
Total Intangible Assets	20,000
Total Assets	$455,000

Liabilities:
Current:

Accounts Payable	25,000
Salaries Payable	10,000
Taxes Payable	4,000
Total Current Liabilities	39,000

Long-term Liabilities:

Notes Payable	100,000
Bonds Payable	150,000
Less Discount	< 10,000>
	140,000
Total Long-term Liabilities	240,000
Total Liabilities	279,000

Owners' Equity:
Paid in Capital:

Common Stock	10,000
Additional Paid in Capital—Common Stock	80,000
Preferred Stock	30,000
Additional Paid in Capital—Preferred Stock	10,000
Total Paid in Capital	130,000
Retained Earnings	46,000
Total Owners' Equity	176,000
Total Liabilities Plus Owners' Equity	455,000

FIGURE 1-4 A Classified Balance Sheet

Best Buy Co. Inc.
Balance Sheet as of 3/1/2008

$ in millions
Assets

Current Assets:

Cash and Short Term Investments	1,502.00
Accounts Receivable, Net	549.00
Inventory	4,708.00
Prepaid Expenses	0.00
Other Current Assets	583.00
Total Current Assets	7,342.00

Property and Equipment

Land and Buildings	732.00
Leasehold Improvements	1,752.00
Fixtures and Equipment	3,057.00
Property Under Capital Lease	67.00
Less: Accumulated Depreciation	2,302.00
Net Property and Equipment	**3,306.00**

Other Non-Current Assets

Goodwill	1,088.00
Tradenames	97.00
Long Term Investments	605.00
Other Non-Current Assets	320.00
Total Other Non-Current Assets	**2,110.00**
Total Assets	**12,758.00**

Liabilities and Stockholders' Equity Liabilities:

Accounts Payable	4,297.00
Accrued Compensation Expense	373.00
Accrued Income Taxes	404.00
Short Term Debt	156.00
Current Portion of Long Term Debt	33.00
Other Accrued Liabilities	1,506.00
Total Current Liabilities	6,769.00

Non-Current Liabilities:

Long Term Liabilities	838.00
Long-Term Debt	627.00
Minority Interest	40.00
Other Non-Current Liabilities	838.00
Total Non-Current Liabilities	1,505.00
Total Liabilities	8,274.00

Stockholders' Equity:

Common Stock	41.00
Additional Paid in Capital	8.00
Retained Earnings	3,933.00
Accumulated Other Comprehensive Income	502.00
Total Stockholders' Equity	**4,484.00**
TOTAL LIABILITIES AND STOCKHOLDERS' EQUITY	**12,758.00**

FIGURE 1-5 Best Buy Co., Inc. Classified Balance Sheet

The Statement of Cash Flows

The final financial statement is the statement of cash flows. The main objective of this statement is to explain how the balance in cash changed from the beginning of the year to the end of the year.

The statement of cash flows is divided into three sections:

1. Cash from operating activities
2. Cash from investing activities
3. Cash from financing activities

The bottom line of this statement shows the change in cash.

The three sections of the statement are quite simple. The first section, **cash from operating activities**, includes the cash generated by the basic operations of the business—sales to customers less various operating expenses. These are, generally, the same numbers that appear in the income statement. But as we shall see in a moment, there are some significant differences between net income and cash from operating activities.

The second section, **cash from investing activities**, involves money coming in or going out due to buying and selling noncurrent assets.

The third section, **cash from financing activities**, includes money coming in or going out when the company issues stock or bonds; signs a long-term note payable with a bank; or pays dividends to the stockholders.

There are two formats, or approaches, to preparing a statement of cash flow:

1. **The direct approach**
2. **The indirect approach**

The only difference between these two approaches involves the first section of the statement of cash flows—cash from operating activities. The direct approach, which looks at all cash receipts less all cash payments from operations, sounds pretty straightforward. But since we normally do accrual accounting (not cash basis accounting), using the direct approach requires converting a lot of numbers from the accrual basis to the cash basis.

The indirect approach, which may sound a bit complicated, is actually easier to use. This approach is based on the premise that with a few exceptions, we have already calculated cash from operating activities. Cash from operating activities is essentially the same number as net income. All we have to do is eliminate the few items that are included in net income but do not involve cash. Once we eliminate these items, the remaining number will be cash from operating activities.

Let's just look at one item. Depreciation expense is a real expense. It is the allocation of the cost of a plant asset over its useful life—a recognition of the gradual "using up" of the asset. Although depreciation does not involve cash, it is subtracted from revenues in calculating net income. Since it did not represent a cash outflow, we eliminate this subtraction by adding it back. To complete this example, assume that the company had revenue of $1,000 and expenses of $700; all revenue and all expenses were in cash, except $100 of depreciation expense. Question: How much cash was generated from operating activities? The calculation is simple:

Net Income	$300 (1,000 − 700)
Plus Depreciation	100 (a noncash expense)
Cash from Operating Activities	$400

Another way to arrive at the same figure:

Revenue	$1,000
Less Expenses Paid for in Cash	<600> (700 − 100)
Cash from Operating Activities	$400

We will cover the statement of cash flows in much more detail in chapter 8. In that chapter, a very complete step-by-step method for preparing a statement of cash flows will be presented.

The Statement of Owners' Equity

This statement shows all the changes in the various individual accounts that make up the total owners' equity. The statement looks very much like a Microsoft Excel spreadsheet. The various owners' equity accounts are listed across the page as column headings. The beginning balance, plus all the transactions affecting owners' equity, as well as the ending balance, are listed down the side of the page. This statement is quite straightforward. Remember that there are just two transactions or events that affect retained earnings. Net income increases retained earnings and dividends decrease retained earnings. Figure 1-6 illustrates the statement of owners' equity.

Company Name
Statement of Owners' Equity for the year ending 12/31/2008

	Common Stock	Additional Paid in Capital	Retained Earnings	Total Owners' Equity
Beginning Balance	$50,000	$100,000	$50,000	$200,000
Issue Common Stock	5,000	20,000		25,000
Net Income			80,000	80,000
Payment of Dividends			<40,000>	<40,000>
Ending Balance	$55,000	$120,000	$90,000	$265,000

FIGURE 1-6 Statement of Owners' Equity

USING FINANCIAL STATEMENT INFORMATION

Accounting information is communicated primarily through financial statements. The income statement and the balance sheet are two of the primary financial statements. If one wants to see how well an entity is performing, calculating return on investment (ROI) may tell a good part of the story. ROI is calculated by dividing net income by average total assets. ROI measures the amount of profit earned by the business compared with how much money has been invested in the business:

$$\text{ROI} = \frac{\text{Net Income}}{\text{Average Total Assets}}$$

To compute ROI, you need to prepare both an income statement **and** a balance sheet.

Knowing the company's net income is important, but it doesn't tell you much at all about the company's performance unless you have some measure of the size of the entity, such as total assets. Two million dollars of income may sound like a lot of money to you. If you were operating a small business in your dorm room, like renting small appliances such as refrigerators, $2 million in income would be huge. However, if a major corporation reported $2 million in income on assets of $500 billion, that would describe serious failure.

REVIEW QUESTIONS

1. *Why is the balance sheet dated on a specific day, while the income statement and statement of cash flows are dated for a period of time, such as a year?*

The balance sheet shows the financial position of the business on a specific date. The items listed on the balance sheet—assets, liabilities, and owners' equity—are referred to as stocks, or things, as opposed to flows. Assets, for example, exist at a point in time. If you go to sleep on December 31 with $10,000 in the bank, when you wake up on January 1, you will have $10,000 in the bank.

Revenues are flows; they occur during a period of time. We would never say "the revenue at this point in time." Instead we refer to the revenues for a period of time, such as a month or a year. Both the income statement and the statement of cash flows comprise flows, events, or transactions that took place over a period of time. On the other hand, the balance sheet shows the financial position on a specific date. For a set of financial statements, the date of the balance sheet is the last day of the period reported on the income statement.

2. *What is meant by owners' equity?*

Owners' equity represents the owner's interest in the business. Since the accounting equation is Assets = Liabilities + Owners' Equity, we know that owners' equity must equal assets less liabilities, or the net worth of the business. If the entity went out of business, all the assets would be converted to cash. All the liabilities would be paid and if there was any money left over, it would go to the owners. That's why the owners' equity is sometimes referred to as the residual equity. The owners get what is left over.

The word "equity" is sometimes difficult for students to understand. This example might help. If you buy a house for $500,000, put 20% down, and borrow 80% from the bank (we would call that a mortgage loan, or simply a mortgage). The house is worth $500,000. You owe the bank 400,000 (80% × 500,000). Thus, your equity in the house is $100,000. Now let's say that a year goes by, the house increases in value to $550,000, and you have paid back $25,000 of principal on your $400,000 mortgage. Now what is your equity in the house? The house is now worth $550,000 and your obligation to the bank is $375,000. So your equity in the house is $550,000 − 375,000, or $175,000.

3. *Are assets the opposite of liabilities?*

Not really. Assets are things that will provide future benefits; liabilities are money or services owed to others. They are not exactly opposites. However, accounts receivable is the exact opposite of accounts payable, and notes receivable and notes payable are likewise opposites.

4. *What do we mean by matching? What is the matching principle?*

The matching principle is a fundamental concept underlying the income statement. This principle says that to determine the net income of the period, we need to do two things. First, we determine the revenue for the period. The second step involves matching. What we are trying to do is to match this years' expenses and losses to the revenues that were earned this year. Some expenses are easy to match. An invoice for a telephone expense for 2008 is certainly going to be matched with 2008 revenue. Cost of goods sold is an expense that represents the cost to the business of the items that were sold during the year. Cost of goods sold is matched against revenue to generate a number that we call gross profit, or gross margin. If the company's product is sold with a 3-year warranty on parts and labor, then we are going to have to estimate the cost of providing services on assets covered by the warranty for all 3 years.

5. *On the statement of cash flows, how does cash from operating activities differ from net income?*

Net income is determined on an accrual basis, not a cash basis. That is, we measure revenue and expenses that took place during a specific period instead of looking to see whether cash came in or went out. Therefore, the net income figure will include some revenue and expense items that did not bring in or use up cash. On the other hand, cash flows from operating activities is exclusively cash—it includes only cash that came in from operating the business less the cash that went out from operating the business. The two numbers are usually quite similar, but they are rarely the same number.

There are two ways to calculate the cash flow from operating activities. One way is to add up all the cash receipts from operating the business and subtract all the cash payments. Another way is to start with net income and eliminate the noncash items, leaving the cash flow from operating activities.

6. *Does the balance in retained earnings mean that the company has that much cash on hand?*

The balance in the retained earnings account is the sum of all the income that the company has earned (since the day it began operating) less any dividends paid to the owners. The dividends are usually cash, but the income of a company is not equal to cash received; therefore, the retained earnings account does not reflect a pot full of cash. Furthermore, even if all the income was for cash, the company could have used the cash to purchase various assets. In short, the balance in the retained earnings account is completely independent of the balance in cash.

7. *Why do we use historical cost to value assets when current market value seems much more relevant?*

First of all, on the day that an asset is acquired, the purchase price (which is the historical cost) is the best measure of the current value of the asset acquired. It is also objective and verifiable—two attributes that accountants like. As time passes, the current value may change, but the historical cost will still be an objective measure.

8. *Does conservatism mean that the goal of accounting is to report the minimum income?*

The goal of accounting is to present the most **accurate** statements of the company's financial position and the results of operations. That is why we sometimes refer to accounting statements as being transparent. The financial statement user can see through the accounting principles and observe the economic reality. Conservatism is a principle that is used as a last resort. If there are two equally valid approaches to a business transaction and one approach is just as good as the other, then, by applying the conservatism principle, the accountant would pick the method that is least likely to overstate assets or income.

9. *Why are there so many choices in accounting principles? Why isn't there just one way to do everything?*

There are a number of choices in accounting principles because all companies are different. A principle being used by one company may accurately reflect the results of its operations, but that same principle applied to another, different company would not properly reflect the results of its operations. Companies need to have choices in the application of accounting principles. However, if a company was not consistent in the application of accounting principles, the auditors would point this out to the readers of the financial statements in the audit opinion. Although companies may choose from a variety of principles, the reader of the financial statement will know if it used the same set of principles from year to year.

10. *How do the three basic financial statements articulate? What does that mean?*

The three basic financial statements articulate or are linked to each other. When the income from the income statement is added to the balance in retained earnings, the balance sheet will balance. The change in cash from the beginning of the year to the end of the year is equal to the bottom line on the statement of cash flows. The three statements are simply three different ways of looking at the same business transactions.

PRACTICE MULTIPLE CHOICE QUESTIONS

1. Material transactions that are both unusual and infrequent are called

    a. changes in accounting principle.

    b. extraordinary items.

    c. discontinued operations.

    d. unusual gains and losses (not extraordinary).

Solution: The correct answer is **b**. A material item that is both unusual and infrequent is called an extraordinary item. Choice **a** refers to when a company changes from one generally accepted accounting principle to another generally accepted accounting principle. Choice **c** refers to a situation where a company disposes of a major segment of the business. Choice **d** refers to items that meet one, but not both, of the criteria to be reported as an extraordinary item.

2. The gain or loss from disposal of a segment of the business is shown as a(n)

    a. unusual gain or loss.

    b. part of discontinued operations.

    c. extraordinary item.

    d. prior period adjustment.

Solution: The correct answer is **b**. When a company disposes of a segment of the business, it is shown as part of discontinued operations. Choice **a** refers to items that meet one, but not both, of the criteria to be shown as an extraordinary item. Choice **c** refers to items that are both unusual and infrequent. Choice **d** refers to the correction of an error in a prior period.

3. Welldone Co. has 200,000 shares of common stock outstanding on January 1. The company has 30,000 shares of preferred stock outstanding, and the company paid the regular $2 per share dividend to the preferred stockholders. On July 1 of the current year, the company issued 100,000 shares of common stock. Net income for the year was $560,000. What is Welldone's earning per share (EPS)?

    a. $1.50

    b. $2.00

    c. $3.00

    d. $3.75

Solution: The correct answer is **b**. The numerator for EPS is net income available to the common shareholders. In this case, that is $560,000 less the preferred dividend of $2.00 × 30,000 shares, or $60,000, equals $500,000. The weighted average number of shares during the year is 250,000 (200,000 for 6 months and 300,000 for 6 months averages to 250,000 for the year): $500,000 ÷ 50,000 = $2.00.

4. Which of the following are elements of the balance sheet?

    a. Assets and expenses

    b. Gains and losses

    c. Assets, liabilities, and owners' equity

    d. Liabilities, gains, and losses

Solution: The correct answer is **c**. Choices **a** and **b** are wrong because expenses and gains are not balance sheet items. Choice **d** is wrong because gains and looses are not a balance sheet items.

5. Argüelles, Inc., had the following events occur during the year:

    A $400,000 loss was incurred upon the closing of one of the company's branches. Due to a competitor's innovation, $500,000 worth of inventory become worthless and was written off. A hurricane damaged one of the branches, causing $1,450,000 in damages. On its year-end income statement, what amount should Argüelles report as extraordinary?

    a. $0

    b. $1,850,000

    c. $2,350,000

    d. $1,450,000

Solution: The correct answer is **d**. Extraordinary items must be both unusual and infrequent. The most common types of extraordinary items are natural disasters and acts of (foreign) governments. The $400,000 loss would be part of discontinued operations. The $500,000 loss would be an unusual, but not extraordinary, loss.

6. Which of the following items would be reported on the right (or credit) side of the balance sheet?

    a. Property, Plant, and Equipment

    b. Long-term investments

    c. Capital stock

    d. Current assets

Solution: The correct answer is **c**. Choices **a**, **b**, and **d** are all asset categories that are shown on the left, or debit, side of the balance sheet.

7. All of the following are elements of the balance sheet except

    a. assets.

    b. liabilities.

    c. revenues.

    d. equity.

Solution: The correct answer is **c**. Choices **a**, **b**, and **d** are all balance sheet accounts.

8. Which of the following is a proper income statement format?

    a. Single step

    b. Multiple step

    c. Consolidated income statement

    d. All of the above

Solution: The correct answer is **d**. We know for sure that the two basic formats for the income statement are the single step and the multiple step. Since both of those are correct, consolidated income statements must also be a proper format, so **d** is the only possible answer, given that **a** and **b** are both proper formats.

9. John's department store was completely destroyed by a fire. How would this event be reported?

    a. Unusual gain or loss

    b. Extraordinary item

    c. Discontinued operations

    d. Prior period adjustment

Solution: The correct answer is **b**. Extraordinary items typically include either natural disasters or acts of (foreign) governments. Choice **a** is wrong because natural disasters are both unusual and infrequent, not just unusual. Choice **c** refers to selling or disposing of a major segment of the business. Choice **d** is wrong because it refers to corrections of errors in prior periods.

10. Which of the following is an objective of financial reporting?

    a. To show the market value of all the assets

    b. To show the investment in all company resources, including human resources

    c. To explain changes in the market value of the company's common stock

    d. To provide information that is useful in investment and credit decisions

Solution: The correct answer is **d**. Choices **a** and **c** are wrong because accounting is based on historical cost, not market value. Choice **b** is wrong because accounting does not attempt to measure human resources.

CHAPTER 2

THE ACCOUNTING CYCLE

LEARNING OBJECTIVES

After studying this chapter, you will understand

- the seven types of accounts
- the rules for debits and credits
- the cash basis and the accrual basis
- the journal and the ledger
- basic journal entries
- adjusting and closing entries and
- how to find and correct errors

HERE IS where we are going in our study of the accounting cycle. This chapter may be the most important chapter in this book. (Make sure that you understand everything in this chapter before you move on to the other chapters.) In this chapter, we cover the complete accounting process—often referred to as the **accounting cycle**. The process begins when an entity engages in economic events or business transactions and culminates with the preparation of the financial statements (see fig. 2-1).

Business transactions are initially recorded in the journal and are periodically trans-ferred (posted) to the ledger. The next steps involve adjusting entries; then closing entries; and, finally, preparing the financial statements.

The first step in the accounting cycle is to analyze and record business transac-tions. Every business transaction is recorded in the journal first, on a chronological basis. The journal is like a diary—everything that happens related to the business must be recorded in the journal. This is where the accountant captures all the data that will be used in preparing the financial statements. These entries (which we re-fer to as **journal entries**) are a very important part of financial accounting. We will emphasize the importance of journal entries throughout this book. The journal entry is the *link* between what a business does and what it reports in its financial statements.

After the business transactions for a period of time have been recorded in the journal, this information is transferred (posted) to the ledger. **Posting** simply means

---

The Accounting Cycle

1. The entity engages in business transactions.
2. All business transactions are entered in the **journal** on a chronological basis.
3. At the end of the period, all the journal entries are posted to the **ledger**.
4. At the end of each period, adjusting entries are recorded in the journal and posted to the ledger.
5. A trial balance is prepared to check that the total debits equal the total credits.
6. Closing entries are prepared to close all the income statement accounts to the income summary account, which is then transferred to the retained earnings account. The balance sheet accounts are not closed; however, their balances are determined.
7. A postclosing trial balance may be prepared.
8. The financial statements are prepared from the balances in the accounts in the ledger.

FIGURE 2-1 Components of the Accounting Cycle

transferring the information from the journal to the ledger. There is a separate page in the ledger for each account. Thus, all the entries made in the journal that either increased or decreased cash are transferred to the cash page or cash account in the ledger. All the entries in the journal that increased or decreased revenue are transferred to the revenue account in the ledger, and so on.

After all the transactions of the period have been entered in the journal and posted to the ledger, various adjusting entries are made. These adjusting entries are needed for two reasons: to make sure that all the revenues and expenses, as well as gains and losses, have been recorded; and to bring the balance sheet accounts up to date. Many adjusting entries are needed simply due to the passage of time (e.g., the inclusion of interest earned on money in a bank account).

After the adjusting entries have been made, a **trial balance** is prepared. This is simply a listing of all the accounts and their debit or credit balance. Debits and credits are explained in detail in chapter 3. For now, what you need to know is that a debit is an entry made on the left side and a credit is an entry made on the right side. We prepare a trial balance to see that all the accounts are in balance (i.e., to see whether the total debits equal the total credits). If the accounts are out of balance, a few tricks can help you find the reason for the imbalance and how to correct it. These tricks will be explained on pages 47–48 of this chapter.

The next step in the cycle is called the **closing process**. All the temporary or income statement account balances are transferred to an account that we call the **income summary account**. After the closing entries have been made, all the income statement accounts will have a zero balance and are closed. The balance in the income summary account (which is equal to the net income of the period) is transferred to the retained earnings account, which is part of owners' equity. You do not have to use an income summary account; the temporary accounts could simply be closed directly to the retained earnings account.

After the closing process has been completed, a postclosing trial balance is prepared, again, simply to make sure that the debits equal the credits.

The final step in the process is the preparation of the financial statements. You will notice that the financial statements are all linked to each other; we refer to this as articulation. When the net income from the income statement is added to the balance in the retained earnings account, the balance sheet will balance. The bottom line on the statement of cash flows represents the change in cash (on the balance sheet) from the beginning of the period to the end of the period.

At the conclusion of this chapter, a demonstration problem is presented that illustrates the complete accounting cycle. Each numbered step in the process refers to the eight steps outlined in figure 2-1. It might be a good idea to try to do this problem once or twice, after you finish reading the chapter, to make sure that you really understand the complete accounting cycle.

TRANSACTION ANALYSIS

The first step in learning about the accounting process is to understand business transactions, often referred to as transaction analysis. **Transaction analysis** is the process of identifying the impact of a business event or transaction on the elements that make up the accounting equation. Because we are dealing with a double-entry system, each business transaction must have an impact on two different elements. Transaction analysis is often done using a "horizontal model," as described next and as illustrated in figure 2-2.

The horizontal model, in its most basic form, simply reflects the accounting equation:

$$\text{Assets} = \text{Liabilities} + \text{owners' Equity}$$

Now, let us populate the equation with some individual asset, liability, and owners' equity elements.

Assets	=	Liabilities	+	Owners' Equity
Cash + Supplies + Office furniture	=	Accounts + Notes payable payable	+	Common + Retained stock earnings

For each economic event or transaction, you determine which accounts were increased or decreased, then you add or subtract the appropriate amount under the account name. For example, if the company purchased office furniture for $5,000 cash, you would put $5,000 under office furniture since office furniture increased, and you would put <$5,000> under cash, since cash decreased.

Because the income in a business goes to the owners, any business transaction that involves income is recorded with the horizontal model as affecting retained earnings, a component of owners' equity that summarizes all the income of the business. The specific transaction details are described to the right of the retained earnings column.

Let us begin with eight simple events or transactions that took place in 2008:

1. Issued common stock for $100,000 cash. As a result of this event, cash—an asset—increased by $100,000, so we put +$100,000 under cash. Common stock, a component of owners' equity, also increased by $100,000, so we put +$100,000 under common stock.

2. Borrowed $50,000 cash from the bank and signed a promissory note. As a result of this transaction, cash increased by $50,000, so we put +$50,000 under cash. (The total cash at this point is $100,000 + $50,000, or $150,000.) Notes payable—a liability—has also increased by $50,000, so we put +$50,000 under notes payable.

3. Purchased $25,000 of office furniture on account. (There are two ways to buy something, as you know. You either pay cash or you charge it. In accounting, we refer to "charging it" as **on account**. The asset office furniture in this case increased by $25,000, so we put +$25,000 under office furniture. Accounts payable—a liability—also increased by $25,000, so we put +$25,000 under accounts payable.

4. Performed services for customers and received payment of $175,000 cash. Here is a transaction that will be part of the company's income. In this transaction, the company has provided a service and therefore has generated revenue or sales. It has also received cash. Therefore, we put +$175,000 under cash and +$175,000 under retained earnings. To the right of retained earnings, we explain that this transaction represented revenue earned, or service revenue.

5. Paid rent expenses of $20,000 cash. This transaction, similar to the previous one, is part of measuring income, but it represents an expense rather than a revenue item. Cash was paid, so we put −$20,000 under cash. Because this expense will reduce income, we put −$20,000 under retained earnings, and to the right, we indicated that this was for rent expense.

6. Salary expenses of $40,000 were paid in cash. A salary expense is the cost of employing people who work for the company and earn a salary. This transaction has exactly the same impact as paying rent, but it is a different expense. We put −$40,000 under cash, since cash went out, and we put −$40,000 under retained earnings and labeled it as salary expense.

7. Paid $15,000 of the balance in accounts payable. **Accounts payable** is a liability account that represents an amount the company owes to other entities. At this point, the total under accounts payable is $25,000. For this transaction, we put −$15,000 under cash because cash was paid out, and we put −$15,000 under accounts payable because by paying cash, we eliminated part of our liability.

Event	Assets		=	Liabilities		+	Owner's Equity	
	Cash	+ Office furniture	= Accounts payable	+ Notes payable		+ Common stock	+ Retained earnings	
1	$100,000					$100,000		
2	$50,000			$50,000				
3		$25,000	$25,000					
4	$175,000						$175,000	service revenue
5	<$20,000>						<$20,000>	rent expense
6	<$40,000>						<$40,000>	salary expense
7	<$15,000>		<$15,000>					
8	<$50,000>	$50,000						
	$200,000	$75,000	$10,000	$50,000		$100,000	$115,000	

Total Assets = $275,000   Total Liabilities + Owners' Equity = $275,000

FIGURE 2-2 Transaction Analysis Using the Horizontal Model

The balance in accounts payable after this transaction is $25,000 less $15,000, or $10,000.

8. Purchased office furniture for $50,000. Here we are exchanging one asset for another; we receive office furniture—an asset—and we give up cash, also an asset. Thus, on the horizontal model, we put +$50,000 under office furniture and −$50,000 under cash.

After we have entered all eight transactions, the completed horizontal model should look like figure 2-2.

After analyzing each transaction and making entries to the horizontal model, we can now accumulate totals and prepare a simple income statement and a simple balance sheet, as shown in figures 2-3 and 2-4.

The horizontal model is simplistic and it works. You could actually use this approach to account for a very small business. However, once the business gets bigger, you are going to need a very, very wide piece of paper to keep track of all

---

Hillcrest Corp.
Income Statement
For the Year Ending 12/31/07

Service Revenue		$175,000
Less Expenses		
Rent	$20,000	
Salaries	40,000	
Total expenses		<60,000>
Net Income		$115,000

FIGURE 2-3 Income Statement

Hillcrest Corp.
Balance Sheet
as of 12/31/07

Assets		Liabilities	
Cash	$200,000	Accounts Payable	$10,000
Supplies	25,000	Notes Payable	50,000
Office Furniture	50,000	Total Liabilities	60,000
		Owners' Equity	
		Common Stock	100,000
		Retained Earnings	115,000
		Total Owners' Equity	215,000
Total Assets	$275,000	Total Liabilities and Owners' Equity	**$275,000**

FIGURE 2-4 Balance Sheet

the various elements. A better way is to make use of accounts, and that is where our presentation of the accounting cycle begins.

THE ACCOUNTING CYCLE

The **account** is the most basic building block in accounting. The account is the basic storage device for accounting data. Information about the company's business transactions is recorded and maintained in the company's accounts. There are seven different types of accounts—three permanent accounts and four temporary accounts. At the end of each period (month, quarter, or year), the balance in each permanent account is determined. These balances are reported on the balance sheet. Also at the end of the period, the balances in the temporary accounts are closed and the company's income is determined. The numbers from the temporary accounts are reported on the income statement.

The reason for closing the temporary accounts at the end of the period is quite simple. We are interested in calculating the net income, or profit, for the period. When the period is over, we calculate the revenue, expenses, gains, and losses for that period. This determines the net income. When the following period begins, the temporary accounts must all have zero balances, because no business transactions for the new period have taken place yet. Closing the temporary accounts at the end of the period ensures that these accounts will begin the next period with a zero balance.

As you have learned, there are seven basic types of accounts. The accounts that make up the balance sheet are *assets, liabilities*, and *owners' equity*. These are the permanent accounts. The accounts that appear on the income statement are *revenue, expenses, gains*, and *losses*. These are the temporary accounts.

SUMMARY OF THE SEVEN TYPES OF ACCOUNTS

Balance Sheet Income Statement

1. Assets
2. Liabilities
3. Owners' Equity
4. Revenue
5. Expenses
6. Gains
7. Losses

The following are brief descriptions of the seven types of accounts that were introduced in chapter 1 and are repeated here:

1. **Assets** are resources that are owned or controlled by the company and will produce future benefits.
2. **Liabilities** are amounts of cash, goods, or services owed to others as the result of a past transaction or event.
3. **Owners' equity** is the owners' interest in the company. Owners' equity is also referred to as the net worth of the business; that is, total assets less total liabilities equals the net worth or the owners' equity.
4. **Revenue** (or sales) are increases in net assets that result from selling goods or services.
5. **Expenses** are the costs of doing business. To determine a company's income, accountants match the revenue earned during a period with the expenses incurred during that period.
6. **Gains** are increases in net assets arising from the sale of something that the entity is not in the business of selling for more than they paid for it.
7. **Losses** are the opposite of gains. Losses represent decreases in net assets that occur when the entity sells something that the entity is not in the business of selling for less than the entity paid for it. Losses can also occur due to a natural disaster such as a fire, hurricane, or earthquake.

THE RULES FOR DEBITS AND CREDITS

The easiest way to think about an account is to picture a T. In fact, we refer to accounts as T-accounts. Every account has two sides. The left side is called the debit side. The right side is called the credit side. The words debit and credit have no other meaning. They just mean left and right, exactly like port and starboard on a boat indicate left and right. Debits are entries made on the left side of an account.

Depending on the type of account, a debit may represent an increase or a decrease. Credits are entries made on the right side of an account. Again, credits may represent an increase or a decrease, depending on the type of account. For example, a debit to an asset account represents an increase. A debit to a liability account represents a decrease. The opposite is true for credits on credit entries: a credit to an asset account would represent a decrease; a credit to a liability account would represent an increase.

Everything we do in accounting is based on the familiar accounting equation:

$$\text{Assets} = \text{Liabilities} + \text{Owners' Equity} \ (A = L + OE)$$

Because assets are shown to the left of the equal sign in the accounting equation, it seems appropriate to have asset accounts increase on the left, or the debit side. Using the same logic, since liabilities and owners' equity are shown to the right of the equals sign: liabilities and owners' equity accounts increase on the right, or the credit side.

Note the vertical line that divides the diagram in figure 2-5. All the accounts on the left side of the diagram increase on the left, or debit, side. All the accounts to the right of the line increase on the right, or credit, side.

The two accounts that will increase net income are revenues and gains. Remember that when a company has net income, the net income increases owners' equity. Since owners' equity increases on the right, or credit, side, it makes sense that revenue and gains should also increase on the right, or credit, side.

By the same logic, expenses and losses reduce net income and thus reduce owners' equity. Expenses and losses, therefore, increase on the left, or debit, side—the opposite of revenues and gains.

Now you may be thinking that this is too difficult to remember—seven accounts, each with two sides. That's 14 individual items to keep track of. Here's an easy way to remember. Only three accounts increase on the left: assets, expenses, and losses. **Everything else** increases on the right, or credit, side.

Another point sometimes bothers students. If assets are a good thing and expenses are a bad thing, why do assets and expense accounts both increase on the left? The simple answer to this question is that asset accounts and expense accounts have a relationship to one another. An *asset* is something that you own or control, an *expense* is a cost of doing business and often represents an asset that has been used up.

Assets		Liabilities	Owners' Equity
+ | −		− | +	− | +
Expenses	Losses	Revenue	Gains
+ | −	+ | −	− | +	− | +

FIGURE 2-5 The Rules for Debits and Credits

Example:

When you pay your next month's rent in advance, you have an asset (prepaid rent). When time passes, that prepaid rent expires and becomes rent expense. When you fill up your gas tank with gasoline, you have an asset. As you drive your car, you use up the gas and the gasoline asset becomes a gasoline expense. Thus, assets and expenses are like two sides of the same coin.

Look at the gasoline example in terms of the T-accounts:

Gasoline Asset		Gasoline Expense	
$45	$30	$30	

On May 1, you fill up your gas tank by buying 15 gallons of gas at $3/gal. You put 15 × $3, or $45, in your asset account for gasoline. You then drive the car for a week and use up 10 gallons: 10 × $3, or $30 worth of gas was used up. An asset that has been used up becomes an expense. Note that some of these numbers are subtractions, but they do not need to be in angle brackets. The debit and credit mechanism takes care of that. For example, the $30 credit to gasoline is a subtraction, but it doesn't need angle brackets because are accountants know that a credit to an asset account represents a subtraction, or a decrease to the account.

The entry to record the using up of $30 worth of gas (which we will learn more about in a few pages) is a debit to gas expense and a credit to gasoline. That journal entry increases an expense and decreases an asset. To be able to do this, both types of accounts must increase and decrease on the same side. For us to be able to increase an expense and decrease an asset in a single journal entry, both types of accounts must increase on the same side (debit) and must decrease on the same side (credit).

Key Takeaway:

You may think of assets as expenses that have not been used up yet, and expenses as assets that have been used up.

Figure 2-5 is very important. Two or three weeks from now, this diagram will have become second nature to you. Just remember that *only assets, expenses, and losses increase on the left, or debit, side*. Everything else increases on the right.

THE CHART OF ACCOUNTS

You have been introduced to accounts and the seven different types of accounts. Question: When a company starts up a business and sets up its accounting system, what accounts does it use? Answer: It sets up the appropriate accounts, depending on the type of information that the company wants to generate from its accounting system. For example, if it just wants a single total for sales, then it just needs only one sales or revenue account. If the company wants to report sales by product line, it may want to set up three different sales accounts: sales revenue for product line A, sales revenue for product line B, and sales revenue for product line C.

The total collection of accounts is referred to as the **Chart of Accounts**. Accounting software programs usually come with several pre-established charts of accounts that can be modified to fit an individual company's information needs. All of the accounts are numbered, so the asset accounts may be assigned numbers from 1,000 through 1,999; liabilities from 2,000 through 2,999; and so on.

Figure 2-6 illustrates a chart of accounts for a service company. Note that the account numbers for the asset accounts are 1,000 through 1,999; liability accounts are 2,000 through 2,999; owners' equity accounts are 3,000 through 3,999; revenue accounts are 4,000 through 4,999; and expense accounts are 5,000 through 7,000.

CASH BASIS VERSUS ACCRUAL BASIS

There are two ways to account for business activities: the **cash basis** and the **accrual basis**. If you are using the cash basis, the accounting is pretty simple. Revenue is recorded when cash comes in, and expenses are recorded when cash goes out. For the purpose of preparing an individual tax return, most taxpayers are on the cash basis. Under the cash basis, revenues are recognized when cash is received from customers, after the company has sold a product or provided a service. Let us say that you are a dentist, and you provide some dental services for a patient in December 2007, but you don't receive payment until January 2008. Because you are on the cash basis for tax purposes, the money that was collected in January 2008 is treated as 2008 revenue, even though you performed the service in December 2007. Under the cash basis, revenue is recognized when the cash is collected.

On the other hand, if you use the accrual basis, the revenue is recognized when the services are rendered. Thus, in our example with the dentist, he or she would recognize revenue in December 2007 for the dental service provided in December 2007. Many individuals and small companies use the cash basis because of its simplicity. However, most medium-sized and large companies use the accrual basis.

There is also the modified cash basis, which reflects most transactions based on cash receipts and disbursements. However, accounting on the modified accrual basis does make some accrual-type adjustments, such as **capitalizing** (recording an expenditure of cash as the acquisition of an asset) expenditures for plant assets and recording depreciation, as well as keeping track of inventory and cost of goods sold. The modified cash basis includes some elements of both the cash basis and the accrual basis. Professional services companies, such as law and accounting firms use the **modified accrual basis**. Your study of accounting will generally focus on the full accrual basis, although you might see a few references to the cash basis.

THE JOURNAL ENTRY

We now turn to the process of recording business transactions. Making a journal entry is very similar to the work we did at the beginning of the chapter when we studied transaction analysis and the horizontal model. Instead of adding or subtracting

Category	Account No	Caption
Current Asset	101	Cash
Current Asset	102	Debt Investments
Current Asset	103	Petty Cash
Current Asset	104	Debt Investments
Current Asset	105	Stock Investments
Current Asset	106	Fees Receivable
Current Asset	107	Accounts Receivable
Current Asset	108	Allowance for Doubtful Accounts
Current Asset	109	Commissions Receivable
Current Asset	110	Notes Receivable
Current Asset	111	Bond Interest Receivable
Current Asset	112	Interest Receivable
Current Asset	113	Merchandise Inventory
Current Asset	114	Prepaid Advertising
Current Asset	115	Supplies
Current Asset	116	Prepaid Insurance
Current Asset	117	Prepaid Rent
Current Asset	118	<<UNDEFINED>>
Property, Plant, and Equipment	119	Land
Property, Plant, and Equipment	120	Buildings
Property, Plant, and Equipment	121	Accumulated Depreciation Buildings
Property, Plant, and Equipment	122	Office Building and Plant
Property, Plant, and Equipment	123	Accumulated Depreciation Office Building Plant
Property, Plant, and Equipment	124	Furniture
Property, Plant, and Equipment	125	Accumulated Depreciation Furniture
Property, Plant, and Equipment	126	Office Equipment
Property, Plant, and Equipment	127	Accumulated Depreciation Office Equipment
Property, Plant, and Equipment	128	Equipment
Property, Plant, and Equipment	129	Accumulated Depreciation Equiprnent
Property, Plant, and Equipment	130	Automobiles

FIGURE 2-6 Service Company Simplified Chart of Accounts (*Continued*)

Category	Account No	Caption
Property, Plant, and Equipment	131	Accumulated Depreciation Automobiles
Intangible Assets	132	Goodwill
Intangible Assets	133	Patent
Intangible Assets	134	Copyright
Intangible Assets	186	<<UNDEFINED>>
Current Liability	200	Notes Payable
Current Liability	201	Accounts Payable
Current Liability	202	Advances from Customers
Current Liability	203	Unearned Revenue
Current Liability	204	Salaries Payable
Current Liability	205	FICA Taxes Payable
Current Liability	206	Federal Income Taxes Payable
Current Liability	207	Federal Income Tax Withholding Payable
Current Liability	208	State Income Tax Payable
Current Liability	209	State Income Tax Withholding Payable
Current Liability	210	Income Taxes Payable
Current Liability	211	Union Dues Payable
Current Liability	213	Federal Unemployment Taxes Payable
Current Liability	214	State Unemployment Taxes Payable
Current Liability	215	Sales Taxes Payable
Current Liability	216	Interest Payable
Current Liability	217	Pension Contributions Payable
Current Liability	218	Income Tax Payable
Current Liability	219	Estimated Warranty Liability
Current Liability	220	Property Taxes Payable
Current Liability	221	Utilities Payable
Current Liability	222	Dividends Payable
Current Liability	223	Notes Payable
Current Liability	224	Discount on Notes Payable
Current Liability	225	<<UNDEFINED>>

FIGURE 2-6 (*Continued*) Service Company Simplified Chart of Accounts

Category	Account No	Caption
Long-term Liability	226	Notes Payable
Long-term Liability	227	Bonds Payable
Long-term Liability	228	Discount on Bonds Payable
Long-term Liability	229	<<UNDEFINED>>
Equity	301	Common Stock
Equity	302	P-I-C in Excess of Par—Preferred
Equity	303	P-I-C in Excess of Par—Common
Equity	304	Retained Earnings
Equity	305	Treasury Stock
Revenue	400	Service Revenue
Revenue	401	Sales
Revenue	401	Admission Revenue
Revenue	402	Sales Returns and Allowances
Revenue	403	Sales Discounts
Revenue	404	Rent Revenue
Revenue	405	Interest Revenue
Revenue	406	<<UNDEFINED>>
Purchase Expenses	500	Cost of Goods Sold
Purchase Expenses	501	Purchases
Purchase Expenses	502	Purchases Returns and Allowances
Purchase Expenses	503	Purchases Discounts
Purchase Expenses	504	Freight-in
Selling Expense	600	Advertising Expense
Selling Expense	601	Bad Debt Expense
Selling Expense	602	Depreciation Expense
Selling Expense	603	Repair Expense
Selling Expense	604	Store Salaries Expense
Selling Expense	605	Sales Salaries Expense
Selling Expense	606	Supplies Expense
Selling Expense	607	Gas & Oil Expense
Selling Expense	608	Cleaning Supplies Expense
Selling Expense	609	Postage Expense
Selling Expense	610	Research and Development Expense
Selling Expense	611	Warranty Expense

FIGURE 2-6 (*Continued*) Service Company Simplified Chart of Accounts

Category	Account No	Caption
Selling Expense	612	Freight-out
Selling Expense	613	<<UNDEFINED>>
Administrative Expense	700	Depreciation Expense
Administrative Expense	701	Interest Expense
Administrative Expense	702	Salaries and Wages Expense
Administrative Expense	703	Insurance Expense
Administrative Expense	704	Patent Amortization Expense
Administrative Expense	705	Copyright Amortization Expense
Administrative Expense	706	Salaries Expense
Administrative Expense	707	Rent Expenses
Administrative Expense	708	Payroll Taxes Expense
Administrative Expense	709	Utilities Expense
Administrative Expense	710	Pension Expense
Administrative Expense	711	Vacation Benefits Expense
Administrative Expense	712	Travel Expense
Administrative Expense	713	Supplies Expense
Administrative Expense	714	Telephone Expense
Administrative Expense	715	Miscellaneous General Expenses
Other Expense and Loss	716	Property Tax Expense
Administrative Expense	717	Office Expense
Administrative Expense	718	Legal Services Expense
Administrative Expense	719	<<UNDEFINED>>
Other Revenue and Gain	800	Dividend Revenue
Other Revenue and Gain	801	Bond Interest Revenue
Other Revenue and Gain	802	Gain on Sale of Stock Investments
Other Revenue and Gain	803	Interest Revenue
Other Revenue and Gain	804	Gain on Sale of Bonds
Other Revenue and Gain	805	Rent Revenue
Other Revenue and Gain	806	Gain on Plant Assets
Other Revenue and Gain	807	<<UNDEFINED>>
Other Expense and Loss	900	Interest Expense
Other Expense and Loss	901	Income Tax Expense
Other Expense and Loss	902	<<UNDEFINED>>

FIGURE 2-6 (*Continued*) Service Company Simplified Chart of Accounts

numbers in a column, we will make use of T-accounts and record increases or decreases using debits and credits.

Two different books are used in the accounting process: the journal and the ledger. (Sometimes these books are referred to as the general journal and the general ledger, because there are also special journals and subsidiary ledgers.) The **journal** is the book of original entry. Each transaction is entered in the journal on a chronological basis; each day's transactions are recorded in the journal for that day. Periodically, all the journal entries are transferred or posted to the ledger. The ledger information is kept in digital form in a computer, but it may be helpful at this stage of your accounting education to think of the process of posting the journal entries to the ledger as updating or adjusting the balance in the various accounts that are maintained in the ledger. The easy way to think of the general ledger is as a book, with page after page of accounts— one page per ledger account. The T-accounts are all included in the general ledger.

Key Takeaway:
Having two books—the journal and the ledger—is very useful. They can be used to keep track of the same transactions in two different ways. The journal is like a diary; it is a chronological listing of all the transactions entered into by the company during a period of time. The ledger maintains a separate page for each account. If we want to know the balance in a given account, we just look at that page in the ledger.

RECORDING JOURNAL ENTRIES

Every business transaction is recorded in the journal on a chronological basis. As you read this book, you will learn about the basic transactions that are related to a particular set of accounts. For example, transactions that affect inventory are discussed in chapter 4; transactions involving Property, Plant, and Equipment are discussed in chapter 5. A summary of the most common transactions for each set of accounts is provided at the conclusion of chapters 3 through 7. At the end of this chapter, you will find a comprehensive illustration of the complete accounting cycle—from analyzing business transactions, to making journal entries and adjusting entries, to posting to the ledger, to taking a trial balance, to closing, and, finally, to preparing the financial statements.

We are doing **double-entry accounting**; therefore, every entry will have at least two parts. Making a journal entry involves three separate steps:

1. Understand the business transaction and determine which accounts are affected and whether each affected account is increasing or decreasing.

2. Apply the rules for debits and credits to determine whether each account is to be debited or credited.

3. Complete the process by listing first, against the left margin, the account(s) to be debited and the amount(s). Then indent and list the account(s) to be credited and the amount(s). Remember, you can have more than one debit or credit, but the amount of the total debits must equal the amount of the total credits.

Let us use the eight transactions that we evaluated with the horizontal model and make journal entries for these transactions.

The first transaction was the issuing of $100,000 worth of common stock. Cash increased and common stock increased. Thus, to increase an asset (cash), we debit the account. To increase an owners' equity account, we credit the account. So, the journal entry is debit cash and credit common stock for $100,000. The standard format for a journal entry is this: List the account or accounts to be debited next to the left margin. Indent the account or accounts to be credited. The total debits must equal the total credits. Our first entry would therefore look like this:

Cash	100,000
Common Stock	100,000

In the business world, the numbers in the journal entry are recorded in columns, so the entry in the journal would look more like this.

	Debit	Credit
Cash	100,000	
Common Stock		100,000

When making journal entries, simply imagine that there are two columns labeled debit and credit, respectively. You don't have to draw the columns all the time. It's perfectly OK to make a journal entry simply by listing the account(s) to be debited, the amount of the debit(s), and the account(s) to be credited and the amount of the credit(s). In a formal journal entry, there would also be an explanation in parenthesis, below the entry. For our first entry, the explanation might be "(issued 5,000 shares of common stock at $20 per share)."

In the second event, the company borrowed money and signed a note. As a result, cash (an asset) increased and notes payable (a liability) increased. Assets increase on the debit side and liabilities increase on the credit side. Thus, the journal entry is as follows:

Cash	50,000
Notes Payable	50,000

In the third transaction, the company purchased supplies on account. Here, supplies (an asset) increased and accounts payable (a liability) also increased. This is just like the previous entry, but with different asset and liability accounts. Assets increase on the debit side and liabilities increase on the credit side. Thus, the entry to buy supplies on account is as follows:

Supplies	25,000
Accounts Payable	25,000

The fourth event involved earning service revenue and receiving cash. Cash (an asset) increased and service revenue (a revenue account) also increased. Assets increase on the debit side and revenues increase on the credit side. Thus, the entry is as shown here:

Cash	175,000	
Service Revenue		175,000

In the fifth event, the company paid rent expenses of $20,000. Rent expenses (an expense account) increased and cash (an asset account) decreased. Expenses increase on the debit side and assets decrease on the credit side. Thus, the journal entry to record paying a rent expense is

Rent Expense	20,000	
Cash		20,000

In the sixth event, the company paid salary expenses of $40,000. This is the same as for the fifth transaction, with a different expense account. Therefore, the journal entry is

Salary Expense	40,000	
Cash		40,000

In the seventh transaction, the company paid $15,000 cash on the balance in accounts payable. Cash (an asset account) decreased and accounts payable (a liability account) also decreased. Liabilities decrease on the debit side and assets decrease on the credit side. Thus, the entry to make a payment on account is

Accounts Payable	15,000	
Cash		15,000

The final entry was for the purchase of office furniture for cash. This is just like the third entry, exchanging one asset for another. Instead of supplies, the company is purchasing furniture; however, the format of the entry is the same: debit the asset that is increasing and credit the asset that is decreasing. Thus, the entry for the purchase of office furniture for cash is shown as follows:

Office Furniture	50,000	
Cash		50,000

That's it! You are now on your way to understanding journal entries—an essential element of accounting. Do not forget the comprehensive illustration on page 49 of this chapter, which will give you an excellent opportunity to review the journal entry process.

POSTING TO THE LEDGER

As we have seen, all business transactions are initially recorded in the journal on a chronological basis. The journal is like a diary. All the transactions that take place are recorded on a daily basis in the journal.

After all the transactions are recorded, we need to transfer the daily transaction data to the ledger. The ledger has a separate page for each account. We refer to the process of transferring the transaction data from the journal to the ledger as posting. Posting use to be done at the end of a period, but with today's computer systems, posting can be done on a daily basis.

Having both a ledger and a journal makes a great deal of sense. If you want to know what happened on a specific date, you would look at the journal. If you wanted to know the balance in a particular account, you would look in the ledger. When the company wants to prepare financial statements, the numbers for the statements come from the balances in the ledger.

THE TRIAL BALANCE

Whenever the accountants want to check whether the bookkeeping has been performed accurately, they produced a **trial balance**. A trial balance is not a financial statement, although it looks like one. A trial balance is simply a listing of all the accounts, along with their debit or credit balances. What we want to see, of course, is that the total debits *equal* the total credits.

ADJUSTING ENTRIES

There are two types of journal entries: journal entries to record business transactions and journal entries to adjust the accounts. We have just looked at some basic journal entries to record transactions. Now we need to shift our focus to adjusting entries. Adjusting entries do two things: (1) they bring the various balance sheet accounts up to date, and (2) they record the proper amount of revenues and expenses in the appropriate accounting period. Virtually all adjusting entries fall into two broad categories:

1. Debits to expense accounts, coupled with credits to either an asset or a liability account

2. Credits to revenue, coupled with debits to a liability or asset account

We can identify four different types of adjusting entries:

1. Prepayments

2. Accruals

3. Depreciation entries

4. Adjustment of the inventory account and a determination of cost of goods sold (a combination of adjusting and closing entries)

The most common type of adjusting entries are prepayments and accruals. Each type of adjustment involves a pair of related journal entries. For prepayments, the first entry involves recording an actual business transaction—either a cash receipt or a cash disbursement. The receipt or payment of cash creates either an asset or a liability. The second journal entry, which is the adjustment, involves recognizing that part or all of the asset or liability created in the first entry has become used up (in the case of an asset) or earned (in the case of a liability).

Here are two sets of journal entries. The first pair represents a prepayment situation; the second pair represents an accrual.

Prepayment:
The company pays $6,000, representing a prepayment of rent on a factory. Three months go by, and one quarter of the prepaid rent has expired.

The journal entries to record these transactions are as follows:

a.	Prepaid Rent	6,000	
	Cash		6,000
b.	Rent Expense	2,500	
	Prepaid Rent		2,500

Note that the adjusting entry consists of a debit to an expense and a credit to a balance sheet account.

Accrual:
The salaries of the employees are $1,000/day, or $5,000 per week, payable on the last day of the week. Assume that December 31 is a Tuesday. Therefore, the company has to accrue, or recognize, 2 days' worth of salaries that were earned in December. The journal entries for this situation are as follows:

a.	Salary Expense	2,000	
	Salaries Payable		2,000
b.	Salaries Payable	2,000	
	Salary Expense	3,000	
	Cash		5,000

On Friday, $5,000 cash is paid for salaries. Two days' worth of salaries were accrued in entry **a**; thus, the expense has already been recognized. We credit salaries payable to indicate that the liability has been paid. Salary expense for the three remaining days (January 1–3) is recognized by debiting salary expense for $3,000.

Note that the adjusting entry consists of a debit to an expense and a credit to a balance sheet account.

Remember that for prepayment adjustments, the adjusting entry is the second entry of the pair of related entries. For accrual adjustments, the first entry is the adjusting entry.

Let us look at some additional prepayment and accrual adjustments.

Prepayment Adjustments:

1.	A 1-year fire insurance policy has been purchased.		
	a. Prepaid Insurance	6,000	
	Cash		6,000

Six months pass and one half of the policy expires.
b. Insurance Expense   3,000
    Prepaid Insurance   3,000
(This is the adjusting entry.)

2. Sell three-year magazine subscriptions for 900.
    a. Cash   900
        Unearned Subscription Revenue   900
    One year passes and one third of the unearned subscription revenue is now earned.
    b. Unearned Subscription Revenue   300
        Subscription Revenue   300
    (This is the adjusting entry.)

Note that a revenue account is credited and a balance sheet account (a liability) is debited. Remember that the most common adjusting entries are either debits to expenses or credits to revenue. Note also that, in the previous example related to prepaid insurance, an expense account is debited and a balance sheet account (prepaid insurance is an asset account) is credited.

Accrual Adjustments:

The company is in possession of a 1-year note receivable in the amount of $2,000, bearing interest of 6% per year. The note was received on June 30, 2008. The company received cash in payment of the note and the accrued interest on June 30, 2008.

    a. Interest Receivable   60
        Interest Revenue   60
    b. Cash   2,120
        Interest Receivable   60
        Interest Revenue   60
        Note Receivable   2,000

Note that for accrual adjustments, the first entry of a pair of related journal entries is the adjustment. This entry is always a debit to an expense account and a credit to a balance sheet account, or a credit to a revenue account and a debit to a balance sheet account. Furthermore, remember that all adjusting entries accomplish two important actions:

1. They recognize revenue and expenses in the proper period.
2. They bring the related balance sheet accounts up to date.

Depreciation Adjustments:

Depreciation is the allocation of the cost of a tangible asset over its useful life. It is an attempt to match the cost of using the asset with the revenues generated by the use of the asset. Depreciation expense is a function of four elements:

1. The cost of the asset
2. The estimated useful life of the asset

3. The estimated salvage value of the asset

4. The depreciation method used

Depreciation:
Assume that the company purchased a piece of equipment for $12,000, with a $2,000 salvage value and an estimated useful life of 5 years.

 The formula for calculating depreciation expense using the straight line method is

$$\frac{[Cost - salvage]}{Life} \frac{\$12,000 - \$2,000}{5} = \$2,000 \text{ per year}$$

Note that depreciation involves recognition that part of the cost of an asset has been used up during the period. Depreciation is the *allocation* of the *cost* of an asset over its useful life. It is not an attempt to measure the asset's current market value.

Depreciation Expense	$2,000
Asset—Accumulation Depreciation	$2,000

 The accumulated depreciation account is a contra-asset account—an account that "goes against" or is subtracted from an asset account. The prefix "contra" means against. The cost of a plant asset less its accumulated depreciation is referred to as the book value or undepreciated cost of the asset.

Adjusting the Inventory Account and Determining Cost of Goods Sold

We will cover accounting for inventory and cost of goods sold in chapter 4. Inventory represents the products that the company is in the business of selling. The cost to the company of all the merchandise that was sold during the period is cost of goods sold. There are two general approaches to accounting for inventory: the periodic method and the perpetual method. We will review these two approaches in greater detail in chapter 4. At this point, we want look at the basic inventory relationships that are part of the cost of goods sold model.

The Cost at Goods Sold Model

Beginning inventory

+ Purchases

Goods available for sale

<Ending inventory>

Cost of goods sold

Let's try this with some small figures:

Beginning inventory	10
+ Purchases	15
Goods available for sale	25
<Ending inventory>	<5>
Cost of goods sold	20

At the end of the year, a company using the periodic inventory method must take a physical count of the ending inventory to be able to compute the cost of goods sold. Here is how an accountant computes a firm's cost of goods sold, which reflects what it cost the company to buy or make the products that they are in the business of selling. The journal entry based on the calculation above looks like this:

Cost of Goods Sold	20	
Ending Inventory	5	
Beginning Inventory		10
Purchases		15

You credit everything that makes cost of goods sold greater (beginning inventory and purchases), you debit everything that makes cost of goods sold smaller (ending inventory), and the difference goes in the box and *is the cost of goods sold*. This entry represents both an adjusting entry and a closing entry. As an adjusting entry, it determines the expense that we call cost of goods sold, which will appear on the income statement, and it establishes the amount of the ending inventory, which will appear on the balance sheet. As a closing entry, it closes the beginning inventory and purchases accounts, so when the next period starts, the balance in the inventory and purchases accounts will be zero.

THE CLOSING PROCESS

At the end of the period (which could be a month or a year), after all the business transactions have been recorded and after all the accounts have been adjusted, we need to complete the accounting cycle by closing the temporary (income statement) accounts and balancing the permanent (balance sheet) accounts. After these tasks are finished, we can prepare the financial statements.

There are two main reasons for closing the temporary accounts:

1. The balances in all the revenue, expense, gain, and loss accounts will be moved to one place—the income summary account. When all of these amounts are combined into one account, the number that makes the income summary account balance equals the net income for the period.

Key Takeaway:

Summary of the closing process.

Close all the revenue, expense, gain, and loss accounts to the income summary account.

We do this in four steps: A, B, C, D

A. Close all revenue and gain accounts to the income summary account.

B. Close all expense and loss accounts to the income summary account.

C. Close the income summary account to the retained earnings account. If income is positive, entry C will be a debit to the income summary account and a credit to retained earnings. (The impact of this entry is to increase the retained earnings account by the amount of the net income.)

D. Close dividends, if any, to the retained earnings account.

The income summary account can then be used to prepare the income statement. Every temporary account that was closed to the income summary account is included in the income statement. Note that you do not have to use an income summary account; the temporary accounts could simply be closed directly to the retained earnings account. However, the closing process described here is very orderly and systematic.

Let's look at a simple example:

Revenue		Expenses		Gains		Losses	
$500(A1)	$500	$300	$300(B1)	$100(A2)	$100	$200	$200(B2)
–0–		–0–		–0–		–0–	

Income Summary		Retained Earnings	
$300(A1)	$500(A1)		$100(C)
$200(A2)	$100(A2)		
$100(C)			
–0–			

In this example, the revenue and gains equal $600 (or $500 + $100); the expenses and losses are $500 (or $300 + $200). Therefore, the net income equals $100. Note that C is the net income.

2. The second reason for closing the temporary accounts is to clear out the accounts and make them zero so that when the next period begins, all the temporary accounts start the new period at zero.

Let us compare temporary accounts with permanent accounts. Cash is a permanent account. If you go to sleep on New Year's Eve with $500 cash in the bank, you will wake up on January 1 and there will still be $500 in the bank. Revenue is a temporary account. On December 31, we can calculate how much revenue was earned during the month of December. However, when January 1 begins, the revenue for the month of January is zero until the first sale is made.

BALANCING THE PERMANENT ACCOUNTS

Balancing the permanent accounts is even easier than closing the temporary accounts. Just add the numbers on the debit and credit sides of each account, find the difference between the two totals, and put the difference on the side that is greater. That is the balance in the account. (Hint: Draw a double line below the last number in each account, write the balance below the double lines on the side that is greater, and put a check mark next to the balance.)

CORRECTING ERRORS

You should know how to correct errors. There are several different types of errors. The first is what we call out-of-balance errors, which occur when the trial balance indicates that the total debits do not equal the total credits. You may also discover this type of error when preparing a balance sheet where the statement does not balance. What can you do to discover the cause of the error and then fix it?

Out-of-Balance Errors

The obvious first step is to look for a transaction that is the same amount as the out-of-balance amount. A second step would be to divide the out-of-balance amount by 2 and look for a transaction of that amount. (If you put $50 on the debit side of a balance sheet and the $50 belongs on the credit side, you will be out of balance by $100.) A third option is to divide the out-of-balance amount by 9. If it divides evenly, you may have transposed two numbers (writing 42 as 24 produces a difference of 18, which is evenly divisible by 9. For example,

$63 - 36 = 27, 84 - 48 = 36,$ and so on). If this occurs, look for a transposition.

Other Bookkeeping Errors

When the trial balance balances, there still may be accounting or bookkeeping errors. Transactions may have been recorded improperly. The three-column approach illustrated in figure 2-7 is a simple way to prepare adjustments for improper accounting entries. To use this approach, prepare three columns with the following headings:

- What They Did
- What They Should Have Done
- The Adjustment

What They Did	What They Should Have Done	The Adjustment
Expense →	Equipment →	Equipment →
Cash	Cash	Expense

FIGURE 2-7   The Three-Column Approach to Correcting Transaction Recording Errors

What They Did	What They Should Have Done	The Adjustment
Cash	Accounts Receivable	Accounts Receivable
Sales	Sales	Cash

FIGURE 2-8   Correcting an Error Made in Recording a Sale

What They Did	What They Should Have Done	The Adjustment
Cash $10,000	Cash $10,000	Sales $10,000
Sales $10,000	Land $6,000	Land $6,000
	Gain $4,000	Gain $4,000

FIGURE 2-9   Correcting an Error in Recording a Sale of Land

Let's say that the company made a sale on account, but recorded it as if it were for cash. Then the company would have debited cash and credited sales. (Put this in the first column.) The correct journal entry would be to debit accounts receivable and credit sales. (Put this into the second column.) Now simply look at both of these entries, and the adjustment is clear. We need a debit to accounts receivable; instead, we have a debit to cash. We can correct this by simply debiting accounts receivable and crediting sales. (See figure 2-8 for the three-column approach to correcting an error regarding a sales transaction.)

Let's say that the company sells a piece of land for $10,000 that it bought for $6,000, but records the transaction as a sale of merchandise. We can correct this error as indicated in figure 2-9.

PREPARING THE FINANCIAL STATEMENTS

Once you have completed the process of closing the temporary accounts and balancing the permanent accounts, you can prepare the financial statements. The financial statements are interrelated. Numbers from one statement are linked to another statement.

We prepare the income statement first. All the numbers on the income statement come from the income summary account. The number from the closing entry (C) should equal the net income.

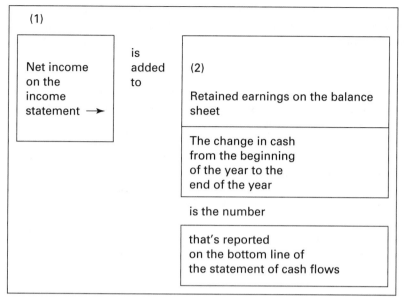

FIGURE 2-10 The Relationships Between the Income Statement, Balance Sheet and Statement of Cash Flows

The net income figure on the income statement is added to the retained earnings account on the balance sheet. We can then produce a statement of retained earnings, which is simply:

Beginning balance of retained Earnings + Net income − Dividends
= Ending balance of retained earnings.

Once we compute the ending balance of retained earnings, we can prepare the balance sheet. When the net income is added to retained earnings and the ending balance of retained earnings is calculated, the balance sheet should balance.

The statement of cash flows is linked to the balance sheet. The bottom line on the statement of cash flows equals the change in the cash account on the balance sheet from the beginning of the year to the end of the year.

Thus, we have three major financial statements, which are all linked as indicated in figure 2-10.

COMPREHENSIVE ILLUSTRATION

Let us now work through a comprehensive problem that illustrates the complete accounting cycle. We begin with business transactions, journal entries, and adjusting entries. Then we post these entries to the general ledger and prepare a trial balance.

The next steps are the closing process and the preparation of the financial statements. There are 15 transactions in this example. The first 11 are business transactions, then there are 4 adjusting entries.

Note: There are several **contra-accounts** in these journal entries. A contra-account is an account that "goes against" or is subtracted from another account. A contra-asset is subtracted from an asset account. A contra-liability is subtracted from a liability account. A contra-account increases on the opposite side from the account it goes against. Thus, a contra-asset account increases on the credit side because assets increase on the debit side. Building—accumulated depreciation is a common contra-account; it is subtracted from the building asset account. The building account increases on the debit side. Building—accumulated depreciation, a contra-asset, increases on the credit side.

We will review these journal entries and more in the next five chapters. Here are just a few comments about these transactions. In transactions 1 and 2 that follow, the company is raising money by issuing stock or borrowing money from a bank. Therefore, the asset cash is increasing and thus we make a debit to cash. In transactions 3 and 4, the company is buying items and paying cash; therefore, we make a credit to cash. In transactions 5, 8, 12, 13, and 14, the company is incurring an expense; therefore, an expense account increases so we debit an expense account. In transaction 9, the company earned revenue; we credit a revenue account.

Transaction	*Journal Entry*		
1. Owners invested $100,000 into the company and received common stock. The business received cash—an asset—so we debit cash $100,000. The owners' equity in the business increased, so we credit common stock—an owners' equity account—$100,000.	Cash Common Stock	100,000	100,000
2. The company borrowed $50,000 from the bank. The company received cash—an asset— so we debit cash $50,000. Notes payable—a liability— increased, so we credit notes payable $50,000.	Cash Note Payable	50,000	50,000

3. The company bought land for $25,000 cash.
Land—an asset—increased, so we debit land $25,000. Cash—an asset—decreased, so we credit cash $25,000.

Land	25,000	
Cash		25,000

4. The company bought a 3-month insurance policy for $3,000.
Prepaid insurance—an asset— increased, so we debit prepaid insurance 3,000. Cash—an asset—decreased, so we credit cash 3,000.

Prepaid Insurance	3,000	
Cash		3,000

5. The company paid salaries for a total of $5,000.
Salaries expense—an expense—increased, so we debit salaries expense $5,000. Cash—an asset— decreased, so we credit cash $5,000.

Salaries Expense	5,000	
Cash		5,000

6. The company purchased supplies on account for $20,000.
Supplies—an asset— increased, so we debit supplies $20,000. Accounts payable—a liability—increased, so we credit accounts payable $20,000.

Supplies	20,000	
Accounts Payable		20,000

7. The company paid a cash dividend. (A dividend represents a distribution of an entity's past earnings to the stockholders.)
Paying a dividend reduces owner's equity. Retained earnings—an owners' equity account— decreased, so we debit retained earnings $3,000. Cash—an asset—decreased, so we credit cash $3,000.

Dividends (R/E)	3,000	
Cash		3,000

8. The company paid rent for the period for a total of $10,000. Rent expense— an expense—increased by $10,000, so we debit rent expense $10,000. Cash—an asset—decreased, so we credit cash $10,000.	Rent Expense Cash	10,000	10,000
9. The company provided services for customers for $50,000. It received $20,000 cash and the balance on account. Cash—an asset—increased by $20,000, so we debit cash. Accounts receivable—an asset—increased by $30,000, so we debit accounts receivable $30,000. Service revenue—a revenue account—increased by $50,000, so we credit service revenue $50,000.	Cash Accounts Receivable Service Revenue	20,000 30,000	50,000
10. The company collected $10,000 from customers on account. Cash—an asset—increased, so we debit cash $10,000. Accounts receivable—an asset—decreased by $10,000, so we credit accounts receivable $10,000.	Cash Accounts Receivable	10,000	10,000
11. The company made a payment of $20,000 on accounts payable. Accounts payable—a liability—decreased by $20,000, so we debit accounts payable $20,000. Cash—an asset—decreased by $20,000, so we credit cash $20,000.	Accounts Payable Cash	20,000	20,000

Here is the information for the adjusting entries:

12. The telephone expense for the period is estimated to be $2,000. Telephone expense—an expense account—increased by $2,000, so we debit telephone expense $2,000. Accounts payable—a liability—increased by $2,000, so we credit accounts payable $2,000.	Telephone Expense Accounts Payable	2,000	2,000

13. A count of the supplies indicated that $5,000 of supplies on hand at the end of the period. The company purchased $20,000 worth of supplies and now $5,000 remain. Therefore, the company must have used up $15,000 worth of supplies. Supplies expense increased by $15,000, so we debit supplies expense. The asset supplies decreased by $15,000, so we credit supplies $15,000.

Supplies Expense	15,000	
Supplies		15,000

14. The company paid $3,000 for 3 months of insurance premium, and now one month's worth of insurance has expired.
Insurance expense—an expense—increased by $1,000, so we debit insurance expense $1,000. Prepaid insurance—an asset—decreased by $1,000, so we credit prepaid insurance.

Insurance Expense	1,000	
Prepaid Insurance		1,000

15. One month's interest accrued on the note payable.
Interest expense—an expense— increased, so we debit interest expense $375. Interest payable—a liability—increased, so we credit interest payable $375.

Interest Expense	375	
Interest Payable		375

Figure 2-11 shows how the 15 journal entries from our comprehensive illustration are posted to the ledger.

At this point in our example, the company's trial balance can be prepared. (See figure 2-12, which shows the trial balance for Hillcrest Corp.) This is simply a listing of all the accounts in the ledger and their balances. We are checking to see if the total debits equal the total credits.

Cash		Accounts Receivable	
$100,000 (1)	$25,000 (3)	$30,000 (9)	$10,000 (10)
50,000 (2)	3,000 (4)		
20,000 (9)	5,000 (5)		
10,000 (10)	3,000 (7)		
	10,000 (8)		
	20,000 (11)		

Supplies		Prepaid Insurance	
$20,000 (6)	$15,000 (13)	$3,000 (4)	$1,000 (14)

Land		Accounts Payable	
$25,000 (3)		$20,000 (11)	$20,000 (6)
			2,000 (12)

Notes Payable		Rent Expense	
	$50,000 (2)	$10,000 (8)	

Interest Expense		Interest Payable	
$375 (15)			$375 (15)

Insurance Expense		Salary Expense	
$1,000 (14)		$5,000 (5)	

Telephone Expense		Supplies Expense	
$2,000 (12)		$15,000 (13)	

Common Stock		Retained Earnings	
	$100,000 (1)	$3,000 (7)	

FIGURE 2-11 Journal Entries Posted to the Ledger

Hillcrest Company Trial Balance as of 12/31/2008			
Cash	$114,000	Accounts payable	$2,000
Accounts receivable	20,000	Notes payable	50,000
Supplies	5,000	Common stock	100,000
Prepaid insurance	2,000	Retained earnings	<3,000>
Land	25,000	Service revenue	50,000
Rent expense	10,000	Interest payable	375
Insurance expense	1,000		
Telephone expense	2,000		
Supplies expense	15,000		
Salaries expense	5,000		
Interest expense	375		
Total debits	$199,375	Total credits	$199,375

FIGURE 2-12   Trial Balance for Hillcrest Corp.

Now let us look at the closing entries. Remember, there are four closing entries, usually labeled A, B, C, and D:

Entry A closes revenues and gains to the income summary.

Entry B closes expenses and losses to the income summary.

Entry C closes the income summary account to retained earnings.

Entry D closes any dividends to retained earnings.

In our illustration, there is one A entry, six B entries, and one C entry.

A	Service revenue	$50,000	
	Income summary		$50,000
B1	Income summary	1,000	
	Insurance expense		1,000
B2	Income summary	5,000	
	Salary expense		5,000
B3	Income summary	2,000	
	Telephone expense		2,000
B4	Income summary	10,000	
	Rent expense		10,000
B5	Income summary	5,000	
	Supplies expense		5,000
B6	Income summary	375	
	Interest expense		375
C	Income summary	16,625	
	Retained earnings		16,625

Cash		Accounts Receivable	
$100,000 (1)	$25,000 (3)	$30,000 (9)	$10,000 (10)
50,000 (2)	3,000 (4)	$20,000	
20,000 (9)	5,000 (5)		
10,000 (10)	3,000 (7)		
	10,000 (8)		
	20,000 (11)		
$114,000			

Supplies		Prepaid Insurance	
$20,000 (6)	$15,000 (8)	$3,000 (4)	$1,000 (14)
$5,000		$2,000	

Land		Accounts Payable	
$25,000 (3)		$20,000 (11)	$20,000 (6)
$25,000			2,000 (11)
			$2,000

Notes Payable		Rent Expense	
	$50,000 (2)	$10,000 (8)	$10,000 (B4)
	$50,000	$0	

Interest Expense		Interest Payable	
$375 (15)	$375 (B6)		$375 (15)
$0		$375	

Insurance Expense		Salary Expense	
$1,000 (14)	$1,000 (B1)	$5,000 (5)	$5,000 (B2)
$0		$0	

Telephone Expense		Supplies Expense	
$2,000 (11)	$2,000 (B3)	$15,000 (13)	$15,000 (B5)
$0		$0	

Common Stock		Retained Earnings	
	$100,000 (1)	$3,000 (7)	$16,625 (C)
	$100,000		$13,625

FIGURE 2-13 T-Accounts After Closing Entries Have Been Posted

You do not have to use the income summary account; the temporary accounts could simply be closed directly to the retained earnings account. We recommend using an income summary account.

Figure 2-13 shows the T-accounts after the closing entries have been posted. The temporary, or income statement, accounts have all been closed. They will begin the next period with a zero balance. The permanent, or balance sheet, accounts have all been balanced. They will begin the next period with the same balance that they have at the end of the previous period.

All of the numbers that were closed to the income summary account in entries A and B (revenue, expense, gain, and loss) are the numbers that will appear in the income statement.

The final element of the accounting cycle is the preparation of the financial statements. In this comprehensive illustration, we have recorded 15 transactions—11 business transactions and 4 adjustments. The entries were recorded in the journal and posted to the ledger. A trial balance was prepared, indicating that the total debits equaled the total credits. Now the financial statements can be prepared. Review figure 2-14, the income statement; figure 2-15, the balance sheet; and figure 2-16, the statement of cash flows.

We have just reviewed a complete illustration of all the elements of the accounting cycle. Practice doing this a few times, and you should have a very firm grasp of the basic accounting process.

Hillcrest Corp.		
Income Statement		
for the Year Ending 12/31/08		
Service Revenue		$50,000
Less Expenses		
Salaries	$ 5,000	
Rent	10,000	
Insurance	1,000	
Telephone	2,000	
Supplies	15,000	
Interest	375	
Total Expenses		33,375
Net Income		$16,625

FIGURE 2-14 Income Statement

Hillcrest Corp.
Balance Sheet
as of 12/31/08

Assets		Liabilities	
Cash	$114,000	Accounts Payable	$ 12,000
Accounts Receivable	20,000	Note Payable	50,000
Supplies	5,000	Interest Payable	375
Prepaid Insurance	2,000		
Total Current Assets	141,000	Total Liabilities	52,375
Property, Plant, and Equipment			
Land	25,000	Owners' Equity	
		Common Stock	100,000
		Retained Earnings	13,625
		Total Owners' Equity	113,625
		Total Liabilities and	
Total Assets	$166,000	Owners' Equity	$166,000

FIGURE 2-15 Balance Sheet

Hillcrest Corp.
Statement of Cash Flows
for the Year Ending 12/31/08

Cash from Operating Activities		
Net Income	$16,625	
Increase in Accounts Receivable	<20,000>	
Increase in Supplies	<5,000>	
Increase in Prepaid Insurance	<2,000>	
Increase in Accounts Payable	2,000	
Increase in Interest Payable	375	
Net Cash from Operating Activities		<8,000>
Cash from Investing Activities		
Purchase Land	<25,000>	
Net Cash from Investing Activities		<25,000>
Cash from Financing Activities		
Issue Common Stock	100,000	
Borrow from the Bank	50,000	
Pay Dividends	<3,000>	
Net Cash from Financing Activities		147,000
Change in Cash		$114,000

FIGURE 2-16 Statement of Cash Flows

REVIEW QUESTIONS

1. *Why is there so much attention paid to journal entries? Why are journal entries so important?*

The journal entry is the link between the business transactions of the company and what the company reports in its financial statement. If you want to know what the impact of a particular transaction will be on the financial statements, you need to know the journal entry to record that particular transaction.

Here's a question that comes up quite a bit: You are asked what the impact of a particular transaction would be on the company's net income. (This happens to be a very popular exam question.) A simple way to answer would be to look at the journal entry for that transaction. If both the debit and the credit are balance sheet accounts, for example, then the impact of that transaction on income would be zero.

2. *Does every company need to make adjusting entries? Why don't they record everything during the period instead of waiting until the end of the period?*

All companies record business transactions during the accounting period. However, some transactions are simply due to the passage of time, and the company must wait until the entire period is over to record the transactions. Earning interest and the expiration of prepaid rent and prepaid insurance, as well as depreciation, are all functions of time passing; thus, these items are adjusted at the end of the period. Note that these adjusting entries do two things: They get the revenue or expense recognized in the appropriate period and they bring the balances in the balance sheet accounts up to date.

3. *What is the purpose of closing entries? Why aren't the balance sheet accounts closed, as well as the income statement accounts?*

There are two purposes to closing entries. One is to gather all information about transactions that affected income in one place in order to determine the income for the period. Most companies close all the income statement accounts into a summary account called income summary. Once all the income statement accounts are closed to the income summary account, we can compute the net income. Net income is equal to the closing entry C, which closes the income summary account to retained earnings. A second purpose of preparing closing entries is to eliminate all balances in the income statement accounts so when the next period begins, all the income statement accounts begin with a zero balance.

Income statement accounts reflect the activity for a specific period. Therefore, they must begin the period with a zero balance. Balance sheet accounts, on the other hand, reflect amounts as of a point in time. As mentioned earlier, if you have $100 in the bank on December 31, then when you wake up on January 1, you will still have $100 in the bank.

4. *If the trial balance balances, does that mean that no errors have been made?*

If the trial balance balances, this just means that the total debits equal the total credits. However, there still may be errors. For example, if a transaction was not recorded, the trial balance would balance, but something would be missing. Also, if a specific transaction was recorded twice, the trial balance would balance, but there would be something wrong. In addition, if a transaction was recorded by debiting cash instead of accounts receivable, the trial balance would balance, but some of the balances would be incorrect.

5. *Why is the journal entry to record cost of goods sold both an adjusting entry and a closing entry?*

Like other adjusting entries, the journal entry to record cost of goods sold puts an expense (in this case, cost of goods sold) into the correct period, and it brings the balance sheet account ending inventory up to date. Like a closing entry, it closes out the beginning inventory and purchases, and makes their balances zero.

6. *Why are the current assets always listed in the same order?*

Current assets are the assets that the company will use to pay current obligations. Obviously, cash is the most liquid current asset and it is listed first. The account that is next in terms of liquidity—marketable securities—is listed second. Marketable securities are not cash, but you can call your broker, sell the security, and get cash very quickly. The other current assets are listed in terms of most liquid to least liquid. Prepaid expenses, the last current asset, will never become cash, but by, prepaying an expense, it means that you don't have to come up with cash to pay for a particular expense item. It has been prepaid.

Other assets are typically listed in a standard manner. For example, Property, Plant, and Equipment assets are usually listed as land, buildings, and equipment. However, the listing of the current assets in order of liquidity is more of a requirement.

7. *On the balance sheet, why do we show the cost of plant assets in one account and the accumulated depreciation in another account? Why not just show the net amount?*

Showing the cost of a plant asset in one account and the accumulated depreciation in a separate account includes more information than if we just showed the net amount in a single account. If I tell you that I have an asset with a balance of $200,000 in the asset account and $50,000 in the accumulated depreciation account, I have told you quite a bit about this asset. You know that I paid $200,000 for it some time ago and that it has used up about one quarter of its service potential. With just the net amount in one account, you wouldn't be able to tell what I paid for the asset and you have absolutely no way of telling how much of the asset had been used up.

8. *What are contra-accounts?*

The word "contra" means against. Contra-accounts go against other accounts. For example, allowance for uncollectibles is a contra-asset account that goes against or is subtracted from accounts receivable. Accumulated depreciation is a contra-account that goes against or is subtracted from an asset account such as building and equipment. Using contra-accounts allows the accountant to communicate more information about a specific account.

9. *What is meant by the phrase "debits by the window and credits by the door"?*

It just so happens that in most classrooms, the room is set up so that as you face the black or white board, the windows are on your left. The debits (left) are by the windows and credits (right) are by the door. Remember that this is true of most classrooms, but certainly not all.

PRACTICE MULTIPLE CHOICE QUESTIONS

1. Which of the following statements about accrual accounting is true?

    a. It provides a poor indication of a company's present and continuing ability to generate positive cash flows.

    b. Revenues are recognized when sales are made.

    c. It is most concerned with the cash receipts and cash disbursements of a business.

    d. It is concerned only with the cash expended by a company and the cash earned by the company, but not the process by which cash is used.

Solution: The correct answer is **b**. Choice **a** is wrong because accrual accounting does provide some indication about the company's ability to generate positive cash flows. Choice **c** is wrong because accrual accounting is not "most concerned" with cash receipts and disbursements, which would be true of the cash basis. Choice **d** is wrong because accrual accounting is not focused on cash receipts and disbursements.

2. All asset and expense accounts are increased

    a. on the right (or credit side).

    b. on the left (or debit side).

    c. on the top of the balance sheet.

    d. at the bottom of the balance sheet.

Solution: The correct answer is **b**. Choice **a** is wrong because asset and expense accounts are increased on the debit, not the credit, side. Choices **c** and d simply don't make any sense.

3. Each general journal entry consists of

    a. the account(s) and amount(s) to be debited.

    b. the account(s) and amount(s) to be credited.

    c. a date and an explanation.

    d. all of the above as they are all are parts of a general journal entry.

Solution: Choice **d** is the correct answer, because **a**, **b**, and **c** are all parts of a journal entry.

4. How would you make an adjusting entry to recognize unearned revenue that has been earned?

    a. Debit unearned revenue and credit revenue.

    b. Debit revenue and credit unearned revenue.

    c. Debit unearned revenue and credit cash..

    d. None of the above.

Solution: The correct answer is **a**. Choice **b** is wrong because it has the debits and credits reversed. Choice **c** is wrong because adjusting entries do not involve cash. Choice **d** is wrong because choice A is the correct answer.

5. A ballet company sells season tickets to 500 people for $450 each cash. The entry for the sale of season tickets is

a. Unearned Ticket Revenue	$225,000	
Ticket Revenue		$225,000
b. Ticket Revenue	$225,000	
Cash		$225,000
c. Cash	$225,000	
Unearned Ticket Revenue		$225,000
d. Accounts Receivable	$225,000	
Ticket Revenue		$225,000

Solution: The correct answer is **c**. Choices **a** and **d** can be immediately eliminated because the sale transaction was for cash and these two choices do not have a cash component. Choice **b** is wrong because the cash account must be debited to record a receipt of cash.

6. The journal entry to accrue an expense is

    a. debit interest expense and credit interest payable.

    b. debit interest payable and credit interest expense.

    c. debit revenue and credit unearned revenue.

    d. debit unearned revenue and credit revenue.

Solution: The correct answer is **a**. The question involves accruing an expense, which requires a debit to an expense account. Choices **b, c,** and **d,** can be eliminated immediately because they do not have a debit to an expense account.

7. An account that reduces an asset, liability, or owners' equity account is called

    a. an adjunct account.

    b. a contra-account.

    c. accounts receivable.

    d. a balance account.

Solution: The correct answer is **b**. Choice **a** is wrong because an adjunct account is added to an asset, liability, or owners' equity account. Choices **b** and **d** are nonsensical.

8. Which of the following statements about a trial balance is incorrect?

    a. Its primary purpose is to prove the mathematical equality of the debits and credits after posting.

    b. It uncovers errors in journalizing and posting.

    c. It is useful in the preparation of financial statements.

    d. It proves that all transactions have been recorded and posted to the ledger.

Solution: The correct answer is **d**. If a transaction took place but was not recorded, the trial balance would still balance. The other choices are all correct statements regarding the trial balance.

9. An adjusting entry would normally not include a debit to
   a. an expense account and a credit to an asset account.
   b. an expense account and a credit to a liability account.
   c. a liability account and a credit to a revenue account.
   d. an asset account and a credit to a liability account.

Solution: The correct answer is **d**. Normally, adjusting entries involve an income statement account such as an expense or revenue account and a related balance sheet account. Choice **d** involves two balance sheet accounts. Choices **a**, **b**, and **c** follow the normal pattern.

10. If the adjusting entry for an accrued expense is not made, then
   a. assets will be overstated.
   b. expenses will be overstated.
   c. liabilities will be understated.
   d. owners' equity will be understated.

Solution: The correct answer is **c**. When an accrual of an expense is recorded, an expense is debited and a liability is credited. If this entry is not made, then there is a missing credit to a liability, which means that the liability account involved will be understated. Choice **a** is wrong because assets are not involved in this transaction. Choice **b** is wrong because if the expense is not accrued, an expense account will be understated, not overstated. Choice **d** is wrong because accrual of an expense does not involve owners' equity.

CHAPTER 3

INTERNAL CONTROLS, CASH, AND RECEIVABLES

LEARNING OBJECTIVES

After studying this chapter, you will understand

- the meaning and the importance of internal controls
- the impact of the Sarbanes–Oxley Act
- how to prepare a bank reconciliation
- credit sales and accounts receivable, and accounting for sales transactions, accounts receivable, and bad debt expense
- accounting for notes receivable

HERE IS where we are going in our study of internal controls, cash, and receivables. The first thing we will look at will be **internal accounting controls,** or simply internal controls. Internal controls represent a comprehensive set of polices, procedures, rules, and so forth that are designed to protect the entity's asset from theft, to make sure that accounting records are complete and correct, and to encourage all employees to follow the company's rules and procedures.

Here's an example of an internal control: Every check written for more than $1,000 must have two signatures. This is a simple control that makes it difficult for the person who has the responsibility for writing checks to write one to himself, which would be theft.

Without internal controls, the following events might occur:

- Employees could simply take away company assets (office supplies, computers, televisions, and so forth).
- The income statement could contain fictitious amounts for sales or net income.

The failure of Enron Corporation and the collapse of Arthur Andersen prompted the U.S. Congress to pass legislation to ensure that these events do not happen again—this legislation is known as the Sarbanes–Oxley Act of 2002.

This is very similar to the congressional reaction to the stock market crash of 1929. The U.S. Congress's response to the events of 1929 was the Securities Act of 1933 and the Securities Exchange Act of 1934. This legislation created a federal agency (the Securities and Exchange Commission [the SEC]) to regulate the securities market and to make sure that we do not have another 1929 type of crash. As it turns out, the SEC has done a pretty good job over the years since it was established. We have seen several major blips in stock market prices, but nothing like the events of 1929.

THE SARBANES–OXLEY ACT REQUIREMENTS

Here are three of the most important elements of Sarbanes–Oxley:

1. The chief executive officer (CEO) and the chief financial officer (CFO) must sign off or certify that the company's financial statements are correct.
2. The CEO and CFO must sign off or certify that the company's internal controls are in place and are working.
3. The company's external auditors (the certified public accountants [CPAs]) must do a special audit and issue an opinion concerning management's assertions about the internal controls.

Cash is quite easy to account for—most of it is simply money in a checking account. (It is interesting to note that although cash represents a very small percentage of the total assets, auditors (the firm's CPAs) generally spend a good bit of time auditing the cash account. Why? The answer is this: It's a lot easier to steal cash than to steal an office building. There are many ways to steal cash, and it generally revolves around checks.

It is interesting to note that a cash account is one of the only accounts where the company receives a monthly statement telling them what the correct balance in the account should be. Of course, I'm refering to the monthly bank statement. By comparing the balance per the bank statement with the balance in the cash account in the ledger, you can verify the accuracy of the cash account. We refer to this process as "preparing a bank reconciliation." I will present a very simple process and standard format for preparing a bank reconciliation. This exercise often appears on the first mid-term exam!

Accounting for **accounts receivable** is an interesting process. Accounts receivable represents the money that the company's customers owe the company for goods and services purchased on account. One of the major elements in this process is estimating **bad debt expense**. This is the cost of being unable to collect money that a customer owes the company.

Here is the problem: A customer buys $100 of merchandise in 2006. The customer never pays the bill, and in 2007 the company gives up and writes the customer's account off, thus creating an expense or a loss in 2007. Note that the sale took place in 2006 and the expense is reported in 2007. That's not the way to match revenues and expenses. We need to reflect the bad debt expense in the *same year* as the sale. How can we do this without a crystal ball? How can we know who will pay their bills and who won't? The answer is that we make an estimate, based on the company's history of collections on accounts receivable.

Accounting for notes receivable is the final topic in this chapter. A note receivable is a more formal version of an account receivable, and is evidenced by a document that we call a promissory note.

I think that this is a good place for a "commercial announcement" from your author. You have probably figured out by now that I believe that understanding journal entries is important. Why is this so? The answer is simple. The journal entry is the *link* between the entity's transactions and what gets reported on the financial statements.

In each chapter, I present and explain all the typical journal entries for each topic. Furthermore, at the end of chapters 3–7, there is a summary of all the journal entries that were covered in that particular chapter. Make sure that you understand these entries and you will be well on your way to mastering financial accounting, as well as getting a high grade in the course.

SARBANES–OXLEY AND INTERNAL CONTROL

As indicated in the previous section, Sarbanes–Oxley requires management to report on the effectiveness of the company's internal controls. The firm's CPAs must issue an opinion as to management's compliance with this reporting requirement.

A company's system of internal controls must follow one of several basic models of internal control. One of the most popular is the COSO (Committee of Sponsoring Organizations) framework. COSO is a private sector organization that was originally formed to sponsor the National Commission on Fraudulent Financial Reporting. The COSO framework defines internal control as

> *"A process affected by the entity's board of directors, management, and other personnel, designed to provide reasonable assurance regarding the achievement of objectives in the following categories:*
>
> *1. Reliability of financial reporting*
>
> *2. Effectiveness and efficiency of operations*
>
> *3. Compliance with applicable laws and regulations"*

The internal controls of a business consist of the organizational plan and related measures that a company adopts to

1. safeguard the firms assets,
2. encourage adherence to company policies,
3. promote operational efficiency, and
4. ensure accurate and reliable accounting records.

A system of internal controls usually includes the following characteristics:

1. Competent, reliable, and ethical personnel
2. Assignment of responsibility
3. Proper authorization of transactions

4. Supervision of employees

5. Separation of duties

6. Internal and external audits

The COSO framework includes the following five components:

1. The control environment

2. The risk assessment process

3. The accounting information system

4. Control activities

5. Monitoring[1]

The Control Environment

The control environment reflects management's commitment to integrity and ethical values. It is determined, in part, by the role played by the board of directors and the audit committee of the board. Do they take an active role in company matters? Does the audit committee work effectively with the external auditors? Do they review the audit findings and ask the right questions?

The organizational structure of the company is another component of the control environment. Has authority and responsibility for decision making been clearly established? Is there a proper segregation of duties? One employee should not have custody of an asset and responsibility for the record keeping related to that asset.

Risk Assessment

Has management reviewed and analyzed the various factors that affect the risk that the company's objectives will not be reached? How have they attempted to deal with these factors? There is a risk that the company's financial statements will not be correct. There is also the risk that the company's assets may be vulnerable to theft and other dangers.

The Accounting Information System

Obviously, the accounting system is a major component of the company's internal controls. There must be adequate controls surrounding the complete accounting process—from the preparation of business documents, to recording transactions in the journal and posting to the ledger, to the preparation of the financial statements.

Control Activities

Control activities are procedures that are performed to make sure that management's policies are being implemented. There are several areas where these control activities are established.

---

[1] COSO information from http://www.COSO.org/publications/executive_summary_integrated_framework.htm.

One set of control activities involves the preparation of budgets and forecasts, and the comparison to actual performance and the calculation of **variances.** A variance is the difference between the budgeted number and the actual number achieved. There are other control activities related to information processing, including restricting an individual's access to computers and restricting the use of specific software applications.

A simple but effective internal control activity is the use of serial numbers on documents such as sales invoices, checks, and stock certificates. Another simple control activity involves requiring two signatures on all checks above a minimum amount; this should help prevent unauthorized cash disbursements.

A company should also have physical controls in place to prevent unauthorized access to specific assets, computer systems, and accounting records. Locks, fences, and security guards are also part of any internal control system.

We have already touched on the notion of segregation of duties. No one individual should perform more than one of the following functions:

1. Authorizing transactions
2. Recording transactions in the accounting system
3. Having custody of specific assets

Another control activity is simply reviewing what has taken place and determining whether the company's controls are in fact being implemented and are working properly. Some of these monitoring activities will be performed by the company's internal auditors. The internal auditors are employees of the company whose function is to review and evaluate compliance with managements' procedures and policies, and then to report their findings to management.[2]

REPORTING CASH

The following topics are discussed in this section:

1. Restricted cash
2. Bank overdrafts
3. Cash equivalents
4. Petty cash

Cash set aside or designated for a specific purpose is *not* a part of the normal cash account. This is called **restricted cash**. Compensating balances consist of money that the bank requires a depositor to maintain at all times. This is also part of restricted cash.

Bank overdrafts occur when a company writes a check for an amount of money in excess of the balance in their checking account. Bank overdrafts should be reported as a current liability, and should not be simply subtracted from the total balance of cash.

---

[2] For more information on internal controls, see http://COSO.org/publications/executive_summary_integrated_framework.htm.

Some companies report **cash and cash equivalents** on their balance sheet instead of just cash. Cash equivalents consist of short-term, highly liquid securities. These securities generally can be converted into a known amount of cash, and are so close to their maturity date (3 months or less) that there is virtually no interest rate risk. The following items are usually considered cash equivalents:

1. **Treasury bills** are short-term obligations of the U.S. government that have a maturity period of 1 year or less and are sold at a discount from face value.

2. **Commercial paper** is short-term, unsecured, discounted, and negotiable notes sold by one company to another in order to satisfy immediate cash needs.

3. **Money market funds** are mutual funds that invest solely in money market instruments. Money market instruments are forms of debt that mature in less than 1 year and are very liquid.[3]

Petty Cash

Large companies often set up and maintain a petty cash fund to make small cash disbursements and to maintain control over these payments. These are the procedures for maintaining a petty cash fund:

1. When the petty cash fund is established, money is taken out of the bank, and actual dollar bills are given to the petty cash custodian who maintains control over the petty cash fund.

2. When someone in the company needs some cash to pay for something, a form (called a petty cash voucher) is filled out, indicating the amount of cash and the purpose of the expenditure. At any time, the petty cash custodian will have cash plus petty cash vouchers equal to the amount of the total petty cash fund.

3. Periodically, the petty cash fund is replenished. The petty cash custodian takes all the petty cash vouchers and presents them to a company official who has responsibility for cash, and he or she gives the petty cash custodian an amount of money equal to the total of all the petty cash vouchers. At that time, a journal entry is made, such as the one below:

Supplies expense	50	
Postage expense	100	
Entertainment expense	150	
Cash		300

Note: Once the petty cash fund is established, there are no more entries debiting or crediting the petty cash fund. Every time the fund is replenished, an entry like the one above is made.

---

[3] See http://bwnt.businessweek.com/Glossary.

THE BANK RECONCILIATION

The bank reconciliation is an element of internal control. Rarely does a business receive a report from an outside entity that permits the company to verify the balance of a particular account. However, each month, the bank sends a statement to the company and this statement can be used to verify the accuracy of the balance in the company's cash account (cash in bank).

The typical *format* for the bank reconciliation is shown in figure 3-1.

It would be a rare event for the balance per bank to equal the balance per books simply because of the time lag between when the company or the bank records a transaction and when the other party records the same information.

There are usually numerous differences between the bank balance and the book balance. We refer to these differences as **reconciling items**. A reconciling item is an item that one party (the company or the bank) knows about (and has recorded) in the current period that the other party doesn't learn about until the following period.

On the bank side, there are usually at least two reconciling items: **deposits in transit** and **outstanding checks**. A deposit in transit occurs when a deposit is made by the company (and added to the balance in the cash account) in one period, but is not recorded by the bank until the next period. An outstanding check occurs when the company writes a check (and deducts it from the balance in the cash account), but the bank doesn't deduct it until it receives the check for payment, which may be several (or more) days later.

Adjustments or reconciling items on the book side include collections made by the bank on the company's behalf: bank service charges (printing checks, etc.) and nonsufficient funds (NSF) checks (checks that bounced).

A completed bank reconciliation appears in figure 3-2.

The bank reconciliation is relatively easy to prepare, and since the adjusted balances must agree, it is very easy to see if you have made a mistake in doing the problem. Most students have little trouble with these problems when all the reconciling items are given to them in the problem (e.g., you are told that the deposits in transit are $500.) But what if the problem doesn't give you all the information directly, but simply gives you a copy of the bank statement and a copy of the cash ledger account and *you* must determine what the basic reconciling items are? This sometimes throws students for a loop, but it is relatively easy to determine the reconciling items. Basically, there are only two steps: First, look at the bank statement and trace every number to the cash account or checkbook. Any numbers that appear on the bank statement, but are not included in the cash account (or checkbook) are candidates to be a reconciling

Bank Reconciliation		
Balance per bank		Balance per books
+/– Adjustments		+/– Adjustments
Adjusted balance	=	Adjusted balance

FIGURE 3-1 Typical Bank Reconciliation Format

Bank Reconciliation			
Balance per bank	$12,030	Balance per book	$6,250
+ Deposits in transit	3,500	+ Collection by bank	1,000
		+ Interest earned	40
<Outstanding checks>	<8,500>	<Bank service charge>	<60>
		<NSF checks>	<200>
Adjusted balance	$ 7,030 =	Adjusted balance	$7,030

FIGURE 3-2 Completed Bank Reconciliation Form

item. The second step would be to look at the cash account and trace every number to the bank statement for the period. Any number on the books, but not on the bank statement, would require review. For example, if the company writes 20 checks during the month and only 17 checks were cleared by the bank by the end of the period, then the 3 checks that did not clear must be outstanding. Similarly, any deposit that appears on the cash account in the current month, but does not show up on the bank statement, must be a deposit in transit.

EXAM TIP

Sometimes a problem may require a separate schedule to compute the deposits in transit and/or the outstanding checks. Consider this problem: Checks written per the books in June amounted to $5,000, and checks that cleared the bank in June totaled $4,000. In addition, you are given the reconciliation for the previous month, which indicated outstanding checks of $1,000. Therefore, the outstanding checks for June consist of the $5,000 in checks written during June less the checks written in June that cleared the bank in June, which would be $4,000 less the $1,000 outstanding from the previous period, or $3,000. Thus, the outstanding checks for June equal $5,000 − $3,000, or $2,000.

DEMONSTRATION PROBLEM 1 *Bank Reconciliation*

The following information relates to Lauro Inc. on December 31, 2007:

Balance in the general ledger for cash in bank	$2,050
Balance per the bank statement	2,322
Collection of a note receivable by the bank	475
Interest earned	25
Customer's check returned with the bank statement marked NSF	150
Deposits made during the month that did not appear on the monthly bank statement	450
Checks written during the month that did not clear the bank by the end of the month (they did not appear on the bank statement)	422
Bank service charge	50

Required: Prepare a bank reconciliation and the year-end adjusting entry that Lauro Inc. will have to make on December 31, 2007.

Solution: The first thing to do after reading this problem is to put the format of the solution on your paper in outline form. It is important for you to know that the solutions to many accounting problems have a standard format. This is one such problem. Begin by putting the outline of the standard bank reconciliation on your paper.

Bank Reconciliation

Lauro Inc.

December 31, 2007

Balance per bank		Balance per books
Reconciling items	=	Reconciling items
Adjusted balance		Adjusted balance

Then it is simply a matter of reading all the data, determining if you need to adjust the bank balance or the book balance, and entering the reconciling item into the reconciliation. In this problem, the reconciling items are pretty straightforward. The deposits that didn't make it into the bank are "deposits in transit" and are added to the bank balance. The checks that were written during the month but did not clear the bank are "outstanding checks" and are subtracted from the bank balance. The customer's check that was returned stamped NSF means that the check bounced and was deducted from our balance. Therefore, it must be subtracted from the book balance. The other items seem pretty straightforward. Your solution should look like this:

Bank Reconciliation

Lauro Inc.

December 31, 2007

Balance per bank	$2,322	Balance per books	$2,050
Deposits in transit	+ 450	Collection by bank	+ 475
		Interest earned	+ 25
<Outstanding checks>	<422>	<NSF check>	<150>
		<Bank service charge>	<50>
Adjusted balance	$2,350	Adjusted balance	$2,350

■

The journal entry related to the reconciliation involves only the items on the right-hand side of the page. Any item with a plus (+) in front of it would result in a debit to cash; any item with a minus (−) in front of it would require a credit to cash. We can net out the debits and credits to cash and show just a single debit or credit. Note that for the customer's check that bounced and was deducted from our balance in the bank, we have to put that amount back in the customer's account, which will require a debit to accounts receivable.

The necessary journal entry based on this reconciliation is:

Cash	300	
Accounts Receivable	150	
Bank Service Charge Expense	50	
Notes Receivable		475
Interest Revenue		25

ACCOUNTS RECEIVABLE

The most common type of receivables are trade accounts receivable or simply, accounts receivable. This account reflects the total amount of money that all the customers currently owe the company for goods and services that have been delivered for which the company has not been paid. That amount is referred to as the gross receivables. We do not show the gross accounts receivable on the balance sheet, because the company will rarely collect the total accounts receivable. They will collect a bit less than that. Why? Because of the simple fact that some people just don't pay their bills, customers pass away without paying, customers file for bankruptcy, customers leave the country, and so forth.

We need to do two things to recognize the fact that we will probably not collect the total of the gross receivables:

1. We need to estimate how much of the total accounts receivable we expect to collect, and how much of the total accounts receivable we expect *not to collect*. The amount shown on the balance sheet for accounts receivable is the **net realizable value**. Net realizable value is the gross receivable less an allowance for uncollected accounts. This is the amount we expect to collect.

2. We need to record the expense related to the accounts receivable that will never be collected.

There are two basic methods used to account for uncollectible accounts (or bad debts). One is hardly used at all, so we will focus our attention on the allowance method (the other method, direct write-off, will be discussed later).

When you use the allowance method, there are two different approaches. The percentage of sales approach is an income statement approach. When you use this approach, you make the bad debt expense or uncollectible account expense to be a percentage of sales based on the company's history. This method is very simple to apply. Assume that accounts receivable equal $100,000, sales equal $2,000,000, and bad debt expense has historically been equal to 2% of sales. The balance in the allowance account is $5,000. Using the percentage of sales approach with these numbers, we simply multiply 2% times the sales of $2,000,000, and the bad debt expense is $40,000. The journal entry to record this is

Bad Debt Expense	40,000	
Allowance for Uncollectibles		40,000

Note that this journal entry is *not* affected by either the balance in the accounts receivable account or the balance in the allowance account. By using this method, you guarantee that *bad debt expense is always a function of sales*, and the related balance sheet account (the allowance for uncollectibles) may fluctuate a bit.

The other approach is a balance sheet approach. Here, we estimate what the balance in the allowance account should be, based on an **aging** of the accounts receivable. An aging is simply a listing of accounts receivable in categories based on their ages (i.e., how long it has been since the date of the purchase that gave rise to the accounts receivable). Companies that use this approach group all their accounts receivable by ages: 0–30 days, 31–61, 90+, and so forth. For each category, multiply the dollar total by the percentage of the total that we expect *not* to collect. Obviously, the older the receivable, the less likely it is that it will be collected. For example, a company may expect to collect 98% of all accounts receivable between 0–30 days, and only expect to collect 40% of all accounts receivable in the >120 days category. Once we calculate how much we expect *not* to collect, we make a journal entry to add or subtract an amount to/from the balance in the allowance account to reflect the net realizable value of the receivables (i.e., exactly how much we expect to collect). The journal entry to record this is the same as the entry above (but the amounts will be different).

Key Takeaway: Note that with the income statement approach, bad debt expense is always a specific percentage of sales and the allowance account is free to fluctuate. With the balance sheet approach, the net realizable value of the receivables accurately reflects what the company expects to collect and the bad debt expense is allowed to fluctuate.

The balance sheet approach is a bit more time consuming, because more calculations are needed. Some companies use both methods. During the year, they use the income statement approach for monthly financial statements. At year end, they do an aging and use the balance sheet approach.

There are several journal entries involved in accounting for uncollectible accounts. We have already seen the first one—the entry that is made to record bad debt expense and to adjust the allowance account. That journal entry is a debit to bad debt expense and a credit to the allowance for uncollectibles, using either the income statement or balance sheet approach.

A second journal entry is made when a specific account receivable is written off. That entry is

Allowance for Uncollectibles	XXX	
Accounts Receivable		XXX

EXAM TIP

Note that writing off a specific bad debt does *not* affect the income statement (this question is often asked on exams). It's the first entry above (where bad debt expense is debited, and the allowance account is credited) that affects the income statement.

A third entry is the collection of an account receivable previously written off. To do this, first we must reverse the entry that was made when the account was written off. Then we record the collection just like any other account receivable. Thus, the two entries are

Accounts Receivable	XXX	
Allowance for Uncollectibles		XXX
Cash	XXX	
Accounts Receivable		XXX

Using either of the two allowance method approaches (income statement or balance sheet), the company is able to report accounts receivable at the net realizable value—the amount that the company expects to collect.

The alternative to the allowance method is the direct write-off method. Using this method, no effort is made to estimate bad debt expense or the allowance for uncollectibles. Therefore, accounts receivable on the balance sheet are grossly overstated; this results in an overstatement of assets. When a specific account is written off, the account is written off directly to bad debt expense—hence the name "direct write-off." Using the direct write-off method, we don't have a proper matching of revenues and expenses since the write-off will most likely not take place in the same period as the sale.

The direct write-off method is rarely used. The income statement derived using this approach will give a relatively true picture of the bad debt expense, but on the balance sheet, assets will be overstated (since accounts receivable will be reported gross—without any allowance account).

DEMONSTRATION PROBLEM 2 *Accounts Receivable Transactions and Balance Sheet Presentation*

On January 1, 2006, accounts receivable were $250,000 and the allowance for bad debts was a credit of $15,000. During the year, credit sales amounted to $500,000 and collections on account were $425,000. For monthly reporting purposes, bad debts were estimated to be 3% of credit sales. Also during the year, $10,000 of accounts receivable were written off and recoveries of previously written off receivables totaled $5,000. On December 31, an aging of the receivables was prepared and is shown below:

Customer names	Age category	Balance	Percentage uncollectible	Total
Aires Company	0–30 days	$100,000	3%	$3,000
Kasten Inc.	31–60 days	80,000	6%	4,800
Chaucer Company	61–90 days	70,000	20%	14,000
Marks Inc.	>90 days	50,000	50%	25,000
Grand total				$46,800

Prepare all the journal entries to record the transactions described above and show how accounts receivable should be presented on the balance sheet.

Solution:

Accounts Receivable	500,000	
Sales		500,000
Bad Debt Expense	15,000	
Allowance for Uncollectibles		15,000
(Monthly provision @ 3% of sales)		
Allowance for Uncollectibles	10,000	
Accounts Receivable		10,000
(Bad debt write-off—writing off a specific bad debt)		
Cash	425,000	
Accounts Receivable		425,000
(Collection on account)		
Accounts Receivable	5,000	
Allowance for Uncollectibles		5,000
Cash	5,000	
Accounts Receivable		5,000
(Recovery of accounts previously written off)		
Bad Debt Expense	21,800	
Allowance for Uncollectibles		21,800
(Adjust the allowance account based on the year-end aging.)		

To do this problem, you need to set up T-accounts for both accounts receivable and the allowance account:

Accounts Receivable				Allowance for Uncollectibles	
Beginning balance	$250,000				$15,000 Beginning balance
Credit sales	500,000	$425,000 Collections			15,000 Monthly provisions ($500,000 × .03)
Recovery	5,000				5,000 Recovery
		$10,000 Bad debt write-off			
Balance	$320,000			Bad debt write-off $10,000	21,800 year-end provision
					$46,800 Required amount (Based on an aging)

Balance Sheet Presentation
Current Assets

Accounts Receivable	$320,000
Less Allowance for Uncollectibles	<46,800>
Net Realizable Value	$273,200

■

Key Takeaway: When working with accounts receivable and the allowance account, it is essential to prepare T-accounts. You must also be familiar with the basic journal entries

1. Estimating bad debt expense,
2. Writing off a specific bad debt, and
3. Collection an account previously written off.

NOTES RECEIVABLE

Notes receivable are similar to accounts receivable, but are more formal. The basic document related to notes receivable is called a **promissory note**. There are two parties. The maker of the note (the debtor) is the party that signs the note, which is simply a promise to pay the other party—the payee—a stated amount of money (the principal) plus interest on the principal. The maker of the note has a note payable; the payee or recipient of the note has a note receivable. When a loan is made in exchange for a note receivable, the bank (payee) records the following (assume a $1,000, 6%, 90-day note):

Note Receivable	1,000	
Cash		1,000

Since the interest isn't paid every month, most companies that report monthly financial statements will have to accrue the interest. Interest on a short-term note receivable is typically simple interest. The formula for simple interest is

$$\text{Amount of interest} = \text{Principal} \times \text{Rate} \times \text{Time}$$

The first month's interest in our $1,000, 6%, 90-day note is calculated as follows:

$$\text{Amount of interest} = P \times R \times T$$
$$= 1,000 \times 6\% \times 30/360 = \$5$$

The journal entry to accrue one month's interest is

Interest Receivable	5	
Interest Revenue		5

Key Takeaway: Interest rates (unless otherwise noted) are for a year. We only understand *annual interest rates*. For example, a credit card company may advertise that interest is only $1\frac{1}{2}\%$. That's for a month! Note that $1\frac{1}{2}\%$ a month $\times$ 12 months $=$ 18% per year. The 18% rate is the number you understand when making interest calculations; the interest rate and the time must be stated in the same context. If the interest rate is per year, then the time must be a fraction of a year.

If the time of the note is specified in days, such as a $1,000, 6%, 90-day rate, then in counting the days for the purpose of computing interest, we count the first day, but not the last day. Also, with notes stated in terms of days, we generally use a 360-day year to simplify the calculations.

The journal entry to accrue the interest for 1 month on our $1,000, 6%, 90-day note is

Interest Receivable	5	
Interest Revenue		5

When accruing interest on a note receivable, some students have an impulse to debit interest receivable and credit note receivable. This is incorrect. The underlying promissory note that gave rise to the note receivable has not changed; in fact, the note will never change, so we only debit the note once—when we receive it. Also, we credit the note only once: when we receive the cash and the note has been fully paid.

The entry to record receipt of payment in full, assuming that 2 months of interest has been accrued is

Cash	1,015	
Interest Receivable		10
Interest Revenue		5
Note Receivable		1,000

(The credit to interest receivable in the entry above is to record the receipt of interest revenue accrued in a previous month. The credit to interest revenue is to record interest earned since the last time it was accrued until the day that the note is paid in full.)

GETTING CASH FOR RECEIVABLES

Sometimes a company has a lot of accounts receivable or notes receivable and can't wait for the customer or maker of the note to make a payment; they need the cash right away. Without getting into too much detail, you should know that accounts receivable can be sold, or the company can borrow cash with the accounts receivable as collateral. Similarly, a note receivable can be discounted at a bank. Companies that buy other companies' receivables or lend money with the receivables as collateral are called factors.

Sales of receivables can be made on a "with recourse" or a "without recourse" basis. With recourse means that if the company that bought the account receivable can't collect the receivable, they have recourse against the company that sold the note and that company will have to pay the buyer. If the receivables are sold without recourse, and the buyer can't collect, then the buyer has incurred a loss.

The typical note receivable is an interest-bearing note. Let us assume that the company borrows $1,000 and signs a $1,000, 12%, 6-month note. Upon signing the note, the bank makes the following journal entry:

Note Receivable	1,000	
Cash		1,000

Every month, the company will accrue a month's interest, calculated as follows:

$$\text{Interest} = \text{Principal} \times \text{Rate} \times \text{Time}$$
$$1{,}000 \times .12 \times 1/12 = 10$$

The journal entry to accrue 1 month's interest is:

Interest Receivable	10	
Interest Revenue		10

After accruing interest for 5 months, the note matures in month 6, and the maker of the note pays the bank back the principal plus 6 months' interest, and the following journal entry is made:

Cash	1,060	
Interest Receivable		$50
Interest Revenue		10
Notes Receivable		1,000

SUMMARY OF JOURNAL ENTRIES

This is a list of the most common transactions and journal entries corresponding to the topics covered in this chapter. I would recommend that you review this list of journal entries several times until you are certain that you understand each one. The journal entry is the link between the actual business transactions that take place and the financial statements that are prepared by the entity.

One technique that I find to be very useful is to take this list of transactions and journal entries, cover the right-hand side of the page with a blank sheet of paper so you can just see the description of the transaction, and then write out each journal entry. After writing out each entry, slide the paper down a bit and check to see that you have made the correct entry. Do this before your exams to test your understanding of the material.

Transaction	**Journal Entry**
Sale for cash	Cash
	Sales Revenue
Collections on account	Cash
	Accounts Receivable
Estimate bad debt expense	Bad Debt Expense
	Allowance for Uncollectibles
Write off a specific bad account	Allowance for Uncollectibles
	Accounts Receivable
Collection of an account	Accounts Receivable
Previously written off	Allowance for Uncollectibles
Then	Cash
	Accounts Receivable

Receipt of note receivable	Notes Receivable
	Cash
Recognize interest earned on	Interest Receivable
note receivable	Interest Revenue
Establish a petty cash fund	Petty Cash
	Cash in Bank
Reimburse petty cash fund	Miscellaneous Expenses
	Cash in Bank
Record reconciling items from	Bank Service Charge
bank reconciliation	Accounts Receivable (NSF)
	Interest Revenue
	Cash

REVIEW QUESTIONS

1. *If you are using the allowance method for uncollectible accounts expense, what difference does it make if you use the balance sheet or the income statement approach?*

When you use the allowance method to estimate bad debt expense, there are two approaches—an income statement approach and a balance sheet approach—and it does make a difference depending on which approach you use. If you use the income statement approach, you will force bad debt expense to be a stated percentage of sales. That means that over time, bad debt expense as a percentage of sales will always be the same (e.g., 3%). However, the allowance for doubtful accounts will fluctuate as a percentage of accounts receivable from year to year.

If you use the balance sheet approach, you will force the allowance for uncollectibles to be a specific percentage of accounts receivable, based on an aging. This approach means that accounts receivable less the allowance account will be an accurate portrayal of what the company should reasonably be able to collect. At the same time, bad debt expense as a percentage of sales will fluctuate.

Some companies use both approaches. They use the income statement approach for monthly financial statements because it is so easy to calculate. (e.g., bad debt expense equals 3% of sales and you're finished). At year end, they use the balance sheet approach. They prepare an aging of the account receivable, and then adjust the balance in the allowance account to reflect the collectibility of the receivables.

Note that the journal entry using either approach is the same—debit bad debt expense and credit the allowance for uncollectibles.

2. *Why are accounts receivable shown at net realizable value?*

We show accounts receivable at net realizable value because that is the amount the company expects to collect from its customers. Without an allowance account, the income would be overstated because there would be no bad debt expense recorded, and the assets would be overstated as well, since very few companies collect 100% of their receivables.

3. *What is an "aging"? What ages are we talking about?*

An aging of accounts receivable is simply a listing of a company's accounts receivable by their age, that is, how long it has been since the customer made the purchase that gave rise to the receivable. We usually lump receivables into age categories: 0–30 days, 31–60 days, and so forth. For each age group, multiply the total receivables by the percentage expected to be uncollectible, based on past experience. The older the receivables, the less likely it is that the company will be able to collect them.

4. *Why is the direct write-off method not used?*

The direct write-off method does not make use of an allowance account. When the company determines that a specific account receivable will not be collected, that account is written off (directly) against bad debt expense. The journal entry is a debit to bad debt expense and a credit to accounts receivable. There are two problems with this approach: First, since it usually takes quite a while to determine that a particular customer is not going to pay, the bad debt expense usually winds up in a different period than when the sale was made that created the accounts receivable; thus, you don't have a proper matching of revenues and expenses. The second problem, which is more serious, is that your accounts receivable will be overstated on the balance sheet since no company collects all of its receivables.

5. *What is the function of internal controls?*

The main function of internal controls is to make sure that the employees are following management policies and procedures; thus, assets are protected from theft, the accounting records are accurate, and the company is operating efficiently and effectively. When the external auditors do their audit, they will test these controls, and if they find that the controls are in place and working, they may be able to reduce the amount of testing that they need to do to verify that the financial statements are fairly presented.

6. *Why was there so much attention placed on internal controls in Sarbanes–Oxley?*

One element of internal control is to ensure that the accounting records are accurate and that the financial statements are not misstated. The events leading up to the passage of the Sarbanes–Oxley included a number of companies that issued financial statements that were misstated. Thus, one major element of Sarbanes–Oxley was to make sure that those companies' internal controls were in place and working effectively to hopefully reduce the number of improper or inaccurate financial statements.

Section 404 of Sarbanes–Oxley requires that each annual report contain an "internal control" report that shall

"1) State the responsibility of management for establishing and maintaining an adequate internal control structure and procedures for financial reporting, and

2) Contain an assessment as of the effectiveness of the internal control structure and procedures for financial reporting."

The company's external auditor shall attest to and report on the assessment made by the management of the company regarding the internal controls. This attestation must follow standards established by the PCAOB. (The Public Companies Accounting Oversight Board was created by Sarbanes–Oxley. This organization regulates the public accounting profession).

7. *What is COSO and what did it do?*

COSO is the Committee of Sponsoring Organizations of the Treadway Commission. It is a private sector organization that was originally formed to sponsor the National Commission on Fraudulent Financial Reporting. COSO issued a document called *Internal Control—Integrated Framework*.

Under Section 404 of Sarbanes–Oxley, the PCAOB requires management to use an internal control framework, such as the COSO framework (which describes how to assess the control environment, determine control objectives, perform risk assessment, identify controls, and monitor compliance). Most companies have elected to use the COSO framework as their standard internal control framework.

8. *What are the main provisions of Sarbanes–Oxley?*

The main provisions of Sarbanes–Oxley are

a. creation of the PCAOB to regulate the public accounting profession;

b. certification of financial statements by the CEO and CFO;

c. auditor independence by means of partner rotation every 5 years;

d. internal controls report by management, attestation by CPA;

e. criminal and civil penalties;

f. jail sentences and fines for company executives who knowingly misstate financial statements;

g. new standards for corporate auditing committees; and

h. prohibits companies from making personal loans to executives.

9. *What is risk assessment and why is it important?*

Risk assessment is the analysis and identification of the factors that affect the risk that the company's objectives will not be achieved, and the attempt to manage these risks.

For the company's internal control system to be effective, management must continuously assess the risks that threaten the achievement of the company's objectives. Management's objectives include proper operation of the company's business activities and accurate reporting of the financial position and results of operations in the financial statements.

PRACTICE MULTIPLE CHOICE QUESTIONS

1. Foxy Company's bank statement shows a balance of $40,000 on February 1, 2007. As of February 1, there are $5,000 of deposits in transit and $6,500 of outstanding checks. The adjusted cash balance on February 1, 2006, is

    a. $51,500.
    b. $28,500.
    c. $38,500.
    d. $41,500.

Solution: The correct answer is **c**. The adjusted balance is found by taking the balance per bank statement ($40,000), adding the deposits in transit ($5,000), and subtracting the outstanding checks ($6,500). The other choices are wrong.

2. On a bank reconciliation, the following items should appear as adjustments to the bank balance:

    a. Deposits in transit
    b. Outstanding checks
    c. Neither a nor b
    d. Both a and b

Solution: The correct answer is **d**. On a bank reconciliation, deposits in transit should be added to the bank balance and outstanding checks should be subtracted from the bank balance. The other choices are wrong.

3. TomKat Corporation estimates from past experience that 4% of credit sales become uncollectible. If the company's credit sales were $452,000 in 2006, the entry to record bad debt expense using the income statement approach would be

a. Allowance for Uncollectibles	18,080	
Bad Debt Expense		18,080
b. Credit Sales	18,080	
Bad Debt Expense		18,080
c. Bad Debt Expense	18,080	
Accounts Payable		18,080
d. Bad Debt Expense	18,080	
Allowance for Uncollectibles		18,080

Solution: The correct answer is **d**. Note that the amounts are all the same, so the dollar amount of the transaction is not an issue. Using the income statement approach, a journal entry is made debiting bad debt expense and crediting allowance for uncollectibles for an amount equal to a percentage (based on past experience) multiplied by the credit sales. Choice **a** is wrong because it has the debits and credits reversed. Choice **b** is wrong because the correct answer must have a debit to bad debt expense, not a credit. Choice **c** is wrong because accounts payable are not involved here.

4. The balance in accounts receivable of the Grant Corp. is $150,000, and the balance in the allowance for uncollectibles is a credit of $5,000. An aging of the receivables at year end indicates that $7,500 of accounts receivable will never be collected. Using the balance sheet approach, what is the year-end adjusting entry that Grant must make on December 31?

a. Bad Debt Expense	7,500	
Allowance for Uncollectibles		7,500
b. Bad Debt Expense	12,500	
Allowance for Uncollectibles		12,500
c. Allowance for Uncollectibles	7,500	
Accounts Receivable		7,500
d. Bad Debt Expense	2,500	
Allowance for Uncollectibles		2,500

Solution: The correct answer is **d**. Using the balance sheet approach to accounting for bad debts, the balance in the allowance account is made to equal an amount that reflects the accounts that the company expects not to collect, based on an aging. In this problem, the current balance in the allowance account is $5,000, and the aging calls for a balance of $7,500. Therefore, the adjusting entry needed is a debit to bad debt expense and a credit to the allowance account for $2,500. Choices **a** and **b** are the correct journal entry, but the wrong amount. Choice **c** is the wrong journal entry and the wrong amount.

CHAPTER 4

INVENTORY

LEARNING OBJECTIVES

After studying this chapter, you will understand

- the cost of goods sold model
- the periodic and perpetual inventory methods
- LIFO, FIFO, and average cost flow assumptions
- the lower of cost or market inventory valuation and
- the impact of inventory-related errors

INVENTORY IS an important topic because it is virtually the only account that has a direct impact on both the balance sheet and the income statement. Inventory is generally the most significant current asset on the balance sheet. Cost of goods sold is usually the first and one of the largest expenses on the income statement. Maintaining the proper level of inventory is an important element of running a business. Minimizing the cost of the merchandise that the company sells is also critical.

Here is where we are going in our study of **inventory**. First of all, exactly what is inventory? Inventory is simply the products that the company is in the business of selling. General Motors' inventory consists of cars and trucks. Hewlett–Packard's inventory consists of computers and printers. (Note, by the way, that GM's computers and printers would be considered Property, Plant, and Equipment. Likewise, Hewlett–Packard's cars and trucks would also be Property, Plant, and Equipment.)

Some companies make their own inventory; these are manufacturing companies. Other companies purchase their inventory from someone else; we refer to these companies as merchandising companies.

When a company buys or manufactures the products that it is in the business of selling, these items become part of the company's inventory. When these items are sold, the cost of these items is transferred out of inventory and becomes part of **cost of goods sold**. Cost of goods sold means exactly what the words indicate. This is the cost to the company of the merchandise that they just sold. When we subtract cost of goods sold from sales, we get gross profit or gross margin. Notice that gross profit is not equal to net income or profit. We have to subtract all the operating expenses from gross profit before we arrive at net income.

There are three basic issues related to inventory:

1. What costs are included in inventory? (Is it just the purchase price, or are there other costs that must be included?)
2. Which units are included in inventory? (For example, what about goods in transit? Who owns the goods while they are sitting in a truck outside of Cleveland, Ohio?)
3. What is the flow of goods into and then out of the company? For accounting purposes, does the company sell the oldest goods first or the ones that they just purchased? And what difference would that make? (In fact, it makes a huge difference, as you will see in this chapter.)

At the end of the period, the inventory is reported on the balance sheet at the **lower of cost or market**. This is a simple calculation which ensures that the inventory on the balance sheet is not overstated. (There is a simple way to make this calculation using Excel, and I will show you how easy it is.)

Because inventory affects both the income statement (cost of goods sold is the second item on the income statement) and the balance sheet (inventory is typically the largest of the current assets), students are often asked to identify the impact of various inventory errors. I'll show you how a simple mini-spreadsheet can make this task fun and easy (well, maybe just easy).

A final topic in this chapter, covered in appendix C, which you might be able to skip because some professors choose not to cover this topic, is a technique used to estimate the ending inventory without counting it. This can come in handy, for example, when you have a fire or flood loss and the entire inventory is destroyed, but you have absolutely no idea how much inventory was on hand before it was destroyed. We call this the **gross profit method**.

BASIC INVENTORY ISSUES

Inventory represents the products that a company is in the business of selling. It consists of merchandise that the company purchases that it is going to resell, or products that the company manufactures and sells. The first issue concerns the **cost** of the inventory, which is included in the inventory account that appears on the balance sheet (before the units of inventory are sold) and as a part of cost of goods sold on the income statement (after they are sold). As you will see, there are several components of inventory cost.

The second issue concerns the **units** that are included in the inventory. The main issues concern goods in transit and goods on consignment.

The third issue concerns the **flow** of inventory items into and out of the business. In most companies, each inventory item looks just like the next inventory item; thus, it is impossible to identify how much was paid for each individual unit. As it turns out, this is information that the company must have to determine ending inventory and cost of goods sold. The easiest way to make this determination is to adopt one of several flow assumptions.

In summary, we need to focus on three issues:

1. What is included in the *cost* of the inventory?
2. Which *units* are included in the inventory?
3. What is the *flow* of units into and out of the business?

Let's look at these three issues:

Inventory Cost

There is a general rule in accounting that the cost of an asset (such as merchandise inventory) includes the purchase price plus all other costs necessary to get the asset to your place of business and ready for its intended use. For merchandise inventory, some of these other costs would include freight-in, packaging, attaching price tags, and anything else you would do to the inventory before it is ready to be sold.

EXAM TIP

Remember this rule about freight because it comes up all the time on exams: **Freight-in** is an inventoriable cost (i.e., it becomes part of the cost of the inventory). When the inventory is sold, the freight-in will be part of the cost of goods sold. **Freight-out**, on the other hand—the cost of shipping merchandise to your customers—is a selling expense. It will appear on the income statement under the caption "selling, general, and administrative expenses."

Terminology Point

When a business spends money, we refer to that as an expenditure. There are three possible outcomes for an expenditure:

1. The company has *acquired an asset.*
2. The company has *incurred an expense.*
3. The company has paid a *liability.*

There are words that are used to describe these first two situations. If the business has acquired an asset, the verb we use to describe how the expenditure is recorded is **to capitalize**. Thus, when an asset is acquired, we capitalize the expenditure. We debit an asset account. If the business has incurred an expense, the verb we use is **to expense**. Thus, when an expense is incurred, we expense the expenditure. We debit an expense account. There is no special verb for the third situation. If you are paying a bill, you are reducing a liability, and we would therefore debit a liability account.

Inventory Units

This is very simple. We have to be concerned with two items: **goods in transit** and **consigned goods**.

Goods in transit represent merchandise that is on the way from the seller to the buyer. Goods in transit are typically shipped either FOB Shipping Point or FOB Destination. (FOB means free on board). Thus, when goods are shipped FOB Shipping Point, the transaction is free to the seller; therefore, the buyer pays the freight. The freight company is working for the buyer, and title passes to the buyer as soon as the goods are loaded on the truck. When goods are shipped FOB Destination, the transaction is free to the buyer; therefore, the seller pays the freight. The freight company is working for the seller, and the goods on the truck still belong to the seller. Title passes when the goods are taken off the truck and delivered to the buyer.

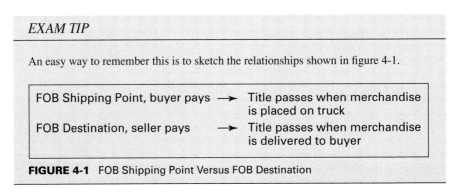

EXAM TIP

An easy way to remember this is to sketch the relationships shown in figure 4-1.

> FOB Shipping Point, buyer pays → Title passes when merchandise is placed on truck
>
> FOB Destination, seller pays → Title passes when merchandise is delivered to buyer

FIGURE 4-1 FOB Shipping Point Versus FOB Destination

Goods on consignment are easy to understand. Let's say that you have a suit that is in good shape, but you simply don't like to wear it anymore. How can you get some money for this suit? One way would be to give it to a "consignment store." The store takes your suit. (They have physical possession of the suit, but you still own it.) If they can sell it, they keep some of the proceeds from the sale and give you the rest. If they can't sell it, they simply give the suit back to you.

Merchandise inventory is sometimes given to another business on consignment; thus, it is not counted when the company takes inventory (because it is not in the company's warehouse). However, the business still owns these goods, and their cost must be included in the final inventory figure.

Inventory Flow Assumptions

Since most inventory consists of homogeneous items (they all look the same), it is virtually impossible to tell how much was paid for each individual item. However, when a company sells its inventory, it needs to know how much it cost, and it also needs to know the cost of the ending inventory—the merchandise that it bought or manufactured but did not sell.

If we could identify each individual unit of inventory and could determine how much was paid for each item, we would do that. That is called the **specific identification** method, and it can be used only in very special circumstances (e.g., a luxury yacht dealer who has only a dozen yachts in inventory and knows the cost of each one).

Every other business has to make an assumption about the flow of goods into and then out of the business. Do we sell the items in the same order that they were purchased—that would be first in, first out—or do we sell the most recently purchased items first—that would be last in, first out.

There are three typical flow assumptions used in business:

1. FIFO (first in, first out)

2. LIFO (last in, first out)

3. Average cost

These three flow assumptions are discussed in great detail later in this chapter. At this point, what you need to know is that most businesses cannot specifically identify the cost of each unit of inventory, and therefore they must make an assumption about the flow of goods into and out of the business.

PURCHASING AND SELLING INVENTORY

Companies that sell a product must have inventory. This is what they are in the business of selling. They either manufacture it themselves or they buy it from someone else. We refer to these companies as either manufacturing or merchandising companies. In this book, our focus is on merchandising companies.

When a company buys inventory, they either pay cash or they "charge it." We refer to "charging it" as **buying on account**.

There is usually some type of written evidence to document a business transaction. If a company purchases inventory for cash, then the check that the company wrote to pay for the goods becomes evidence of the transaction. If the goods are purchased on account, the sales invoice (or bill) becomes the document that is evidence of the transaction. The invoice shows a description of the items purchased, as well as the quantities and prices.

Sometimes there is something wrong with the merchandise; it may have been raining when the merchandise was delivered and everything is wet. In a case like this, generally one of two things happens: (1) The buyer returns the merchandise and we record a **purchase return**, or (2) the seller encourages the buyer to accept the merchandise, keeping the wet stock, by offering to discount the purchase price, and we record a **purchase allowance**. These two events—purchase returns and purchase allowances—are usually combined in one account called, what else?... **purchase returns and allowances**. The journal entry for recording these events is

Accounts Payable	XXX
Purchase Returns and Allowances	XXX

In an attempt to encourage customers to pay their bills on time (or maybe early), the customer may be offered a discount. Typical credit terms are 2/10, n/30, which means you get a 2% discount if you pay the bill within 10 days; otherwise, the entire bill is due in 30 days.

Key Takeaway: The credit terms **2/10, n/30** sound like a 2% discount, but it is really much more than that. Note that when a company is given credit terms of 2/10, n/30, the likelihood is that the company will either take the discount and pay on the 10th day, or skip the discount and pay on the 30th day. In other words, you get a 2% discount if you give up your money for 20 days (30 − 10). Since there are roughly eighteen 20-day periods in a year, then 2/10, n/30 translates into 18 × 2, or 36%, on an annual basis.

EXAM TIP

We tend to understand interest rates only when they are expressed on an annual basis. The annual interest rate or discount associated with the credit terms of 2/10, n/30 is 36%. That's quite a bit more than 2%.

When you get an offer in the mail to sign up for yet another credit card, and the bank tells you that the interest on any unpaid balance is only $1\frac{1}{2}\%$, that's $1\frac{1}{2}\%$ *per month*, or 18% per year. **Remember that!**

If a company takes the discount and pays their invoice within 10 days, we call that a purchase discount. One hundred percent of the accounts payable is eliminated. The net cost of the merchandise is 98% of the invoice or list price. The journal entry for recording payment for a purchase and taking the discount is

Accounts Payable	1,000	
Purchase Discount		20
Cash		980

Note that by paying only $980, the customer has paid off the entire $1,000 invoice; thus, accounts payable is reduced by $1,000.

Selling Inventory (Sales Revenue)

Selling inventory is just like buying inventory, except that you are on the other side of the counter. When you make a sale of merchandise to a customer, it is very much like purchasing inventory, only now you are the seller rather than the buyer. When you sell merchandise, you give the merchandise to the customer, and the customer either gives you cash or "charges" the transaction and promises to pay you sometime in the future. These charge sales are called **sales on account**, and the customer's promise to pay you in the future is called accounts receivable.

The basic journal entry for recording a sale is

Accounts Receivable	XXX	
Sales		XXX

Just like with purchases, there are sales discounts, as well as sales returns and allowances—they work the same way as purchase discounts and purchase returns and allowances. Here is a brief example with the appropriate journal entries.

ABC Company sells $1,000 of merchandise to XYZ Company on account; credit terms are 2/10, n/30. XYZ returns half of the merchandise and pays for the goods on the 10th day.

Accounts Receivable	1,000	
Sales		1,000
Sales Returns and Allowances	500	
Accounts Receivable		500
Cash	490	
Sales Discount	10	
Accounts Receivable		500

THE COST OF GOODS SOLD MODEL

A basic relationship in dealing with inventory is sometimes called **the cost of goods sold model**. This is how we compute cost of goods sold:

> Beginning inventory
> + Purchases
> Goods available for sale
> <Ending inventory>
> Cost of goods sold

Inserting some numbers into this model yields the following computation:

Beginning inventory	$5,000
+ Purchases	20,000
Goods available for sale	25,000
<Ending inventory>	<7,000>
Cost of goods sold	$18,000

Looking back at chapter 1, page 9, note that the first three numbers on a company's income statement are:

Sales revenue

<Cost of goods sold>

Gross profit

THE PERIODIC METHOD VERSUS THE PERPETUAL METHOD

As I indicated in the introductory section, there are two methods for accounting for inventory—the **periodic method** and the **perpetual method**. Both methods accomplish the same thing—keeping track of the purchase and sale of merchandise inventory. The periodic method relies on a physical count of the inventory on hand at the end of the period (hence the name periodic) to determine the ending inventory and cost of goods sold. The perpetual method keeps track of all the inventory coming in and going out on a daily basis (hence the name perpetual, which could also be called the daily method). You might ask, if thousand of units of inventory come in and go out on a daily basis, how in the world can we keep track of all this stuff? And the answer is simple: We use the universal product code (UPC), or bar code, a scanning device, and a computer.

You see the perpetual method at work every day, you're just not aware of it. Think about going into a Safeway store and buying a box of Wheaties. When the checkout clerk rings up your purchase, he or she scans the box of cereal. The scanning device tells the computer which item you just purchased, and the computer deletes one box of Wheaties from inventory at *cost*, and also records the sale of a box of Wheaties at the *selling price*.

Let's look at these two methods in more detail.

The Periodic Method

As inventory is acquired for resale, the company debits an account called purchases. When merchandise is sold, just the sale at the selling price is recorded. There is no accounting for the cost of the merchandise that was sold. That is done at the end of the period (remember, this is the *periodic* method). When we get to the end of the period, a physical count is made of all the inventory on hand. Then we use the cost of goods sold model to determine the cost of goods sold.

Using the numbers from our earlier example, here is how we compute cost of goods sold:

Beginning inventory	$5,000
+ Purchases	20,000
Goods available for sale	25,000
<Ending inventory (per the count)>	<7,000>
Cost of goods sold	$18,000

EXAM TIP

An easy way to make the journal entry to record cost of goods sold is to set up the entry in blank (just account names, no numbers), with a box to the right of cost of goods sold:

    Cost of goods sold   ☐▭▭☐
    Ending Inventory
      Beginning Inventory
      Purchases

Note that when you make this entry, you credit everything that makes cost of goods sold larger; you debit everything that makes cost of goods sold smaller; and the missing number, the number that makes the journal entry balance, goes into the box and represents the cost of goods sold.

To summarize accounting for inventory using the periodic method, keep the following concepts in mind:

1. All purchases of merchandise inventory are recorded in a purchases account.

2. Freight-in, packaging, and all other costs incurred to get the inventory to your place of business and ready for its intended use become part of the cost of the inventory. We refer to these costs as **inventoriable costs** or **product costs**.

3. Purchase returns and purchase allowances are also adjustments to the cost of the inventory.

4. The beginning inventory plus the net purchases equals the cost of the goods available for sale.

5. When inventory is sold, the sale is recorded at the selling price. The cost of the inventory that has been sold is not recorded until the end of the period. (Remember, this is the *periodic* method.)

6. At the end of the period, a **physical inventory** is taken. The entire inventory on hand is counted; the units are multiplied by the cost per unit, using one of the three flow assumptions, to determine the total cost of the ending inventory; and the ending inventory is then subtracted from the goods available for sale to determine the cost of goods sold.

7. A combination adjusting and closing entry is made. Everything that makes cost of goods sold larger is credited (e.g., beginning inventory, purchases, freight-in); everything that makes cost of goods sold smaller is debited (e.g., ending inventory); and the number that makes the journal entry balance is debited to cost of goods sold.

Facts:

Beginning inventory	$10,000
Purchases	$40,000
Ending inventory, per physical count	15,000
Sales, at selling price	75,000

Transaction	Periodic Method		Perpetual Method	
Buy Inventory	Purchases	40,000	Merchandise Inventory	40,000
	Accounts Payable	40,000	Accounts Payable	40,000
Sale of Merchandise Inventory	Accounts Receivable	75,000	Accounts Receivable	75,000
	Sales Revenue	75,000	Sales Revenue	75,000
			Cost of Goods Sold	35,000
			Merchandise Inventory	35,000
Year-end Adjusting/ Closing Entry	Cost of Goods Sold	35,000	None Needed	
	Ending Inventory	15,000		
	Beginning Inventory	10,000		
	Purchases	40,000		

Calculation of Cost of goods sold:

Beginning inventory	$10,000
+ Purchases	40,000
Goods available for sale	50,000
<Ending Inventory>	<15,000>
Cost of goods sold	$35,000

FIGURE 4-2   The Periodic Method Versus the Perpetual Method

The Perpetual Method

There are two major differences between the periodic method and the perpetual method. First, when using the perpetual method, purchases of inventory are recorded directly into the merchandise inventory account. *A purchases account is not used.* Second, when inventory is sold, two journal entries are made:

1. An entry is made to record the sale of merchandise at the selling price. This entry is usually a debit to accounts receivable or cash, and a credit to sales.

2. A second entry is made to record the cost of the inventory that was sold. This second entry removes the inventory that was sold from the merchandise inventory account at cost, and adds this amount to cost of goods sold. Since we make these two entries every time that inventory is sold, we do not need to make an adjusting entry at the end of the period to record cost of goods sold. Cost of goods sold is recorded every day, as sales are made.

When we look at the journal entries for the two methods side by side, the differences are obvious (see fig. 4-2 on p. 94).

Every company takes inventory at the end of the year; that's a part of generally accepted accounting principles (GAAP). Note that when you are using the periodic method, this is a blind count; you have no idea how much inventory should be there. With the perpetual method, you know exactly how much inventory should be there. If the physical count indicates a smaller amount, then you know that there must have been some theft or shrinkage.

The perpetual method is clearly superior. The additional costs to implement this approach are minimal, and you get much more useful information. Knowing how much inventory is on hand at all times helps you manage the inventory.

TAKING INVENTORY AND THE COST FLOW ASSUMPTIONS

Taking inventory actually involves two separate tasks:

1. Counting the physical units.
2. Multiplying the physical units by a cost per unit to determine the total cost.

Counting the physical units is a simple task (unless you are the one doing the counting; then it becomes a boring task). Once you determine the number of units on hand, each unit must be multiplied by the cost per unit to determine the total cost. This would seem to be a rather straightforward process, but in fact, it is not as simple as it sounds. Why not? The answer is that most companies buy inventory throughout the year at different prices. Since all the inventory items generally look exactly the same, it is impossible to tell how much was paid for a specific unit of ending inventory.

In a few isolated instances, units of inventory have a unique identification number stamped on each unit. An automobile is such an item. Every car has a unique vehicle identification number (VIN). Therefore, automobile dealerships know the cost of every car in their inventory. Unfortunately, very few products have identification numbers.

Look around where you are sitting right now. Look at the chair that you are sitting on, the table or desk next to you. These items probably do not have an identification number. Therefore, in almost all situations, the only way to determine the cost of the inventory on hand at the end of the period is to assume a flow. There are three typical flow assumptions:

1. FIFO (first in, first out): This assumes that the oldest units—the first ones purchased—are sold first.
2. LIFO (last in, first out): This assumes that the newest units—the last ones purchased—are sold first.
3. Average cost: This assumption requires that you calculate an average cost per unit.

Notes:

- The actual physical flow of units into and out of the business is irrelevant. Any business can adopt any flow assumption, regardless of the actual physical flow.
- When we speak of the "oldest" units, we are referring to an old cost; the units are probably very fresh.

Let's try a simple question to make sure that you understand what LIFO and FIFO mean. What is the actual flow of inventory in a grocery store? Let's use milk as our example. What is the actual flow of cartons of milk in a Safeway store? I certainly hope that the store where you shop for milk has a FIFO flow. (The oldest units are sold first; otherwise, we are going to have a lot of stale milk on our hands.) Even though the actual flow is FIFO, as I indicated above, Safeway can adopt any flow assumption that it wants.

Let us look at the most basic example. Assume no beginning inventory, and suppose that the business buys five inventory items: one at $1, one at $2, one at $3, one at $4, and one at $5. Furthermore, during the period, they sell three units and have two units on hand at the end of the year. Calculate the ending inventory and cost of goods sold.

EXAM TIP

When you are asked to make this calculation (this will happen quite often during class, on homework questions, and certainly on exams), calculate the goods available for sale first, then calculate the ending inventory. Once you have these two figures, simply subtract the ending inventory from the goods available for sale to determine the cost of goods sold. *Do not calculate the cost of goods sold directly.* It is much quicker to get cost of goods sold by subtracting ending inventory from goods available for sale; one reason for this is that the number of units on hand at the end of the period is usually a much smaller number than the units that were sold during the period.

In this example, the goods available for sale equal $1 + $2 + $3 + $4 + $5, or $15.

Flow assumption	Ending inventory	Cost of goods sold
FIFO	$4 + $5 = $9	$15 − $9 = $6
Average Cost	2 units @ $3 = $6	$15 − $6 = $9
LIFO	$1 + $2 = $3	$15 − $3 = $12

Note the following:

1. When prices are going up, *LIFO gives you the highest cost of goods sold* and the lowest ending inventory. This turns out to be both good and bad. Having a high cost of goods sold means that the income you report to the stockholders will be lower. That's bad. The good news is that when you report your income to the IRS on your tax return, lower income means lower taxes. This impact on taxes is one of the main reasons that companies adopt LIFO.

2. When prices are rising, using LIFO will cause the ending inventory to be significantly understated, thus understating current assets, net working capital, and the current ratio as well. When prices are rising, *FIFO gives you the lowest cost of goods sold*, hence the highest reported net income and the highest income tax expense. FIFO also has the effect of showing the highest ending inventory.

3. Some accountants suggest that FIFO permits the reporting of **phantom profits**. What they mean is that the business is reporting high profits because the cost of goods sold consists of very old (and hence lower) costs. It is a phantom profit because there is no way that the company can repeat this level of income, simply because they cannot buy merchandise inventory at those old (and very low) prices anymore.

4. If a business has been using LIFO for some time, the ending inventory consists of very old units (old prices, that is). What would happen if they were forced to sell all of these units at the old prices? (Remember, the physical units aren't old; it's just the cost in dollars that are old.) The answer to the question is that they would report a huge profit and would have to pay a huge income tax.

    We refer to these situations as a **LIFO liquidation**. Sometimes a company has no choice, they are simply forced into selling their entire old inventory. This could happen, for example, if their entire inventory was manufactured in a foreign country. If a war broke out and all manufacturing plants were closed, the business would be unable to get additional inventory, and they would wind up selling their entire existing inventory. Thus, the tax that they would have to pay on this large profit would essentially wipe out all the tax savings that they achieved by adopting LIFO.

5. From a theoretical point of view, *LIFO does the best job of matching current costs with current revenues*. Cost of goods sold using LIFO consists of the most recently acquired merchandise; thus, the current costs are matched with the current revenue.

6. The flow assumption does not have to match the actual physical flow of merchandise. A business may have an actual FIFO flow of merchandise and elect to report using a LIFO flow assumption. By the way, can you think of a real-life situation where the physical flow is LIFO? You will probably have to think about that one for a minute or two.

   I'll give you one example: building materials like bricks at a Home Depot store. A truck comes to the store and dumps a load of bricks in a pile. When the next delivery truck comes, it dumps more bricks on top of the ones that were already there. Now, you come along to buy a few bricks; which ones will you buy—the new ones or the old ones? Well, the old ones are buried deep under the pile, so you will buy some new ones, which are on the top of the pile. The physical flow is LIFO.

7. What about LIFO and FIFO using the periodic and perpetual methods? If you are using FIFO, will you get the same results for ending inventory and cost of goods sold using the periodic and perpetual methods? And, if you are using LIFO, will you get the same results using the periodic and perpetual methods?

   Here are the answers: When you are using *FIFO*, the first unit in is the first unit out, regardless of when you make the calculation—at the end of the day or the end of the period. Thus, *you get the same results using the periodic and perpetual methods*. However, when you are using *LIFO, the results you get for cost of goods sold and ending inventory will be different*. If you are buying inventory throughout the year, the last unit in, if you make the calculation daily, is not the same as the last unit in if you make the calculation at the end of the year.

DEMONSTRATION PROBLEM 1 *Inventory Flow Assumptions*

On January 1, 2007, Hillcrest Inc. had the following in their inventory:

200 units @ $10
300 units @ $12

During the year, they made the following purchases:

February 1	2,000 units @ $14
April 1	500 units @ $15
June 1	800 units @ $16

Hillcrest Inc. uses the periodic inventory method. On December 31, 2007, a physical count of the inventory indicated that there were 300 units on hand.

Required: Calculate the ending inventory on December 31, 2007, and cost of goods for the year 2007 using LIFO, FIFO, and average cost. Also, prepare the year-end adjusting/closing entry for Hillcrest Inc.

Solution: The first thing you need to do is calculate the beginning inventory and the purchases, which will tell you the goods available for sale, which is the sum of those two numbers. When you calculate the cost of goods sold, do it the easy way. First, calculate the ending inventory. That is usually an easy computation because there are usually very few units on hand, compared to the number of units sold during the period.

The beginning inventory is	200 units @ $10 =	$2,000
	300 units @ $12 =	3,600
Beginning inventory =		5,600
The purchases are	2,000 units @ $14 =	28,000
	500 units @ $15 =	7,500
	800 units @ $16 =	12,800
Purchases =		48,300
Goods available for sale are	Beginning inventory	5,600
	+ Purchases	48,300
	Goods available for sale	53,900

Now calculate the ending inventory using each of the three flow assumptions. The cost of goods sold then is the goods available for sale (which I calculated above) less the ending inventory, which I am about to do.

With FIFO, the first units in are the first units out. Therefore, the ending inventory will consist of the most recently acquired units. In this problem, the ending inventory using FIFO is 300 units at the price of the last purchase, which was at $16 per unit. So my FIFO ending inventory is 300 × $16 = $4,800. Cost of goods sold is a snap—it's $53,900 less 4,800, or $49,100.

With LIFO, the opposite is true. LIFO means last in, first out; thus, the ending inventory is made up of the oldest units. In this problem, the ending inventory using LIFO is simply 200 units @ $10 = $2,000 + 100 units @ $12, or $1,200, for a total of $3,200. Cost of goods sold is easy: $53,900 − $3,200 = $50,700.

Average cost requires computing an average cost, so all we do is take the goods available for sale and divide by the total number of units. In this problem, the average cost per unit is $53,900 ÷ 3,800 units, or $14.18/unit. The ending inventory is 30 units × $14.18, or $4,254, and cost of goods sold is once again $53,900 less the ending inventory of $4,254, or $49,646.

Before you turn your exam paper in, check to see if your answers make sense and are "in the ballpark." With all the flow assumptions, the average cost should be in between the other two numbers. And it is: $49,646 is between $49,100 and $50,700. In addition, I know that during periods of rising prices, LIFO produces the highest cost of goods sold and the lowest gross profit. That's why companies use LIFO to reduce income and thus reduce income taxes. Is that the case here, did LIFO produce the highest cost of goods sold? Yes, $50,700 is the highest of the results.

This problem appears on many mid-term and final exams. It is really very easy—practice a few times, check your calculations to make sure you are in the ballpark, and you should be able to get full credit on this problem.

DEMONSTRATION PROBLEM 2 *Inventory: LIFO Versus FIFO Perpetual and Periodic Methods*

The following information is available regarding Hillcrest Incorporation's inventory for May 2006:

May 1	Beginning Balance	500 units	@	$10
May 10	Sold	100 units	@	$25
May 12	Purchased	2,000 units	@	$12
May 15	Sold	500 units	@	$28
May 20	Purchased	1,000 units	@	$15
May 25	Sold	1,400 units	@	$30

Required: Compute ending inventory and cost of goods sold using FIFO periodic and perpetual methods and LIFO periodic and perpetual methods.

Solution: Begin with the FIFO periodic method. Calculate the ending inventory first (there are usually much fewer units in ending inventory than cost of goods sold, and thus there are fewer calculations and fewer chances to make a mistake.

Compute the units first. The company had a beginning balance of 500 units. They purchased 3,000 units and sold 2,000 units; thus, the ending inventory consists of 500 + 3,000 − 2,000 = 1,500 units.

Using FIFO, the ending inventory is made up of the most recently acquired units, or

$$
\begin{array}{ll}
1,000 \text{ units } @ \ \$15 = \$15,000 \\
\underline{+ \ 500 \text{ units } @ \ \$12 = \ \ \ \underline{6,000}} \\
\text{Total} \qquad\qquad\qquad \$21,000
\end{array}
$$

Next, calculate cost of goods sold. There are two ways to calculate cost of goods sold. It will usually be a lot easier to simply take the cost of goods available for sale (the beginning inventory plus the purchases) and subtract the ending inventory, rather than computing the cost of all the units sold (in this problem, that would have been the sale of 100 units plus the sale of 500 units plus the sale of 1,400 units).

In this problem, the cost of the goods available for sale is

$$
\begin{array}{ll}
500 \text{ units} & @ \ \$10 = \ \ \$5,000 \\
+ \ 2,000 \text{ units} & @ \ \$12 = \ \ 24,000 \\
\underline{+ \ 1,000 \text{ units}} & @ \ \$15 = \ \ \underline{15,000} \\
\text{Goods available for sale} & \$44,000
\end{array}
$$

Therefore, the cost of goods sold is simply

Goods available for sale	$44,000
<Less ending inventory>	<21,000>
Cost of goods sold	$23,000

Now use the FIFO perpetual method. That's easy; the answer is the same. Using FIFO, the first items in are the first items out. It doesn't matter when you make that determination— every day, at the end of the month, or at the end of the year. The first item in is going to be the same whenever you make the calculation. Thus, we have the results for both the FIFO periodic and perpetual methods.

Now for LIFO. Begin with the periodic method, using the same approach as above. The ending inventory is made up of

500 units	@ $10	=	$5,000
+1,000 units	@ $12	=	12,000
Ending inventory		=	$17,000
Cost of goods sold:			
Goods available for sale			$44,000 (same number as above)
<Less ending inventory>			<17,000>
Cost of goods sold		=	$27,000

For the LIFO perpetual method, we have to make a schedule (or listing) of each purchase and sale. The key here is to be very careful.

Beginning inventory 500 @ $10

Sold 100 units; therefore, the remaining inventory consists of

400 units @ $10

Purchased 2,000 units; therefore, the inventory consists of

400 units @ $10
+ 2,000 units @ $12

Sold 500 units; therefore, the remaining inventory consists of

400 units @ $10
+ 1,500 @ $12

Purchased 1,000 units; therefore, the inventory consists of

400 units @ $10
+ 1,500 units @ $12
+ 1,000 units @ $15

Sold 1,400 units; therefore, the remaining inventory consists of

400 units @ $10	=	$4,000
+ 1,100 units @ $12	=	13,200
Ending inventory	=	$17,200

Cost of goods sold, therefore, is

$$
\begin{array}{lll}
\text{Goods available for sale} & = & \$44,000 \text{ (same as above)} \\
\underline{<\text{Ending inventory}>} & = & \underline{<17,200>} \\
\text{Cost of goods sold} & = & \$26,800
\end{array}
$$

Problem-Solving Takeaway:

- The FIFO periodic method and the FIFO perpetual method yield the same results for ending inventory and cost of goods sold. The LIFO periodic method and the LIFO perpetual method will most likely produce different results for ending inventory and cost of goods sold.
- When making perpetual computations, be very careful: lots of calculations usually are involved. ■

LOWER OF COST OR MARKET (LCM)

For our purposes, the lower of cost or market (LCM) principle involves a very simple computation. You take the cost of each inventory item, the market value (defined as the replacement cost) of each item, and you value the item on the balance sheet at the *lower* of these two numbers. If the total value of the inventory using LCM is less than the total cost, the inventory is written down to the LCM number using the following journal entry:

$$
\begin{array}{lll}
\text{Cost of Goods Sold} & \text{XXX} & \\
\quad \text{Inventory} & & \text{XXX}
\end{array}
$$

Note: In the real world, the computation of LCM is a little more complex—the number that is used for "market" has upper and lower limits. (The upper limit, or "ceiling," is **net realizable value**, which is calculated by taking the selling price and subtracting the cost to complete and dispose. The lower limit, or "floor," is **the net realizable value less a normal profit.**) Thus, there are three possible market values: replacement cost, net realizable value, and net realizable value less a normal profit. The market value that we use to compare to the cost is referred to as the designated market value. The designated market value number, which is the middle value of the three market value numbers, is compared against the cost. We then simply select the lower of cost or market.

EXAM TIP

Excel is very useful in making these calculations. If you have three numbers and you want to find the middle value, you can use the Median function in Excel. Note that with only three numbers, the median is the middle value. If you take Intermediate Accounting, you will study this computation.

DEMONSTRATION PROBLEM 3 *Inventory—Lower of Cost or Market*

The following information concerns Geraldine Inc.'s ending inventory on 12/31/07:

Item	Qty	Cost	Replacement cost	Selling price	Cost to complete & dispose	Normal profit
A	36	$20	$25	$40	$5	$3
B	30	22	18	38	6	2
C	35	33	32	39	5	3
D	34	24	36	41	7	4
E	40	25	33	40	5	3
F	50	26	30	44	8	4

Required: Prepare the required computations to disclose the inventory at the lower of cost or market.

Solution: The only thing you need to know to solve this problem is that market is defined as the replacement cost and that the upper limit is the net realizable value (selling price less cost to complete and dispose), and that the lower limit is net realizable value less a normal profit. The designated market value (the number you will compare to cost to find the lower of cost or market) is simply the middle value of these three values:

1. Replacement cost
2. The upper limit
3. The lower limit

Here are the computations for this problem:

Item	Qty	Cost	Replacement cost	Net realizable value	NRV— normal profit	Designated market	LCM	Total
A	36	$20	$25	$35	$32	$32	$20	$720
B	30	22	18	32	30	30	22	660
C	35	33	32	34	31	32	32	1,120
D	34	24	36	34	30	34	24	816
E	40	25	33	35	32	33	25	1,000
F	50	26	30	36	32	32	26	1,300
Total Inventory at the Lower of Cost or Market								$5,616

Key Takeaway:

1. When making lower of cost or market calculations, you must know the definition of market value, as well as the methods for calculating the upper and lower limits.

   Market is defined as replacement cost.

   The upper limit is net realizable value, defined as selling price less cost to complete and dispose.

   The lower limit is net realizable value less normal profit.

   The designated market value is the middle value of the three market measures.

2. If you were doing this problem in Excel, you can have the computer select the designated market by having it find the median of the three market measures (in the case where there are only three numbers, the median is, by definition, the middle value).

IMPACT OF INVENTORY ERRORS

Since inventory is an account that directly affects both the income statement (cost of goods sold is the second line on the income statement) and the balance sheet (ending inventory is usually the largest current asset on the balance sheet), accounting professors like to ask exam questions to see if you can determine what the impact would be for various errors in accounting for inventory.

An easy technique for solving this type of question is to use the following diagram:

	1	2		1	2		1	2
Beginning inventory			Sales					
+ Purchases			<CGS>					
Goods available			Gross Profit					
<End Inventory>								
Cost of goods sold (CGS)			Net income			Retained		
						Earnings		

You have seen all these relationships before. On the left is the cost of goods sold model. In the middle are selected items from the income statement, and then retained earnings. Our job is to determine what the impact of a particular error would be on these various numbers. (The 1 and 2 represent periods of time.) All we have to do is to put a + or a − next to the appropriate item, follow the computations, and discover the impact of a particular error on all of these variables.

Let's take a simple error. When taking inventory on December 31, the workers forgot to count Warehouse No. 20, thus the ending inventory is understated. Let's see how the other variables are affected. We will do this by putting a + or a − next to the appropriate item.

	1	2		1	2		1	2
Beginning inventory		−	Sales					
+ Purchases			<CGS>	+	−			
Goods available		−	Gross Profit	−	+			
<End inventory>	−							
Cost of goods sold (CGS)	+	−	Net income	−/+		Retained Earnings	−	OK

Look at the pluses and minuses. Since the ending inventory wasn't counted completely, it is understated at the end of year 1; hence, the cost of goods sold is overstated at the end of year 1. (If the item is not in the ending inventory, the cost of goods sold model assumes that it was sold. Remember, at the end of a period, either you still have it or you sold it). Since cost of goods sold is overstated in year 1, gross profit is understated and net income is also understated.

Since net income goes to the owners (it increases the retained earnings account), retained earnings is also understated at the end of year 1.

The end of year 1 is the beginning of year 2. Since the ending inventory in year 1 was understated, the beginning inventory in year 2 is also understated. This causes goods available for sale in year 2 to be understated and hence cost of goods sold is also understated. If cost of goods sold is too low, then gross profit in year 2 will be overstated, and net income also will be overstated. How about the retained earnings balance at the end of year 2? Retained earnings is a running total of all the income of the firm. If the net income in one year is too small, and the next year the net income is too large by the same amount, then, after 2 years, the balance in the retained earnings account will be just right. Accountants refer to this situation as a **counterbalancing error**.

Let's try one more:

Assume that the ending inventory was counted properly, but that the purchases were understated in year 1. Let's fill in the pluses and minuses and see the impact of this error.

	1	2		1	2		1	2
Beginning inventory		OK	Sales		OK			
+ Purchases	−		<CGS>	−	OK			
Goods available	−	OK	Gross Profit	+				
<End inventory>	OK							
Cost of goods sold (CGS)	−	OK	Net income	+	OK	Retained Earnings	+	+

The error only affected year 1. All the numbers are correct in year 2. However, since retained earnings is a running total of all the income that the company has earned, retained earnings is overstated at the end of year 1, and it is still overstated at the end of year 2.

DEMONSTRATION PROBLEM 4   *Impact of Inventory Errors*

The following transactions may have been recorded erroneously:

1. Goods costing $20,000 were purchased and shipped FOB Shipping Point and were in transit on 12/31/07. These goods were not included in the year-end inventory.

2. Goods costing $50,000 were out on consignment on 12/31/07 and were not included in the year-end inventory.

3. Goods costing $10,000, which were sold for $25,000 FOB Shipping Point were included in 2007 sales. At the end of the day on 12/31/07, the goods were still on the loading dock (and not included in the physical count of the year-end inventory) waiting to be picked up by the local UPS truck.

4. Goods purchased for $30,000 were shipped FOB Destination. The invoice was received on December 31, but the merchandise was not included in inventory because it was not received until January 4, 2008.

5. When taking inventory on 12/31/07, Warehouse No. 7 was counted twice.

Required: For each transaction above, indicate the impact of each item on the following variables:

No.	Purchases	End inventory	CGS	Gross profit	Net income	R/E (07)	R/E (08)
1	OK	Understated	Over	Understated	Understated	Under	OK
2	OK	Understated	Over	Understated	Understated	Under	OK
3	OK	Understated	Over	Understated	Understated	Under	OK
4	OK	Understated	Over	Understated	Understated	Under	OK
5	OK	Overstated	Under	Overstated	Overstated	Over	OK

Problem-Solving Takeaway: When trying to determine the impact of an inventory error, use the simple worksheet in figure 4-3 with pluses and minuses. Once you fill in the appropriate plus or minus next to the amounts that are erroneously stated, you should be able to see the impact on the other variables.

```
Beginning inventory         Sales
+ Purchases                 <Cost of goods sold>
Goods available for sale    Gross profit
<Ending inventory>
Cost of goods sold          = Net income  ⟶  Retained earnings
```

FIGURE 4-3   Computing the impact of an inventory error   ■

REVIEW QUESTIONS

1. *What is the major difference between the periodic method and the perpetual method?*

The major difference is that when using the perpetual method, the cost of all merchandise inventory purchased, as well as merchandise inventory sold, is recorded on a daily basis. With the periodic method, the cost of inventory purchases is recorded every day that there is a purchase, but the cost of inventory sold is only recorded at the end of the period (that's why we call it the periodic method). Thus, with the perpetual method, the merchandise inventory account is always current, and the balance in the account is equal to the cost of the inventory on hand. With the periodic method, the inventory account does not reflect the cost of the inventory on hand until a year-end adjusting entry is made.

2. *If LIFO saves the company money on income taxes, why do more companies use FIFO?*

Some companies would rather report higher earning to the stockholders than save money on income taxes. Also, some companies operate in industries where prices are going down. Companies in these industries elect FIFO for the same reason that companies in industries where the prices are rising elect LIFO—to reduce taxes.

3. *Why is it necessary to take inventory at the end of the year?*

First, if you are using the periodic method, you must take inventory to be able to determine the cost of goods sold. This is done by counting the ending inventory and subtracting the cost of the ending inventory from the goods available for sale (beginning inventory plus purchases). Second, if the company is using the perpetual method, it is still a good idea to count the ending inventory and compare the cost of that inventory with the perpetual inventory records. If the count indicates a lower amount, then there must be some theft or "shrinkage" occurring, which should be investigated. (An unexplained decrease in inventory is referred to as shrinkage.)

4. *What is the impact of overstating or understating the ending inventory?*

The goods available for sale (beginning inventory plus purchases) can only go to one of two places—either you sold the merchandise or you still have it. If the ending inventory is overstated, then cost of goods sold must be understated, and therefore net income is overstated. If the ending inventory is understated, then cost of goods sold must be overstated, and net income is understated.

Note that retained earnings is affected by these errors, but the errors are counterbalancing. If the error causes income to be overstated in year 1, then income will be understated in year 2. Retained earnings will also be overstated in year 1. However, because net income is understated in year 2 (balancing out the overstatement of net income in year 1), the ending balance in retained earnings at the end of the second year is correct.

5. *What is the LIFO reserve?*

The LIFO reserve is simply the difference between the value of the inventory using LIFO and the value of the inventory if the company had been using FIFO or average cost.

6. *What is inventory shrinkage and how do we measure it?*

Inventory shrinkage is the difference between what the company's perpetual inventory records show as the cost of the ending inventory, and the cost of that inventory as determined by the physical count. There may be several causes of shrinkage; theft is the most common reason. Another is that inventory in a liquid state, such as beer or wine, might evaporate. Note that you can only measure shrinkage if you are using the perpetual method. If you are using the periodic method, when you take the physical count and determine the cost of the ending inventory, you have no number to compare it to, and thus you are unable to measure shrinkage.

7. *When prices are rising, which company will report the higher net income—the one using LIFO or the one using FIFO? And which company will report the higher current ratio?*

When prices are rising, the LIFO method matches the most recent costs to the revenue, and thus will report the highest cost of goods sold and the lowest net income. (That's why companies in industries where prices are rising like LIFO—it reduces their reported net income and hence their federal income tax.) Using FIFO would match the oldest costs against current revenues, and therefore the entity would report a higher net income. The current ratio, as well as total current assets and net working capital (current assets less current liabilities), will all be higher using FIFO. With FIFO, the oldest costs go on the income statement, and the most recent costs (which are the most expensive) will appear on the balance sheet as ending inventory.

8. *What is inventory turnover and how do we measure it?*

Inventory turnover reflects how often during the period all the inventory came in and went out. The higher the number, the better. Of course, companies in different industries will have very different turnovers. The turnover at a store selling groceries will be much larger that the turnover at a business selling very expensive jewelry or custom yachts. We calculate inventory turnover by dividing the cost of goods sold by the average inventory. For example, if cost of goods sold was $100,000 and the average inventory is 5,000, then the turnover is 20 times ($100 \div 5 = 20$). The numerator is cost of goods sold rather than sales revenue, because the inventory is stated at cost, so we need the numerator to indicate the cost of the goods we sold rather than the selling price of the goods we sold

9. *What are the problems associated with having too much inventory on hand? What about having too little inventory on hand?*

There are costs associated with keeping inventory on hand, such as depreciation or rent expense on a warehouse to keep it in, paying insurance on the inventory, and so forth. Thus, you don't want to have too much. On the other hand, if you have too little, and you can't fill a customer's order, there is a cost associated with that problem; we call it a **stock-out cost**. This cost does not appear on the income statement, but it is a real cost. Stock-out cost refers to the lost profit due to being out-of-stock on a particular item, and thus you lose the sale and the profit on that sale. If the customer goes to another company to buy the merchandise that you don't have, and they are treated nicely, you may also lose future purchases from that customer, which may be a significant amount.

10. *What is the benefit of reporting inventory at the lower of cost or market?*

When a business reports their inventory on the basis of the lower of cost or market, they avoid the possibility of overstating the value of the inventory. If the replacement cost of an inventory item drops significantly, a company using the lower of cost or market will show that as a loss in the period when the price decreased. If they reported the inventory at cost, rather than at the lower of cost or market, the loss would wind up being reported in a later period—when the inventory is sold. You get a much better matching of revenues and expenses if you report using the lower of cost or market.

PRACTICE MULTIPLE CHOICE QUESTIONS

1. If the beginning inventory is understated,

    a. the current ratio is understated.

    b. cost of goods sold is overstated.

    c. net income is overstated.

    d. working capital is overstated.

Solution: The correct answer is **c**. Because the beginning inventory is understated, goods available for sale will be understated. If ending inventory is correct, then cost of goods sold will be understated and gross profit, as well as net income, will be overstated. Choice **a** is wrong since the ending inventory will be correct. Choice **b** is wrong since cost of goods sold will be understated. Choice **d** is wrong because the ending inventory will be correct (only the beginning inventory is wrong); therefore, working capital will be correct.

2. The ending inventory and cost of goods sold will be the same whether a perpetual or a periodic system is used under the

    a. weighted-average method.

    b. moving average method.

    c. LIFO method.

    d. FIFO method.

Solution: The correct answer is **d**. No matter when you calculate cost of goods sold and ending inventory, the first unit in will always be the first unit out; therefore, the FIFO perpetual method and the FIFO periodic method give the same results. All of the other choices are wrong because each of those methods will produce a different result, depending on when the calculation is made.

3. When prices are rising, the inventory method that gives you the highest cost of goods sold is

    a. FIFO.

    b. LIFO.

    c. average cost.

    d. MILO.

Solution: The correct answer is **b**. LIFO matches the most recent purchases with sales. If prices are rising, the most recent purchases will the most costly, and hence LIFO will produce the highest cost of goods sold. Choice **a** is wrong because it is the opposite of LIFO, and will produce the lowest cost of goods sold. Choice **c** is wrong because it will produce a cost of goods sold in between LIFO and FIFO, and thus will not be the lowest. Choice **d** is a nonsense answer.

4. The inventory system that continuously records changes in inventory (as purchases and sales occur) is the

    a. LIFO system.

    b. FIFO system.

    c. perpetual inventory system.

    d. periodic inventory system.

Solution: The correct answer is **c**. A perpetual inventory system records inventory purchases and sales continuously. Choices **a** and **b** are wrong because LIFO and FIFO can be used with either perpetual or periodic inventory systems. Choice **d** is wrong because cost of goods sold and ending inventory is only calculated at the end of the period, not continuously.

5. Meaghan Co. has the following data from October:

Beginning inventory: 2,000 units @ $4.75

Purchases: 4,000 units @ $4.40

Sales during October: 1,000 units

Determine the cost of goods sold using the FIFO method.

    a. $17,600

    b. $4,750

    c. $22,350

    d. $27,100

Solution: The correct answer is **b**. This is a question where you can take a shortcut and save time. With FIFO, cost of goods sold is made up of the oldest units. Thus, in this problem, since only 1,000 units were sold, they must have come from the beginning inventory. Therefore, cost of goods sold is simply 1,000 units at $4.75, or $4,750. The other choices are not correct.

6. Under the perpetual inventory system,

    a. the quantity of inventory on hand is determined continuously.

    b. all purchases and sales of goods are recorded directly into the inventory account as they occur.

    c. both of the above occur.

    d. neither of the above occur.

Solution: The correct answer is **c**. Under a perpetual inventory system, the quantity of inventory is adjusted daily, and all purchases and sales are recorded directly into the merchandise inventory account. Thus, both choices **a** and **b** are correct, making **c** the right answer. Choice **d** is clearly wrong.

7. When goods in transit are shipped FOB Destination,

    a. title does not pass until the buyer receives the goods from the common carrier.

    b. they are included in the inventory of the buyer.

    c. they are included in the inventory of the shipping company.

    d. title passes to the buyer when the seller delivers the goods to the common carrier.

Solution: The correct answer is **a**. When goods are shipped FOB Destination, the seller is paying for freight. Therefore, all the time that they are in transit, they belong to the seller. Title passes when the goods are delivered to the buyer, which is choice **a**. Choices **b** and **d** are clearly wrong. Choice **b** is wrong because the goods are included in the inventory of the seller, not the buyer. Choice **c** makes no sense and choice **d** is wrong because title passes to the buyer when they are received from the shipping company.

8. In a period of rising prices, the inventory method that produces the lowest ending inventory is the

    a. average cost method.

    b. FIFO perpetual method.

    c. LIFO periodic method.

    d. LIFO perpetual method.

Solution: The correct answer is **c**. Under LIFO, the last goods in are the first goods out; therefore, the ending inventory is made up of the oldest, and hence least costly goods, since prices are rising. If you want the absolutely lowest ending inventory, you want to have the ending inventory consist of the oldest units; therefore, you want to use the LIFO periodic method since that will guarantee that the ending inventory is made up of the oldest units. The other choices are simply not the correct answer.

9. When making a lower of cost or market calculation, the lower limit (the floor) value is defined as the selling price less

    a. the normal profit margin.

    b. the estimated cost of completion and disposal.

    c. the estimated cost of completion and disposal and a normal profit margin.

    d. the net realizable value.

Solution: The correct answer is **c**. This is a question that tests a definition. You simply must know how to calculate the upper and lower limits for the purpose of making the lower of cost or market calculation. The lower limit is net realizable value (which is selling price less costs to complete and dispose) less a normal profit. That is choice **c**. The other choices are wrong.

10. The Cell Phone Co. uses the periodic inventory system. The following data are available for April:

Beginning inventory: 2,000 units @ $4.00

Purchases: 4,000 units @ $4.40

Goods available for sale: $25,600

Sales: 1,000 units

Ending inventory: $21,600

Cost of goods sold: $4,000

Based on your knowledge of the periodic inventory system, what cost flow assumption has the Cell Phone Co. adopted?

   a. LIFO

   b. FIFO

   c. Specific identification

   d. None of the above

Solution: There is no magic involved in answering this type of question. You simply have to try each method. However, since the numbers are quite small, you should be able to make the calculation very quickly. Sales were 1,000 units, and if FIFO is used, these 1,000 units must have come from the beginning inventory; therefore, cost of goods sold is simply 1,000 × $4.00, or $4,000. That's it. Choice **b** is the answer. The company uses FIFO. The other choices are wrong.

CHAPTER *5*

NONCURRENT ASSETS AND DEPRECIATION

LEARNING OBJECTIVES

After studying this chapter, you will understand

- the three categories of marketable securities
- accounting for property, plant, and equipment
- how to calculate depreciation expense
- accounting for intangible assets, and
- how to assess and measure impairments in value

HERE IS where we are going in our study of marketable securities; Property, Plant, and Equipment; and intangible assets.

The FASB (Financial Accounting Standards Board) recently changed the accounting procedures for marketable securities—the first topic that we will cover in this chapter. The board divided marketable securities into three categories: **held to maturity**, **trading**, and **available for sale**.

The held-to-maturity category consists of bonds. Bonds, of course, have a maturity value.

Trading and available-for-sale securities consist of equity securities—the common stock of other corporations. Trading securities are held as an alternative to cash. It is assumed that the company will actively trade these securities. They are considered a part of the company's current assets and are listed on the balance sheet at current market value.

Available-for-sale securities are assumed to be held for the long-term instead of being actively traded. They are listed on the balance sheet as part of long-term investments at current market value. We will go over the relevant journal entries for all marketable securities.

A firm cannot conduct business without some form of plant assets. In this chapter, we will also cover accounting for property, plant, and equipment, and intangible assets.

Property, plant, and equipment includes just what you would expect: land, buildings, equipment, vehicles, computers, and so forth.

Depreciation is the next topic in this chapter. Depreciation is simply the *allocation* of the cost of the asset over its useful life; it is not an attempt to measure loss in value.

This might be the perfect place to introduce a few terms. **Amortization** is the gradual writing off of an amount. In accounting, we amortize such items as intangible assets, plant assets, and bond discounts and premiums, to name a few. **Depreciation** is a specific type of amortization; it is used to amortize plant assets. **Depletion** represents the amortization of a wasting asset, such as an oil field or a coal mine.

Property, Plant, and Equipment assets, other than land, are assumed to depreciate. In addition to recording depreciation of plant assets, sometimes these assets decline in value due to the introduction of new technology or other market forces. In these cases, we record an **impairment** of value. An impairment is recognition that the carrying value of an asset may not be fully recoverable.

Accounting for intangible assets is the final topic in this chapter. We will review the three different types of intangibles: limited-life intangibles, unlimited-life intangibles, and goodwill.

There are two special topics related to plant assets: capitalization of interest and nonmonetary exchanges. Capitalization of interest refers to classifying as an asset some of the cost of borrowed money when constructing an asset for use by the company. A second topic—nonmonetary exchanges—involves acquiring a new asset and exchanging an old asset as part or all of the payment. The rules regarding nonmonetary exchanges have been changed quite recently. We will cover the new rules.

These two topics—capitalization of interest and nonmonetary exchanges— are both advanced topics and are not necessarily covered in every introductory financial accounting course. Therefore, these two topics are covered in appendix D as optional reading.

NONCURRENT ASSETS

On a typical balance sheet, following the current assets, there are three sections of noncurrent assets:

1. Long-term investments
2. Property, plant, and equipment
3. Intangible assets

There is a good deal of similarity in accounting for the assets that are included in these three sections, so all three will be discussed in this chapter.

LONG-TERM INVESTMENTS

Let us begin with long-term investments. Several different assets are reported in this category:

- Long-term investments in debt and equity securities
- Cash surrender value of a life insurance policy
- Land held for future use
- Bond sinking fund

The most interesting assets in this category (and also the most revolutionary or controversial) are long-term investments in debt and equity securities. These assets include shares of common stock and bonds of another corporation. The accounting rule that governs the accounting for these assets is FASB Standard 115, "Accounting for Certain Investments in Debt and Equity Securities." This accounting standard represents a revolutionary standard because it was the first time that a significant asset was required to be reported at *fair market value* instead of historical cost (sometimes referred to as original cost). In FAS (Financial Accounting Standard) 115, the FASB created three categories of securities:

1. Held to maturity
2. Trading
3. Available for sale

Held-to-maturity securities consist of corporate bonds, which are securities that have a maturity date. These securities are shown on the balance sheet at amortized cost (original cost plus or minus any unamortized premium or discount). A bond is essentially a loan. For example, the bondholder gives the company issuing the bond approximately $1,000, and the company gives the bondholder a bond that consists of a promise to pay back $1,000 on the maturity date and a promise to pay a stated rate of interest each year. If the stated rate of interest on the bond is greater than the market rate of interest, the bond will sell for a premium, that is, more than $1,000. If the stated rate of interest is less than the market rate, the bond will sell at a discount, that is, less than $1,000. Accounting for bonds is covered in detail in chapter 6. Gains or losses on the sale of held-to-maturity securities are shown on the income statement in the period that the securities are sold.

Trading securities consist of shares of common stock of other corporations, which the company owns and plans to actively trade. While held-to-maturity securities and available-for-sale securities are listed in the long-term investments section of the balance sheet, trading securities are listed in the current asset section of the balance sheet at their current market value. Unrealized gains and losses (increases or decreases in the market value of securities that are held and have not been sold) are included in net income. (Showing a gain that has not been realized as part of net income is a revolutionary concept.)

Assume that the company buys 1000 shares of XYZ Corp. for $10,000, and that on December 31, the current market value is $12,000. These securities would be listed on the balance sheet at $12,000. The difference between the $10,000 cost and the $12,000 market value is referred to as an **unrealized gain**. An unrealized gain occurs when you buy an asset; it increases in value, but since you still own it, you have not realized the gain. It is an unrealized gain. This gain is included in the calculation of net income even though the company still owns the stock. When the stock is eventually sold, a gain or loss is computed by comparing the selling price with the most recent market value listed on the balance sheet. This would be referred to as a **realized gain**.

Available-for-sale securities are just like trading securities, except that available-for-sale securities are shares of stock the company plans to hold rather than actively trade. These shares are also listed on the balance sheet at fair market value. However, unrealized gains and losses on these securities are *not* included in net income, but are reported as "other comprehensive income," which is a part of owners' equity.

Let us look at a simple example (refer to fig. 5-1). We will use the same numbers for both trading and available-for-sale securities. Note the similarities (the securities are shown on the balance sheet at current market value) and the differences (the treatment of unrealized gains or losses). For **trading securities**, unrealized gains and losses are reported on the income statement. For **available-for-sale securities**, unrealized gains and losses are included in other comprehensive income that is a part of owners' equity and is shown on the balance sheet.

Key Takeaways: The shares of stock in this example were purchased for $10,000 and eventually sold for $25,000, so there is a total profit of $15,000. When classified as trading securities, the $15,000 profit is divided into three pieces and appears on the income statement in all 3 years—$2,000 in year 1, $3,000 in year 2, and $10,000 in year 3. In other words, as the shares of stock increase in value, the gain is reported on the income statement in the year that the increase in value takes place. When the stock is classified as available-for-sale securities, the $15,000 gain is all reported on the income statement in the year in which the shares were sold, which is year 3. Regardless of how the shares are classified, the balance sheet treatment is exactly the same. The shares are shown at their market value.

PROPERTY, PLANT, AND EQUIPMENT

The next section on the balance sheet is **property, plant, and equipment**. Assets shown in this section include

- land,
- buildings,
- machinery,
- computers, and
- vehicles.

These assets are listed on the balance sheet at acquisition cost—sometimes referred to as historical or original cost. The acquisition cost includes all the expenditures made to acquire the asset and get it ready for its intended use. (This is a basic rule of accounting and applies to all asset acquisitions.) Thus, when a large piece of

Transaction	Trading Securities			Available-for-Sale Securities		
		Balance Sheet	Income Statement		Balance Sheet	Income Statement
Bought 100 shares of XYZ common stock	Trading Securities	$10,000	0	Available-for-Sale Securities	$10,000	0
At the end of year 1, market value = $12,000	Trading Securities	$12,000	$2,000 (unrealized gain)	Available-for-Sale Securities Accumulated Other Comprehensive Income	$12,000 $2,000	0
At the end of year 2, market value = $15,000	Trading Securities	$15,000	$3,000	Available-for-Sale Securities Accumulated Other Comprehensive Income	$15,000 $5,000	0
At the end of year 3 12/31/XX, all shares sold for $25,000			$10,000 (realized gain)			$15,000 (realized gain)

FIGURE 5-1 Comparison of Accounting for Trading and Available-for-Sale Securities.

equipment is purchased, the acquisition cost includes the purchase price, freight to get it to the company's place of business, and installation. Even trial runs to calibrate the equipment are part of the acquisition cost.

For land, the acquisition cost includes the purchase price plus the costs incurred to tear down any existing structures and to get the land ready for its intended use (typically a vacant lot on which the company plans to build a building). Accountants make the assumption that land does not depreciate, however, improvements to land do. Therefore, we record land improvements separately. Land improvements would include such items as paved parking lots, exterior lighting, fences, and so forth.

Occasionally, several plant assets are acquired for a single lump sum of money. This is sometimes referred to as a **basket purchase**. The total lump sum paid is allocated to the individual assets acquired in proportion to their relative fair market values (or appraisal values).

EXAMPLE 1

Assume that the following assets, were acquired for $5 million.
These assets had the following appraisal values:

Land	$3,000,000
Building	2,000,000
Equipment	1,000,000
Total	$6,000,000

The total appraisal value of these three assets is $6 million. The $5 million lump sum price would be allocated to those assets as follows:

Land	$3,000,000/6,000,000 × 5,000,000 = $2,500,000
Building	$2,000,000/6,000,000 × 5,000,000 = $1,666,666
Equipment	$1,000,000/6,000,000 × 5,000,000 = $833,000

Appraisal values *are* objective enough to use in allocating the lump sum paid for the assets acquired in a basket purchase. ∎

Costs Subsequent to Acquisition

The items in this category represent expenditures made after a plant asset has been in service for some time. The basic rule that applies here is rather simple, although there is a degree of subjectivity involved. The rule states that if the expenditures makes the asset better than new in some way (goes faster, requires less maintenance, produces fewer defects, gets better mileage, etc.), then the expenditure should be recorded as an asset. On the other hand, if the expenditure just keeps the asset in a condition as good as new, but not better, the expenditure should be recorded as an expense.

Depreciation

Many people do not really understand the concept of depreciation. Some think that it is a measure of the loss in the market value of an asset; others view depreciation as some sort of fund that will be used to replace the asset. Neither of these concepts is correct. Furthermore, the word "depreciation" in standard English does not mean the same thing as the accountant's concept of depreciation.

In standard English, when a person says, "I just bought a new BMW, drove it home, and the car has just depreciated," they mean that the car's value has decreased. However, as accountants, our focus is on *costs* instead of values. To an accountant, depreciation is a method of allocation, not valuation. In financial accounting, depreciation refers to the allocation of the cost of an asset over its useful life in a systematic and rational manner. Allocating the cost of an asset over its life permits accountants to match the revenue generated by the use of the asset with part of the cost of the asset.

EXAM TIP

This definition is often tested. Depreciation is a process of allocation, not valuation.

Although there are a number of different ways to calculate depreciation (all of which are systematic and rational), we will focus on *four* basic methods:

1. Units of activity
2. Straight line
3. Sum of the year's digits
4. Declining balance

Depreciation is a function of four variables:

1. Cost (C)
2. Estimated salvage value (S)
3. Estimated service life (N)
4. Method

The cost less the estimated salvage value is referred to as the **depreciable base**.

Units of Activity Method   The units of activity method allocates the cost of the asset based on a measure of use or activity. The activity may be the number of units produced, the number of miles driven, or the number of hours in the air (e.g., a Boeing 747).

Assume that we purchased a truck for $55,000 which has an estimated useful life of 10 years or 100,000 miles and an estimated salvage value of $5,000.

Using the units of activity method, we will depreciate the truck based on an estimated life of 100,000 miles. The depreciation rate is

$$\frac{\text{Cost} - \text{Salvage value}}{\text{Life}} = \frac{\$55,000 - \$5,000}{100,000} = 0.50/\text{mile}$$

If we drove the truck 15,000 miles in year 1, the depreciation would be $0.50 × 15,000, or $7,500. The depreciation expense is a function of the use of the asset or its activity. The depreciation expense will be different each year depending on how many miles the truck was driven during the period.

Straight-line (SL) Method   The formula for straight-line depreciation is similar to the activity method, except that the life of the asset is expressed in terms of years. The formula for straight line depreciation is

$$\frac{\text{Cost} - \text{Salvage value}}{\text{Life (in years)}}$$

Using the numbers in our example, the depreciation expense will be

$$\frac{\$55,000 - \$5,000}{10 \text{ years}} = \$5,000 \text{ per year}$$

Note that with the straight-line method, the depreciation expense is the *same amount* each year.

These first two methods are proportional. That is, the depreciation is in direct proportion to either the use of the asset or the passage of time. The next two methods are not proportional, but rather accelerated. That is, they produce an accelerated amount of depreciation—much more depreciation in the early years of an asset's life, much less depreciation in the later years.

Sum of the Year's Digits (SYD) Method   This is one of two accelerated depreciation methods. It is simply a mathematical computation that will generate larger numbers in the early years of an asset's life and smaller numbers in the later years of an asset's life.

The sum of the year's digits calculation is simple. You multiply the depreciable base (cost−salvage value) times a fraction. The numerator begins with the life of the asset in years, and is reduced by 1 each year. The denominator is the sum of the digits in the life. A 5-year asset contains the digits 1, 2, 3, 4, and 5. A 10-year asset contains the digits 1, 2, 3, 4, 5, 6, 7, 8, 9, and 10. There is a formula for computing the denominator. The formula is $N(N + 1)/2$. For an asset with a 5-year life, the denominator is $5(6)/2 = 15$. For an asset with a 10-year life, the denominator is $10(11)/2 = 55$.

Most textbook problems have assets with either 5- or 10-year lives, so you might just remember the numbers 15 and 55, although the formula is quite easy to remember.

For the truck, the sum of the year's digits depreciation would be

$$\text{Year 1: } \$55,000 - \$5,000 \times 10/55 = \$9,090$$
$$\text{Year 2: } \$55,000 - \$5,000 \times 9/55 \ = \$8,182$$

$$\text{Year 9: } \$55,000 - \$5,000 \times 2/55 \ = \$1,818$$
$$\text{Year 10: } \$55,000 - \$5,000 \times 1/55 = \$909$$

DECLINING-BALANCE METHOD

Declining balance is the other popular accelerated depreciation method. This method also produces greater depreciation in the early years and less depreciation in the later years. The method is to multiply a stated rate (percentage) times a balance that declines each year, hence the name declining balance. This method has a few variations. The most common variant is to use a rate that is twice the straight-line rate (the straight-line rate is simply 1/life). This is referred to as double-declining balance (DDB). Another variant is to only multiply the straight-line rate by 1.5 or 150%. This is referred to as a 150% declining balance.

In making the calculations, the rate percentage is multiplied by an ever-declining balance. The balance begins with the cost of the asset. Remember that *salvage value is ignored initially*. Once the depreciation for year 1 is calculated, that number is subtracted from the cost, and the remaining number (cost less the first year's depreciation) becomes the new balance.

Let us look at the calculations for the truck:

Year 1: $55,000 \times (1/10 \times 2)$, or $20\% = \$11,000$

Year 2: $\$55,000 - \$11,000 = \$44,000 \times 20\% = \$8,800$

Year 3: $\$44,000 - \$8,800 = \$35,200 \times 20\% = \$7,040$

When using the declining balance method, the estimated salvage value is ignored *initially*; however, it comes into play as you get to the end of the asset's life. You cannot depreciate an asset below its salvage value. Thus, in the case of the truck, we would stop taking depreciation once we get to an accumulated total of $50,000.

For all the depreciation methods, the journal entry to record depreciation expense is the same.

Depreciation Expense   XXX

    Accumulated Depreciation (name of asset)   XXX

In this journal entry, all the depreciation expense for all the company's different assets will go on a single line on the income statement, thus there is no need to identify the debit to depreciation expense. However, the accumulated depreciation will be subtracted from the individual asset's cost on the balance sheet, thus the credit to accumulated depreciation must identify the asset being depreciated.

Depreciation is a very real cost, and it is subtracted on the income statement in determining net income. However, cash is not involved. Depreciation is an expense that does not "use up" cash. This is an important point to remember. When we look at the statement of cash flows in chapter 8, we will make a special adjustment for depreciation because it is a noncash expense item. Figure 5-2 summarizes the depreciation on the truck for the first 2 years using all four methods.

Method	Formula	Calculation Year 1	Calculation Year 2
Units of Activity	$\dfrac{\text{Cost} - \text{Salvage value}}{\text{Life in miles}}$	$\dfrac{\$55,000 - \$5,000}{100,000} = \$0.50/\text{mile}$	$\dfrac{\$55,000 - \$5,000}{100,000} = \$0.50/\text{mile}$
		$15,000 \times 0.50 = \$7,500$	$12,000 \times \$0.50 = \$6,000$
Straight Line	$\dfrac{\text{Cost} - \text{Salvage value}}{\text{Life (in years)}}$	$\dfrac{\$55,000 - \$5,000}{10} = \$5,000$	$\dfrac{\$55,000 - \$5,000}{10} = \$5,000$
Sum of the Year's Digits	$C - S\,n/n\,(n+1)/2$ (year 1) $C - S\,n/n\,(n+1)/2$ (year 2)	$55 - 5 \times 10/55 = \$9,091$	$55 - 5 \times 9/55 = \$8,181$
Double-Declining Balance	$\text{Cost} \times 1/\text{life} \times 2$ $\text{Cost} \times 1/\text{life} \times 2 - $ first year's depreciation	$\$55,000 \times 20\% = \$11,000$	$55,000 - 11,000 \times 20\% = \$8,800$

FIGURE 5-2 Calculating Depreciation Expense Using Four Different Methods.

Basic Data

Cost = $55,000
Estimated salvage value = $5,000
Estimated life in miles = 100,000
Estimated life in years = 10
Actual miles driven, year 1 = 15,000
Actual miles driven, year 2 = 12,000

DEPRECIATION CONVENTIONS

The calculation of depreciation is obviously an estimate. Different depreciation methods produce very different numbers for a given asset. Accordingly, it is certainly not necessary to calculate depreciation expense to the nearest penny. In fact, many companies simplify the depreciation calculation by using one of the following "depreciation conventions":

1. The half-year convention—Regardless of the date of purchase, take one half the year's depreciation in the year of acquisition and one half the year's depreciation in the year of disposition (when the asset is sold or simply "thrown away").

2. Alternatively, take a full year's depreciation in the year of acquisition and no depreciation in the year of disposition, or vice versa.

Partial Year's Depreciation   A minor computational problem arises when an asset is being depreciated using one of the accelerated methods (sum of the year's digits or double-declining balance) and the asset is acquired on a date other that January 1.

For example, assume that the asset is acquired on April 1, 2007, for $130,000; the estimated salvage value is $20,000; the estimated life is 10 years; and the company is using the sum of the year's digits depreciation. Referring to figure 5-3 below, we can see that the first year's depreciation calculated using SYD actually overlaps 2 calendar years—2007 and 2008. The second year of depreciation also spans 2 calendar years.

So, if the question calls for the depreciation expense in 2008, here is how it is calculated:

$$\text{First year of SYD depreciation} = 130 - 20 \times 10/55 = \$20,000$$

$$\text{Second year of SYD depreciation} = 130 - 20 \times 9/55 = \$18,000$$

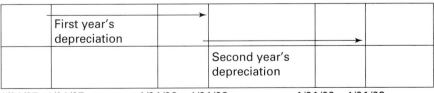

1/01/07 4/01/07   1/01/08   4/01/08   1/01/09   4/01/09

FIGURE 5-3 Partial Years' Depreciation Illustrated.

Depreciation expense for 2008:

$$\$20,000 \times 9/12 = \$15,000 \text{ (April 1–Dec. 31 = 9 months)}$$
$$+\,\$18,000 \times 3/12 = \quad 4,500 \text{ (Jan. 1–March 31 = 3 months)}$$
$$\text{Total} \qquad\qquad \$19,500$$

Disposal of a Depreciable Asset

Eventually, assets get old; newer, more efficient models are available; and the old assets are either sold or traded in on a new asset. When this happens, the key is to remember that this transaction is recorded in two steps:

1. Bring the depreciation up to date. Since the depreciation is usually recorded only once a year on December 31, the first thing we have to do is record the depreciation from January 1 to the date of sale or trade-in.

2. The second step is to record the sale or trade-in. The journal entry is going to look like one of the following two entries:

Cash		Cash	
Accumulated Depreciation	or	Accumulated Depreciation	
Loss			Old Asset
	Old Asset		Gain

The gain or loss is simply the difference between the cash received and the book value of the old asset.

EXAM TIP

Remember that a depreciable asset's book value or carrying value is contained in two accounts: *the asset account and the accumulated depreciation asset account.* When you sell the asset, both accounts must be written off.

DEMONSTRATION PROBLEM 1   *Property, Plant, and Equipment—Record various transactions*

The following transactions took place during 2007:
1. A parcel of land, a building, and a piece of equipment were purchased for $600,000. The appraisal values of the assets acquired were as follows:

Land	$400,000
Building	$300,000
Equipment	$100,000

2. A building was acquired on July 1 in exchange for 10,000 shares of $10 par value common stock. The stock had a market value of $30 per share.

3. Land was purchased for $500,000 to be used for the site of a new building. Two old buildings on the land were torn down at a cost of $50,000 (bricks from the old buildings were sold for $5,000).

4. On July 1, equipment was purchased for $120,000 (estimated salvage value is $20,000).

5. An old building that cost $300,000, was purchased January 1, 2001, and was sold for $200,000 on June 30, 2006.

Required: Prepare journal entries for all the transactions above, including year-end depreciation. The buildings are depreciated using the straight-line method, assuming an estimated life of 10 years and a 10% salvage value. The equipment is being depreciated using the sum of the year's digits method, assuming a 10-year life and a salvage value of 5% of cost.

Solution:

1. Land   300,000   (400/800 × 600,000)

   Buildings   225,000   (300/800 × 600,000)

   Equipment   75,000   (100/800 × 600,000)

      Cash $600,000

(to record a lump sum acquisition of land, buildings, and equipment, with cost allocated based on relative fair market value)

2. Building   300,000

     Common Stock   100,000

     Additional Paid in Capital   200,000

(to record the acquisition of the building by issuing common stock)

3. Land   545,000

     Cash   545,000

(to record the purchase of the land and the cost of tearing down the old building on the land as part of the cost of the land)

4. Equipment   120,000

     Cash   120,000

5. Depreciation Expense   13,500

     Accumulated Depreciation   13,500

   Cash   200,000

   Accumulated Depreciation   175,500

     Building   300,000

     Gain on Sale   75,500

(to bring depreciation on building up to date and to record the sale of the building)

6. Depreciation Expense   33,204

     Accumulated Depreciation—Building   20,250

     Accumulated Depreciation—Equipment   12,954

(to record depreciation on the assets purchased on January 1)

7. Depreciation Expense   13,500
      Accumulated Depreciation—Building   13,500
8. Depreciation Expense   5,700
      Accumulated Depreciation—Equipment   5,700

(to record depreciation of equipment purchased on July 1)
Computations:

$$225{,}000 - 22{,}500 = 202{,}500/10 = 20{,}250$$
$$75{,}000 - 3{,}750 = 71{,}250 \times 15/55 = 12{,}954$$
$$300{,}000 - 30{,}000 = 270{,}000/10 = 27{,}000/2 = 13{,}500$$
$$120{,}000 - 6{,}000 = 114{,}000/10 = 11{,}400/2 = 5{,}700$$

■

Problem-Solving Takeaway:

- Whenever a fixed asset is sold, you must bring the accumulated depreciation up to date before you record the sale of the asset.

- When several assets are acquired for a single lump sum price, the amount paid is allocated among the various assets in proportion to their *relative market values*.

INTANGIBLE ASSETS

Intangible assets are characterized by two factors:

1. They lack physical substance.
2. There is a great deal of uncertainty regarding the future benefits to be derived from these assets. If you were (or are) taking your accounting class in law school, we would be referring to these assets as "intellectual property." The typical intangible assets are as follows:
   a. Patents
   b. Copyrights
   c. Trademarks and trade names
   d. Franchises and licenses
   e. Goodwill

The basic accounting for intangibles is to debit an asset account for the cost of acquisition and then amortize the cost (typically on a straight-line basis) over the legal life or the estimated useful life, whichever is shorter.

There are three types of intangible assets:

1. Limited-life intangibles
2. Unlimited-life intangibles (other than goodwill)
3. Goodwill

Limited-life intangibles are amortized over their legal life or useful life, whichever is shorter. Unlimited-life intangibles are not amortized, but are subject to impairment (more on that later).

Patents

Patents are granted by the United States Patent and Trademark Office. The patent gives the holder an exclusive right to sell a specific product or service covered by the patent. The legal life of a patent is 20 years. The patent account usually is a very nominal amount, reflecting primarily the legal costs involved in filing documents with the U.S. Patent Office in Washington, D.C.

The basic research that was performed in developing the product or service that was patented is required to be expensed as incurred. It is entirely possible that a company spent $500 million dollars in research costs over a 2-year period to develop a product that is protected by a patent, yet their patent account may only have $10,000 to $20,000 in it.

Legal fees incurred in defending a patent (patent infringement lawsuits) are properly capitalized (added to the patent account) if there is a successful outcome. If the outcome is not favorable, the legal fees should be expensed, and whatever balance exists in the patent account should be written off.

The journal entry to amortize a patent would be:

Patent Amortization Expense	XXX	
Patent		XXX

Most companies do not use an "accumulated patent amortization account" (similar to the accumulated depreciation account); they just credit the patent account directly.

Copyrights

A copyright gives an artist, composer, and others the exclusive right to sell his or her art, music, film, and so forth. The legal life of a copyright is the life of the creator plus 70 years. Copyrights are usually amortized over their useful life, which tends to be much shorter than the legal life.

Trademarks and Trade Names

Trademarks and **trade names** are original, distinctive symbols, logos, or other items that serve to identify a company's product. Here is an interesting story about a trademark. One of my friends is the former president of the Jeans division of Levi Strauss & Co. Every now and then, a customer would mail him a blank red tab from a pair of Levis jeans, claiming that it was defective because it did not have the name Levis on it. As it turns out, the trademark is the red tab itself, not a red tab that says Levis on it. Furthermore, to protect the trademark, Levi Strauss had to sell a minimum number of jeans with a blank tab each year.

Trademarks can be renewed indefinitely and therefore they are not required to be amortized.

Franchises and Licenses

A franchise or license is granted to permit the franchisee to operate a specific business, such as a McDonald's restaurant or a Radio Shack store. Some franchises and licenses are established for a limited life and are to be amortized. Other franchises and licenses provide for an unlimited life and are not amortized.

Goodwill

Goodwill is another concept (like depreciation) where the term has several different meanings. Of course, there is "Peace on earth, goodwill to men," which has absolutely nothing to do with accounting. Then there is what we call "internally generated goodwill." This tends to reflect the results of

- many years of advertising the brand or product name,
- many years of providing outstanding customer service, or
- operating in a prime business location.

Because of these events or conditions, the company is able to earn superior profits. This internally generated goodwill is real; it does exist, but it is *not* reflected on the balance sheet.

There is another type of goodwill that is reflected on the balance sheet— "purchased goodwill." This type of goodwill arises when one company purchases another company and pays more money for the company than the fair market value of the net assets acquired.

Let us look at an example
ABC Corporation purchases XYZ for $8 million cash. The fair market values of XYZ's assets and liabilities are

- current assets at $2 million,
- noncurrent assets at $6 million, and
- current liabilities at $1 million.

The net asset value is $7,000,000 ($2,000,000 + $6,000,000 − $1,000,000). ABC paid $8 million cash to acquire all the assets (and assume XYZ's obligations), which had a net fair market value of $7 million. Question: Why would they do this? Answer: Because the XYZ Corp. has a value that is greater than the sum of its parts! There is something there that is valuable, and that allows the company to generate superior earnings.

The journal entry to record this transaction is

Current Assets	2,000,000	
Noncurrent Assets	6,000,000	
Goodwill	1,000,000	
	Current Liabilities	1,000,000
	Cash	8,000,000

The box next to the goodwill account indicates that this is the plug-in amount. Do the journal entry— fill in all the other numbers and the missing number; the number that makes the journal entry balance is the value of the goodwill.

Until recently, goodwill was amortized using the straight-line method over a period not to exceed 40 years. That rule has been changed. Goodwill is no longer amortized. It remains on the balance sheet indefinitely. However, it is subject to impairment.

IMPAIRMENT

Impairment occurs when an asset's fair market value has decreased below the asset's carrying value. Tangible fixed assets should be evaluated on an annual basis to determine if any assets have become impaired.

Recording impairment can be either a one-step or a two-step process. Figure 5-4 below indicates the method used to account for impairments.

Asset Category	Method	Tests
1. Tangible fixed assets	Two-step method	1. Recoverability test: Is expected future cash flow less than the carrying value? If yes, an impairment has occurred. 2. Fair market value test: Is the fair market value of the asset less than the carrying value? If yes, the impairment loss equals the difference between the fair market value and the carrying value of the asset.
2. Limited-life intangibles	Two-step method	Same as (1) above
3. Indefinite-life intangibles	One-step method	1. Fair market value test: Is the fair market value of the asset less than the carrying value of the asset? If yes, an impairment has occurred and the amount of the impairment loss is the difference between the fair market value and the carrying value of the asset.
4. Goodwill Note: The rule for impairment of goodwill involves two separate fair market value components.	Two-step method	Is the fair market value of the business unit less than the carrying amount of the business unit? If yes, there is impairment. Is the fair market value (or implied value) of the goodwill less than the carrying value of the goodwill? If yes, the impairment loss is the difference between the fair market value and the carrying value of the goodwill.

FIGURE 5-4 Calculating Impairment.

EXAMPLE 2

Building cost	$20,000,000
Accumulated depreciation	$8,000,000
Carrying value	$12,000,000

Expected future cash flows $15,000,000 ($15,000,000 is greater than $12,000,000; therefore, there is no impairment)

Expected future cash flows $10,500,000 ($10,500,000 is less than $12,000,000; therefore there is an impairment)

The measure of the impairment (excess of the carrying value over the fair value) is

Fair market value	$10,500,000
Carrying value	$12,000,000
Impairment loss	$1,500,000

■

DEMONSTRATION PROBLEM 2   *Intangible Assets—A Single General Ledger Account*

Browdy Inc. maintains a single general ledger account for intangible assets.

During 2007, the intangible asset account had the following transactions:

January 1	Legal costs associated with obtaining a patent $500,000
February 1	Research and development costs $200,000
March 1	Advertising costs $200,000
April 1	Additional paid-in capital—common stock $100,000 (issued 10,000 shares of $5 par common stock for $15 per share)
July 1	Prepaid rent (paid for 1 year's rent at $2,000 per month) $24,000
August 1	Improvements to land $20,000
September 1	Leased asset (signed a capital lease on a large piece of equipment. The present value of the minimum lease payments is $150,000. The bookkeeper credited cash for this transaction.)
October 1	Legal fees associated with a successful defense of a patent infringement lawsuit $250,000
December 31	Balance in the account $1,244,000

Prepare one or more adjusting entries to present these transactions in accordance with generally accepted accounting principles (GAAP).

Solution: This is a classic textbook problem. A company takes a number of related transactions and posts them all to a single general ledger account. The problem requirements typically ask for a number of adjusting entries. However, there is an easier way to approach these problems. Make one compound entry, close out the single general ledger account, and then put all the items that were in that account into their proper place. In this problem, we have a single account called intangible assets, with a debit balance of $1,244,000.

Begin your solution by making up a compound journal entry. Start the entry with a credit to intangible assets, which closes the intangible asset account. Now just find a place for all the items that were in the account, which is usually quite simple.

Patent ($500,000 + $250,000)	750,000		
Research and Development Expense	200,000		
Advertising Expense	200,000		
Prepaid Rent	24,000		
Land Improvements	20,000		
Leased Equipment	150,000		
Cash	150,000		
Additional Paid-in Capital on C/S		100,000	
Obligation Under Capital Lease		150,000	
Intangible Asset		1,244,000	(This credit closes out the balance in the intangible asset account.) ∎

ACCOUNTING FOR RESEARCH AND DEVELOPMENT

Related to the accounting for intangible assets is the problem of accounting for research and development (R&D) expenditures. Prior to the issuance of FAS 2, "Accounting for Research and Development," some companies capitalized their R&D expenditures and then amortized them over a reasonable period of time. Other companies treated these expenditures as an expense the moment that the money was spent. The fact that there were two acceptable approaches made it difficult to compare two companies' performances. The central issue in accounting for R&D concerns the uncertainty of the future benefits to be obtained from the R&D expenditures. Obviously, when a firm spends $50 million or $100 million or $500 million per year on R&D, it expects that some of these expenditures will lead to increased future revenues or a reduction in operating expenses.

The problem is that it is very difficult to predict the future revenues to be generated by today's R&D. In response to this uncertainty, the FASB concluded that all R&D should be expensed as incurred, simply because it is impossible to come up with an objective measure of the future benefits. This rule thus says, in effect, that since we don't know with certainty what the future benefits will be, we will give them a value of zero! The good aspect of the rule is that now all companies treat R&D in the same manner.

Many textbook authors are critical of FAS 2 because it ignores the economic reality of what is going on in business. Assigning a value of zero to a company's R&D program is misleading for the readers of the financial statements, especially if a new product or service has been developed.

SUMMARY OF JOURNAL ENTRIES

This is a list of the most common transactions and journal entries corresponding to the topics covered in this chapter. I would recommend that you review this list of journal entries several times until you are certain that you understand each one. The journal entry is the link between the actual business transactions that take place and the financial statements that are prepared by the entity.

One technique that I find to be very useful is to take this list of transactions and journal entries, cover the right-hand side of the page with a blank sheet of paper so you can see the description of the transaction, and then write out each journal entry. After writing out each entry, just slide the paper down a bit and check to see that you made the correct entry. Do this before your exams to test your understanding of the material.

Transaction	Journal Entry
Purchase plant assets for cash	Land
	Buildings
	Cash
Sale of plant asset	
Two steps:	
1. Bring the depreciation up to date.	Depreciation Expense
	Asset—Accumulated Depreciation
2. Write off the old asset and	Cash
the accumulated depreciation.	Asset—Accumulated Depreciation
	Loss*
	Asset
	Gain*
Record depletion	Depletion Expense
	Wasting Asset
Acquire intangible asset	Patent
	Cash
Record amortization cost on the patent	Patent Amortization Expense
	Patent

Note: Accounting for capitalization of interest and nonmonetary exchanges is covered in Appendix D

*There may be a gain or a loss.

Capitalization of interest on a self-constructed asset	Building Interest Expense
Acquire asset by issuing Common stock	Land Common Stock (at par) Additional Paid-in Capital
Nonmonetary exchange (has commercial significance)	New Asset Accumulated Depreciation—Old Asset
(You may give or receive cash; you may record a gain or a loss measured by the difference between the book value and the fair value of the old asset).	Cash* Loss* Old Asset Cash* Gain*
Nonmonetary exchange (lacks commercial significance)	New Asset Accumulated Depreciation—Old Asset Cash* Loss*
(You may give or receive cash; no gain or loss recorded.)	Old Asset Cash* Gain*

*The company may either give or receive cash. If the transaction has commercial significance, any gain is recognized. If the transaction lacks commercial significance, a gain is only recognized when cash is received. Losses are always recognized, regardless of the commercial significance of the transaction.

REVIEW QUESTIONS

1. *Why does the cost of an asset include much more than just the purchase price?*

The cost of an asset includes the purchase price plus all the other costs necessary to get the asset to the company's place of business and ready for its intended use. These other costs might include freight costs, installation, calibration, and so forth. One reason to include these items in the cost of the asset is to be able to spread these costs over the period of the asset's use instead of having them be expensed in the year that the asset was acquired (and the year that these costs were incurred).

For example, assume that the freight bill to get a piece of equipment to the company's plant is $10,000, incurred in 2005. If this item is not included in the cost of the equipment, it will appear in its entirety as an expense on the 2005 income statement. In fact, however, if the equipment has a life of 10 years, all 10 years will benefit from this expenditure. By adding the $10,000 to the cost of the equipment, the $10,000 will be reported as depreciation expense over the life of the asset, which will produce a more accurate reflection of the cost of using the asset.

2. *Why don't we record depreciation on land?*

Accountants assume that land does not depreciate. This assumption is usually an appropriate one. Buildings and equipment typically get to the point where they cannot be used. However, this rarely happens to land.

3. *What is meant by impairment and why do we record it?*

An impairment occurs when an asset's cost is determined not to be recoverable. This occurs when the carrying value of the asset is greater than the fair value of the asset. There are two separate steps or tests in evaluating an impairment. First, there is a recoverability test. We compare these future cash flows attributed to the asset with its carrying value. If the future cash flows are less than the carrying value, an impairment has occurred. The second step is to calculate the amount of the impairment. The amount of the impairment is the excess of the carrying value over the future market value of the asset. The journal entry to record an impairment is to debit impairment loss and credit accumulated depreciation.

4. *What is the rationale for expensing all research and development?*

According to FASB Standard 2, all research and development is to be expensed as incurred. There are two reasons to treat research and development this way. This first reason is due to the uncertainty surrounding any future benefits to be derived from the expenditure. We just do not know if the research will result in increased future income. Secondly, by requiring all companies to expense research and development, we gain comparability among companies; everyone does it the same way. In reality, companies do get benefits from research and development (that is why they do it in the first place). However, since we really cannot be certain about any of the future benefits, an easy solution is to consider the future benefits to be zero.

5. *What is the reason for using accelerated depreciation? Why doesn't everybody use straight line?*

Many assets provide most of their utilization early in their life. A new truck can be on the road every day and an old truck is often in the shop being repaired. Thus, we get most of the asset's benefits in the early years of its life, so the depreciation expense should reflect this by having more depreciation in the first few years and less depreciation in the last few years. Accelerated depreciation methods such as double-declining balance and sum of the year's digits yield just this pattern—more depreciation in the early years, less in the later years. Consider an asset that costs $10,000, with a 5-year life and no salvage value.

$$\text{Sum of year's digits} = \$10,000 \times 5/15 \quad \$3,333$$
$$10,000 \times 4/15 \quad \$2,666$$
$$10,000 \times 3/15 \quad \$2,000$$
$$10,000 \times 2/15 \quad \$1,333$$
$$10,000 \times 1/15 \quad \underline{\$666}$$
$$\$9,998$$

Note that 60% of the total depreciation is recorded in the first 2 years.

6. *Why doesn't a company's internally generated goodwill get reported on their balance sheet?*

GAAP states that purchased goodwill is recorded, but internally generated goodwill is not. The reason for this rule is fairly obvious. With purchased goodwill, we have an objective measure. It is the difference between the purchase price and the fair value of the assets acquired. That number is easy to calculate.

Internally generated goodwill would be very difficult to measure. We know that it exists, but we would be hard-pressed to say that the value is $50,000 or $500,000 or $5,000,000.

7. *Why do we call certain transactions "nonmonetary exchanges" when there is cash exchanged as well?*

The term "nonmonetary exchange" is really the exchange of nonmonetary assets, so what is happening is that one nonmonetary asset is being exchanged for another nonmonetary asset. For example, a truck is exchanged for another truck; a piece of land is exchanged for a building. The label "exchange of nonmonetary assets" is appropriate, even if one company gives some cash to the other company.

8. *If I spend money "fixing" a plant asset, how do I know whether to record an asset or an expense?*

Expenditures made subsequent to acquisition are divided into two types. If the expenditure is just to keep the asset running as good as new, we would call that an expense. However, if the expenditure makes the asset better in some way (have a longer life, go faster, produce fewer defective units, etc.), then we would call that an asset and capitalize the expenditure.

PRACTICE MULTIPLE CHOICE QUESTIONS

1. Mindy Co. sells a used truck for $20,000. The cost of the truck was $40,000 and the accumulated depreciation at the time of sale was $12,000. What is the gain on disposal?

    a. $8,000

    b. There is no gain

    c. Not enough information

    d. $20,000

Solution: The correct answer is **b**. The gain or loss on disposal is computed by comparing the selling price and the book value. The selling price is $20,000 and the book value is $28,000 ($40,000 − $12,000). Thus, there is a loss of $8,000 on this transaction. Be careful when you do multiple choice questions. Choice **a** may look good, but the question asked what the *gain* was. There is no gain; thus, **a** cannot be the right answer.

2. An asset is being depreciated using the double-declining balance method with a 5-year life. The book value at the end of the first year is $500,000. What is the book value at the end of the second year?

    a. $300,000

    b. $400,000

    c. $380,000

    d. Not enough information

Solution: The correct answer is **a**. Using the double-declining balance method, you multiply the book value times a rate that is twice the straight-line rate, in this case, $1/5 \times 2 = 40\%$. Thus, the depreciation for the second year is $500,000 \times .4$, or $200,000. Therefore, the book value at the end of the second year is $300,000, or choice **a**. All the other choices are wrong.

    3. A machine was purchased for $500,000, with an estimated life of 5 years and an estimated salvage value of $50,000. Using the sum of the year's digits method, calculate the book value at the end of year 3.

    a. $360,000

    b. $90,000

    c. $315,000

    d. $180,000

Solution: The correct answer is **b**. There is a shortcut you can take when using the sum of the year's digits depreciation. You can accumulate the numbers in the numerator. Thus, for an asset with a 5-year life, the denominator is 15 $[(N\ (n + 1)/2]$. Depreciation for the first year is $5/15 \times$ Cost $-$ Salvage value. Depreciation for the second year is 4/15, and so forth. Therefore, for 3 years, the accumulated depreciation is $5 + 4 + 3$, or $12/15 \times$ Cost $-$ Salvage value. In addition, the book value, or undepreciated cost, is simply $2 + 1$, or $3/15 \times$ Cost $-$ Salvage value, or $3/15 \times \$450 = \$90,000$. The other choices are wrong.

    4. The major characteristics of property, plant, and equipment are

    a. they are acquired for use in operations and not for resale.

    b. they are long term in nature and usually subject to depreciation.

    c. they possess physical substance.

    d. all of the above.

Solution: The correct answer is **b**. Here is a question that is based on the textbook definition of property, plant, and equipment. If you know the definition, the question is simple. You might also note that because choice **d** is "all of the above," if any two of the choices look good, then **d** must be the right answer.

    5. To an accountant, depreciation is

    a. a matter of valuation.

    b. a means of cost allocation.

    c. a means of loss allocation.

    d. a matter of impairment of value.

Solution: The correct answer is **b**. Here is another definition-type question. Accountants consider depreciation to be a process of allocation instead of valuation. Your professor probably mentioned this several times in the lecture on depreciation. Therefore, choice **b** is the right answer. We could also eliminate choice **a** and choice **d**, since they deal with valuation and our accounting system is based on cost. Choice **c** makes no sense.

    6. Melbourne Co. purchased a machine that was installed and put into service on January 1, 2006, at a cost of $480,000. The salvage value was estimated at $80,000. The machine is being depreciated over 10 years using the double-declining balance method. For the year ending December 31, 2007, what amount should Melbourne report as depreciation expense?

a. $96,000

b. $76,800

c. $64,000

d. $61,440

Solution: The correct answer is **b**. Remember that salvage value is ignored initially with the double-declining balance method. So, the first year's depreciation will be $480,000 × 1/10 × 2 = $480,000 × .2 = $96,000. The second year's depreciation will be $480,000 − $96,000, or $384,000 × .2 = $76,800, which is choice **b**. Notice that choice **a** is the first year's depreciation, and the question asks for the second year's depreciation. Also, note that choice **c** is what you would get if you subtracted the salvage value: $480,000 − $80,000 = $400,000 × .2 = $80,000 for the first year and $400,000 − $80,000 = $320,000 × .2 = $64,000. So, the lesson is to be careful and read the question carefully.

7. Erin Corp. purchased a new machine with a 20-year life for $100,000 on January 1, 2000. The estimated salvage value is $8,000. On January 1, 2010, it is estimated that the machine will be able to remain in use for an additional 20 years (making its total life 30 years). Depreciation is recorded using the straight-line method. What will be the depreciation expense recorded on December 31, 2010?

a. $41,250

b. $5,000

c. $3,333

d. $2,300

Solution: The correct answer is **d**. The straight-line depreciation for the first 10 years is $100,000 − $8,000, or $92,000 × 1/20 × 10 = $46,000. On January 1, 2010, they changed their estimate of the useful life. Therefore, the new depreciation for the remaining 20 years will be the cost of the asset, less the estimated salvage value, less the depreciation already taken, that is, $100,000 − $8,000 − $46,000/20, or $46,000/20 = $2,300, or choice **d**. The other choices are not correct.

8. When a business is acquired, the goodwill associated with the acquisition is the difference between the purchase price and the

a. fair value of the net assets acquired.

b. fair value of the net tangible assets acquired.

c. fair value of all assets.

d. none of the above.

Solution: The correct answer is **a**. This is another question based on a definition. The definition of goodwill is the excess of the purchase price over the net assets acquired. Choices **b** and **c** ignore the company's liabilities, which makes no sense.

9. The expiration of intangible assets is called

a. depletion.

b. depreciation.

    c. amortization.

    d. restoration.

Solution: The correct answer is **c**. Writing off an intangible asset is called amortization. Choice **a** refers to depletion, which is used for wasting assets, and choice **b** refers to depreciation, which is used for tangible assets. Choice **d** makes no sense.

10. The assumption that depreciation is a function of use rather than the passage of time is associated with which method?

    a. straight line

    b. activity

    c. double-declining balance

    d. decreasing charge

Solution: The correct answer is **b**. The other three choices, **a**, **c**, and **d**, are all depreciation methods that are based on the asset's life and the passage of time. Only with the activity method is the depreciation a function of the asset's use.

CHAPTER 6

CURRENT AND NONCURRENT LIABLITIES

LEARNING OBJECTIVES

After studying this chapter, you will understand

- how to account for current liabilities
- how to determine the issue price of a bond
- how to prepare the journal entries associated with bonds, and
- how to distinguish between an operating lease and a capital lease

HERE IS where we are going with our study of current and noncurrent liabilities. Current liabilities refer to obligations to deliver cash or provide services within 1 year, or the current operating cycle if longer than 1 year. Typical current liabilities are accounts payable, notes payable, salaries payable, interest payable, and taxes payable. Accounting for current liabilities is rather straightforward and should present few problems, if any.

Accounting for long-term liabilities is another story. The major long-term liability that you will study in this course is bonds payable. First of all, there is a great deal of terminology associated with accounting for bonds. As a preview, consider the following:

- Coupon (or stated rate of interest) versus the yield (or market interest rate)
- Mortgage bonds versus debentures
- Term versus serial bonds

We will cover all of these terms and a great many more in this chapter.

Another element in your study of bonds is determining the issue price of a bond. The typical problem describes the features of a bond (face amount, stated rate of interest, and the term, as well as the yield or market rate of interest). Based on the difference between the stated rate of interest and the market rate of interest, the bond will either sell at par (which is the face value of the bond, usually $1,000), at a discount (less than $1,000), or at a premium (more than $1,000). We will review the calculations in this chapter; they are also covered in appendix B, which deals specifically with the time value of money, present values, and future values.

A final topic in this chapter involves leases. The two types of leases are accounted for in very different manners. If a lease is accounted for as an operating lease, the lessee simply records rent expenses. No asset or liability is recorded. If the lease is accounted for as a capital lease, then the lessee records both an asset and a liability. Furthermore, the lessee records depreciation on the leased asset and, to make things interesting, the lease payments must be divided into an interest component and a repayment of principal component. As you can see, for companies with a significant amount of leased assets, the balance sheet will look very different if the leases are treated as operating or capital leases. These differences will directly affect the computation of two important financial ratios: ROI (return on investment) and debt to equity. We will cover all these issues, as well as the appropriate journal entries in this chapter.

LIABILITIES

In the FASB's conceptual framework, a **liability** is defined as an obligation of the entity to make a payment or provide a service to another entity, based on a past transaction or event. This definition contains three essential elements:

1. It refers to a present obligation.
2. It is based on a past transaction or event.
3. It is unavoidable.

Liabilities are usually divided into two categories: current and noncurrent.

CURRENT LIABILITIES

A current liability is one that will require payment within 1 year (or the operating cycle if it is longer than 1 year) and will be paid with assets that are classified as current, or will create another current liability).

The following list contains the most typical current liabilities:

1. Accounts payable
2. Notes payable
3. Salaries payable
4. Interest payable
5. Sales tax payable
6. Advances from customers
7. Current portion of long-term debt
8. Estimated liability for warranties

Accounts payable represent a liability based on a "purchase on account." When one business buys something from another business, we say that the purchase is "on account," similar to buying something with a credit card. The company making the purchase "charged it," and they will eventually receive an invoice, or a bill, for the transaction that they will have to pay.

The journal entry for the transaction is

Purchases   XXX
   Accounts Payable   XXX

Accounts Payable

The terms for the typical purchase on account can be 2/10, n/30; 2/10, end of month (EOM); or some variation of these terms. The terms 2/10, n/30 mean that the buyer is entitled to a 2% discount if the invoice is paid in 10 days or less; the total is due in 30 days. The terms 2/10, EOM mean that the buyer is entitled to a 2% discount if paid within 10 days; the total is due at the end of the month.

Two percent sounds like a minimal amount, but 2/10, n/30 represents a significant discount. A company making a purchase with these terms will typically do one of two things:

1. Take the 2% discount and pay on the 10th day, or
2. Pay the full amount on the 30th day.

If you take the discount, you get a 2% reduction, and you give up your money for 20 days (30th day − 10th day). There are approximately eighteen 20-day periods in a year ($365/20 = 18+$); thus, the total savings as an annual rate is $2\% \times 18 = 36\%$. That is why most companies keep track of their purchases on account and attempt to pay early to be sure to get the discount. (These discounts are often labeled "purchase discounts" and are subtracted from purchases when computing cost of goods sold, which is the first major expense on the income statement.)

Notes Payable

Notes payable are very much like accounts payable, with two significant differences:

1. Notes payable refer to a *note* that is a separate legal document (sort of a formal IOU).
2. Notes payable generally include interest.

There are two principal types of notes: interest bearing and non-interest bearing. They both include interest, but the interest is not specifically indicated on a non-interest-bearing note.

Interest-Bearing Notes   Figure 6-1 illustrates a $1,000, 8%, 1-year note.

There are three separate journal entries involved in accounting for notes payable:

1. Signing the note,
2. Accruing interest, and
3. Paying the face amount of the note plus the accrued interest.

Date: 1/01/07
   I promise to pay to
   _____ The sum of $1,000 plus
   interest at 8%, due on 12/31/07.

FIGURE 6-1 Interest-Bearing Note Payable

Assume that the note was signed on January 1, 2007; 6 months' interest was accrued on June 30; and the total due was paid on December 31, 2006.

1/01	Cash	1,000	
	Note Payable		1,000
6/30	Interest Expense ($1,000 × .08 × 6/12)	40	
	Interest Payable		40
12/31	Interest Expense	40	
	Interest Payable		40
	Note Payable	1,000	
	Interest Payable	80	
	Cash		1,080

A non-interest-bearing note would look slightly different. See figure 6-2 below. The interest is deducted from the face amount of the note, so the borrower receives an amount of cash that is less than the amount of the note. At maturity, the full amount of the note is paid back to the lender.

Non-Interest-Bearing Notes   Assume that in exchange for this note, the maker of the note receives $920 cash. The journal entries are similar; however, with a non-interest-bearing note, the accrual of interest is recorded by debiting interest expense and *crediting discount instead of crediting interest payable.*

1/01	Cash	920	
	Discount	80	
	Note Payable		1,000
6/30	Interest Expense	40	
	Discount		40
12/31	Interest Expense	40	
	Note Payable	1,000	
	Discount		40
	Cash		1,000

1/01/07
   I promise to pay
   _____ the sum of
   $1,000, due on 12/31/07.

FIGURE 6-2 A Non-interest-Bearing Note

Salaries Payable

Salaries payable is a typical current liability. It appears on most year-end balance sheets because December 31 does not always fall on the last day of the week. Assume that the weekly salary expense is $5,000 and that the employees are paid every Friday. Assume further that December 31 happens to be a Wednesday, which means that on December 31, employees have worked for 3 days (Monday through Wednesday), but will not be paid until Friday, which happens to be in January (next year). To make sure that the salaries earned in December are recorded in the correct period, we accrue the 3 days of salaries, which have been earned but not paid.

12/31	Salary Expense	3,000	
	Salaries Payable		3,000

On Friday, the full $5,000 payroll is paid, and this entry is recorded:

1/02	Salary Expense (Thursday–Friday)	2,000	
	Salaries Payable (Monday–Wednesday)	3,000	
	Cash		5,000

DEMONSTRATION PROBLEM   *Payroll Accounting*

The MGM Company has the following employees whose earning for the past week (and cumulative earnings for the year) are as follows:

B. Crosby	$2,000	($5,000)
B. Hope	$2,500	($5,500)
G. Marx	$3,500	($6,000)
M. Monroe	$3,000	($7,000)

The federal income tax withholding rate is 15%; the state income tax withholding rate is 5%. Federal unemployment tax is 0.8%, and the state unemployment tax rate is 2.5%, both limited to the first $7,000 of income earned.

Required: Prepare the journal entry to record payroll expense, and the journal entry to record payroll tax expense.

Solution: Recording a payroll involves two separate journal entries. The first entry records the salary expense and the amounts withheld from the employees. The second entry records the employer's payroll taxes and the related liabilities. The Federal Insurance Contributions Act (FICA) tax is a United States payroll (or employment) tax imposed by the Federal government on both employees and employers to fund Social Security and Medicare.[1] Accountants generally refer to Social Security and Medicare taxes simply as FICA. For this problem, the two journal entries are:

---

[1] http://en.wikipedia.org/wiki/Federal_Insurance_Contributions_Act_tax

Salary Expense	11,0000	
FICA Taxes Payable		841.50
Federal Income Tax Withheld		1,650.00
State Income Tax Withheld		550.00
Salaries Payable		7,958.50
Payroll Tax Expense	1,122.00	
FICA Taxes Payable		841.50
Federal Unemployment Taxes Payable		68.00
State Unemployment Taxes Payable		212.50

Problem-Solving Takeaway Remember that several of the payroll tax items are assessed only on an individual's first $7,000 of earnings or first $80,000 of earnings. For example, in 2007, FICA was deducted from employees on their first $87,900 of salary, none after that amount. In this problem, M. Monroe had already reached the limit of $7,000; therefore, both federal and state unemployment taxes were based on $8,500 of the salaries, not the total of $11,000.

Interest Payable

Interest on current obligations is computed using the following formula:

$$\text{Interest} = \text{Principle} \times \text{Rate} \times \text{Time}$$

Note that the rate and the time must reflect the same unit of measure. If the rate is per month, time must be stated in months. If the rate is per year, time must be stated in terms of a year (6 months would thus be stated as 6/12 or 1/2 a year).

EXAM TIP

This is a key point. We only understand interest rates when they are stated in terms of an *annual rate*. For example, if you receive a solicitation in the mail for yet another credit card, and the interest is stated as only $1\frac{1}{2}\%$, what does that mean? It means $1\frac{1}{2}\%$ per month, which translates to 18% per year ($1\frac{1}{2} \times 12 = 18$). Do not be fooled by monthly interest rates; make sure that you convert every interest rate into an annual rate.

We have seen the entry to accrue interest several times already, but here it is again:

| 12/31 | Interest Expense | XXX | |
| | Interest Payable | | XXX |

Sales Tax Payable

When you go into Macy's or Sears and buy a shirt or a sweater, the store charges you sales tax. The sales tax is *collected* by the store, but it *belongs* to the state and local government, the store simply collects the money from you and sends it off to the appropriate government agency.

Assume that Macy's sells you a sweater for $100 and the sales tax where you live is 8.25%. Macy's would record the sale as follows:

Cash	108.25	
Sales		100.00
Sales Tax Payable		8.25

When Macy's sends off the money to the state, they simply debit sales tax payable and credit cash. Note that the sales tax has no impact on Macy's income statement. They are simply a conduit—or a middleman—collecting the sales tax from the customer and sending it to the government.

Advances from Customers

In most instances, money is collected from customers at the time of the sale or some days after the sale. However, in some instances, cash is collected *before* the product or service is delivered.

Assume that *TIME* magazine sells a 1-year subscription for $75 and receives a check for $75 before any magazines are mailed or delivered. *TIME* has the customer's money, but the customer hasn't received any product yet. In this case, *TIME owes* the customer $75 worth of *TIME* magazine. That is a current liability. It is usually referred to as unearned revenue or advances from customers. These are account titles for a current liability.

Assume that *TIME* collects $75 for a 1-year subscription, and on April 30, they recorded 4 months worth of subscription revenue. The sale would be recorded as follows:

1/01	Cash	75	
	Unearned Subscription Revenue		75
4/30	Unearned Subscription Revenue	25	
	Subscription Revenue		25

(One third of a year's revenue has been earned.)

Current Portion of Long-Term Debt

Most long-term liabilities mature on a specific date, which determines the *term* of the loan or obligation. We will see an example of this in a moment when we go over accounting for bonds. Most bonds are term bonds; however, there is another type of bond—a serial bond.

Serial Bonds Versus Term Bonds

A 10-year term bond in due is due in exactly 10 years.

A 10-year serial bond provides that 1/10th of the total face amount of the bond is due each year.

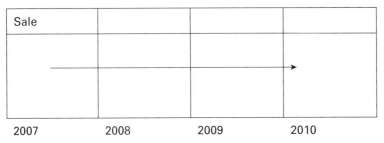

FIGURE 6-3 Warranty Expense as a Function of Time

If a company issues a 10-year serial bond on 1/01/07, it represents a long-term liability, but the amount due at the end of 2007 is a current liability (remember the definition) and must be shown in the current liability section of the balance sheet.

Estimated Liability for Warranties

The accounting issue associated with warranties is getting the total expense in the same period as the revenue (see fig. 6-3).

Assume that Sony sells a color television for $5,000 on 6/30/07 that includes a 3-year warranty on parts and labor. How do we record the warranty expense, and how does it show up on the financial statements?

The television was sold in 2007, but it is covered by the warranty until June 30, 2010. We will not know the total cost to repair all televisions sold in 2007 until the middle of 2010, but we have to make up an income statement for 2007. What do we do? We estimate the total cost of repairing all televisions sold in 2007 during the 3-year period covered by the warranty. Based on past experience, comparing warranty costs and sales, we come up with a figure of 3% of sales. We then simply multiply the annual sales by 3%, and there you are. We get the 3% figure by comparing prior years' actual warranty repairs with prior years' annual sales.

Year	Actual Warranty Expense	Annual Sales
2003	$4,500	$100,000
2004	3,000	110,000
2005	1,600	95,000
	$9,100	$305,000

The calculation is $9,100 ÷ $305,000 = 3%. This is the actual company experience, so we use 3% in estimating this year's expense. If sales for 2007 were $150,000, and actual warranty repair costs incurred were $3,000, Sony would make the following entries:

Cash	150,000	
Sales		150,000
Warranty Expense	3,000	
Cash		3,000
Warranty expense ($4,500 − $3,000)	1,500	
Estimated Liability for Warranties		1,500

(In this last entry, warranty expense is debited for the total estimated warranty expense of $4,500 [which is equal to 3% × Sales of $150,000] less the actual expenses [$3,000] already incurred.)

Short-Term Debt Expected to Be Refinanced

If a company has some short-term debt that they plan on refinancing, they can actually reclassify the debt into the long-term liability section of the balance sheet if two criteria are met:

1. There is an intention to refinance, and
2. There is a demonstrated ability to consummate the refinancing.

A demonstrated ability to consummate the refinancing is usually met by either completing the refinancing after the year-end but before the financial statements are issued, or by having an approved loan from a financial institution during the same period.

LONG-TERM LIABILITIES

There are five typical long-term liabilities on a corporation's balance sheet:

1. Long-term bank loans or notes payable
2. Pension liabilities
3. Other postretirement benefit obligations
4. Bonds
5. Obligations under capital leases

I want to make a few points about the first three items on this list and then spend a good deal of time on the last two items—bonds and leases.

Bank Loans and Long-Term Notes Payable

Long-term bank-loans and long-term notes payable are both noncurrent liabilities. They are recorded much like short-term notes payable.

Long-term notes payable are considered to be financial instruments and must be reported on the balance sheet at fair market value.

Pensions and Other Postretirement Benefit Obligations

Although liabilities created by pension plans and health care plans are beyond the scope of this book, it is important for you to know that these liabilities exist and that some information regarding obligations related to pensions and health care plans must be reported on the balance sheet, with details presented in the notes to the balance sheet.

Among the information presented in the notes is the **projected benefit obligation** of the company's pension plan, which is the present value of the future pension payments that the company is obligated to pay. These are all payments that the company is obligated to make to their employees based on their pension plan. Each employee is entitled to specific payments, and the present value of all these payments is the projected benefit obligation. For a large company, such as General Motors, this obligation is a very large number. The pension plan assets are also disclosed. The majority of the disclosures related to these two liabilities (pensions and health care) are reported in detail in the notes to the financial statements. Note that the FASB has recently changed the disclosure requirements associated with pension plans.

Bonds

Bonds represent a common way for a corporation to obtain financing. A company may need to obtain a large amount of cash and the amount may simply be too big for any one financial institution. So, they issue bonds to the public, where individuals, other corporations, and even mutual funds may buy them.

There is a good deal of accounting nomenclature or technical jargon related to bonds. Here are a few terms that you should understand before you read the material on bonds.

Bond Terminology

Principal amount

Stated (coupon) rate of interest

Market (effective) rate or yield

Discount

Premium

Maturity date

Bond indenture

Convertible bond

Term bond

Serial bond

Mortgage bond

Debenture

Principal Amount   The face value of the bond is called the *principal*. When the bond matures, this is the amount of money that the issuing company will pay the bondholder.

Stated (Coupon) Rate of Interest   The rate of interest that will be paid each period is the stated, or coupon, rate. This rate is multiplied by the principal to determine the actual interest paid. It is often called the coupon rate, which refers to an old practice of attaching actual coupons to the bonds. When an interest payment was due, the bondholders cut the coupon off the bond and mailed it to the financial institution involved, and they would then receive a check for the interest. Today, most bonds are registered; the company has the name and address of each bondholder in its computer. When interest payments are due, the computer system generates a check for the interest for each bondholder.

Market (Effective) Rate or Yield   The effective rate of interest (or yield) is the going rate of interest in the market for bonds of a specific risk profile. When a company is about to issue bonds, they attempt to make the stated rate (which appears on the face of the bond) as close to what they expect the market rate of interest to be when the bonds will be issued. Since very little time elapses between the time that the bonds are printed and when they are issued, the difference between the stated rate and the yield is usually very small.

Maturity Date   This is the date that the bonds mature. On this date, the entire principal, as well as the interest, is due.

Discount and Premium   If the stated rate of interest is 8% and the market rate is 9%, how many bonds would we expect to sell? Answer: None. Who would buy an 8% bond when you can go across the street and buy a bond with the same risk profile for 9%? Nobody. So, how can we sell these 8% bonds? Answer: Sell them at a *discount*. We use interest tables to compute the price of the bond that will guarantee the bondholder a rate of return equal to the market rate.

EXAM TIP

This computation is tested quite often. Learn it here and you will always be able to answer these questions.

DEMONSTRATION PROBLEM

The company issues $500,000, 10-year bonds with a stated interest rate of 8% paid annually when the market rate is 9%. Compute the issue price.

The issue price is the present value of the two cash flows that the bondholder will receive:

Present-value calculations are covered in appendix B. The basic equation that we use to make these calculations is: Amount × Interest Factor = Answer.

Stated Rate of Interest	Market Rate of Interest	Issue Price
8%	9%	Discount
8%	8%	Par
8%	7%	Premium

FIGURE 6-4 Interest Rates and Bond Prices

1. The present value of the principal amount or face value—a sum.
2. The present value of the stream of interest payments—an annuity.
   Note that both present values are calculated at the market rate of interest.

   Present value of the principal

   (Amount × Interest Factor = Answer) $500,000 × .42241 = $211,205

   Present value of the interest $40,000 × 6,41766 = $256,706

   Issue price of bonds $467,911 ∎

Figure 6-4 above summarizes the relationship among the stated rate of interest, the market rate of interest, and the issue price.

When the company's bond pays a higher interest rate than the market, the bond sells for a premium. If the company's bond pays a lower rate of interest than the market, the bond will sell at a discount. If both interest rates are the same, the bond sells at par.

Bond Indenture   The agreement between the corporation issuing the bonds and the bondholders. It specifies all the rights and obligations of both parties.

Convertible Bond   Some bonds are convertible; at the option of the bondholder, the bonds can be converted into shares of the corporation's common stock at a predetermined conversion rate, such as 10 shares of common stock per $1,000 bond. The conversion feature makes the bond more attractive; therefore, the corporation issuing the bonds may be able to issue the bonds at a lower rate of interest.

When you purchase a convertible bond and the corporation whose bonds you own is profitable, its common stock may increase in value, and you may be able to profit from this increase by converting your bonds to shares of common stock.

EXAMPLE

You purchase ten $1,000 convertible bonds at par, paying $10,000. Each bond is convertible to 40 shares of common stock, which have a current market value of $20 each. Thus, initially, it would not make sense to convert, since one $1,000 bond is worth more than 40 shares of a $20 common stock. However, if the stock increases in value to $30, then it would be worthwhile to convert, since each bond would be converted into 40 shares of a $30 stock having a market value of $1,200.

The corporation issuing the convertible bonds may actually be planning on people converting their holdings. Their goal may be to issue common stock, but at a price of $20 per share, they may be concerned that there would be too much dilution of the stockholders' interest. By issuing a convertible bond, the stock only gets issued if the market price increases; therefore, the stock will be issued at the higher price and thus there will not be as much dilution of the existing stockholders' interest. ■

Term Bonds Versus Serial Bonds

It would seem that a 10-year bond would mature in 10 years, but actually it depends on whether it is a term bond or a serial bond. A 10-year term bond does mature in 10 years. A 10-year serial bond matures 1/10 each year for 10 years; thus, a $1,000,000 10-year serial bond would have $100,000 of face value bonds maturing each year for 10-years.

Mortgage Bond Versus Debenture

A mortgage bond is backed by some form of collateral, such as a plant asset. This is similar to the mortgage on your home, where the house is the collateral for the loan.

A debenture, on the other hand, is an unsecured bond; there is no collateral.

EXAM TIP

Every now and then, this "trick" question appears on an exam:

Is a debenture always more risky than a secured bond? The answer is *no*. A debenture from a very strong company may be much less risky than a secured bond from a marginal company.

We know how to compute the issue price of a bond, now we need to review the journal entries for a bond.

Assume that the corporation issued $500,000 of 8%, 10-year bonds for $468,000, issued when the market rate of interest was 9%. (These are the numbers from our earlier example.)

The journal entry to issue the bonds would be

Cash	468,000	
Discount	32,000	
Bonds Payable		500,000

The bond discount must be amortized or written off over the life of the bond. There are two methods for calculating the amortization: the **straight-line** and **effective interest methods**. The straight-line method is quite simple; you just divide the discount by the term of the bond, and that is the annual amortization. In our example, the amortization would be $\dfrac{\$32,000}{10} = \$3,200$, and the journal entry would be

Interest Expense	43,200	
Discount		3,200
Cash (8% × $500,000)		40,000

Note that the amortization of the discount increases the interest expense so that it is more than the cash interest paid to the bondholders. It makes the interest expense reflect the market rate of interest instead of the stated rate of interest.

Date	Interest Expense	Interest Paid	Amortization of Discount	Bond Carrying Value
1/01/01				$468,000
12/31/01	$42,120	$40,000	$2,120	470,120
12/31/02	42,311	40,000	2,311	472,431
12/31/03	42,519	40,000	2,519	474,950
12/31/04	42,745	40,000	2,745	477,695
12/31/05	42,993	40,000	2,993	480,688
12/31/06	43,262	40,000	3,262	483,950
12/31/07	43,556	40,000	3,556	487,506
12/31/08	43,875	40,000	3,875	491,381
12/31/09	44,224	40,000	4,224	495,605
12/31/10	44,604	40,000	4,604	500,207*

*Difference due to rounding. This amount should be $500,000

FIGURE 6-5 Amortization of Bond Discount

The effective interest method involves a slightly more complex calculation, and some professors and some textbooks do not even cover this method. In an effort to be complete, the effective interest method is described here.

Using the effective interest method, you calculate the interest expense each year by multiplying the bond's carrying value (face amount less unamortized discount) by the market rate of interest. The difference between the interest expense and the cash interest paid (which is always $40,000 in this example) is the amortization of the discount. A bond discount amortization table is used to make these calculations (see fig. 6-5).[2]

GAAP says that the preferred method is the effective interest method, but the straight-line method is acceptable if it approximates the effective interest method.

Regardless of how you amortize the discount, at the end of 10-years, it will be completely amortized, and the final journal entry will be

Bonds Payable   500,000
    Cash   500,000

Leases

There are two types of leases: an **operating lease** and a **capital lease**. If a lease meets *any one* of the following criteria, it is capital lease; otherwise, it is an operating lease:

1. The lease transfers ownership.

2. The lease contains a bargain purchase option.

[2] Look at year 2. The interest expense equals the bond carrying value of $470,120 × the market rate of interest of .09. $470,120 × .09 = $42,311. The difference between the interest expense, and the cash interest paid is the amortization; $42,311 − 40,000 = $2311. The new carrying value is $470,120 + $2311 = 472,431.

3. The term of the lease is ≥75% of the life of the asset.

4. The present value of the minimum lease payments is ≥90% of the value of the asset at the inception of the lease.

If the lease does not meet any of the criteria, it is an operating lease, which is essentially a rental. No asset value is created. The journal entry to record an operating lease is:

Rent Expense	XXX	
Cash		XXX

If the lease meets any one of the four criteria, it qualifies as a capital lease, and both an asset and a liability are created. There are three journal entries to be recorded with a capital lease:

1. Signing the lease

2. Making the lease payments

3. Recording depreciation on the leased asset

Consider the following (sample) lease:

Term: 5 years

Annual payments due on 12/31 of $10,000 interest at 8% on the unpaid balance

The present value of the minimum lease payments is

$$\$10,000 \times .68058, \text{ or } \$68,058$$

1. Upon signing the lease

Leased Equipment	68,058	
Obligation Under Capital Lease		68,058

(The amount of this entry is the present value of the minimum lease payments.)

2. Making the annual lease payment

Each payment must be divided into the interest expense part and the reduction of principal (or obligation) part. The interest expense is the interest rate multiplied by the outstanding obligation. (Note the similarity to recording bond discount or premium amortization. The remaining part is the reduction of principal.)

Interest Expense (Interest rate × Outstanding obligation)	5,444	
Obligation ($10,000 − $5,444)		4,556
Cash		10,000

3. Recording depreciation expense

Depreciation Expense	13,612	
Accumulated Depreciation − Leased Equipment		13,612

Depreciation on leased assets is calculated using the same depreciation method that the company uses for the other assets that they own. Assuming straight-line depreciation over 5 years with no salvage, the annual depreciation would be $68,058 \div 5 = $13,612$.

One of the problems related to accounting for leased assets is that the rules are very specific. Some companies want to avoid reporting a capital lease; therefore, they create a lease that does not meet any of the four criteria, which is relatively easy to do. The current rule is essentially "form over substance;" the form of the transaction determines the accounting treatment instead of the economic substance. Most accountants would prefer to have the *substance* of the transaction determine how it is recorded instead of the form.

The reason companies want to avoid recording a capital lease is that they do not want to add an asset and a liability to their balance sheet.

Adding an asset to the balance sheet makes their profitability, as measured by return on investment (net income $\div$ total assets) look worse. Adding a liability to the balance sheet, increases the debt/equity ratio as measured by debt $\div$ total equity, and makes the company look riskier.

SUMMARY OF JOURNAL ENTRIES

This is a list of the most common transactions and journal entries corresponding to the topics covered in this chapter. I would recommend that you review this list of journal entries several times until you are certain that you understand each one. The journal entry is the link between the actual business transactions that take place and the financial statements that are prepared by the entity.

One technique that I find to be very useful is to take this list of transactions and journal entries, cover the right-hand side of the page with a blank sheet of paper so you can just see the description of the transaction, and then write out each journal entry. After writing out each entry, just slide the paper down a bit and check to see that you made the correct entry. Do this before your exams to test your understanding of the material.

Transaction	**Journal Entry**
Borrow money, sign interest-bearing note payable	Cash
	Notes payable
Accrue interest on notes payable	Interest Expense
	Interest Payable
Pay interest and retire note	Notes Payable
	Interest Payable
	Cash
Record sale and collection of sales tax	Cash or Accounts Receivable
	Sales Revenue
	Sales Tax Payable
Remit sales tax to state or county	Sales Tax Payable
	Cash

Record payment of salaries less payroll deductions	Salaries Expense
	    Federal Income Tax Withheld
	    FICA Taxes Payable
	    Union Dues Payable
	    Cash

Record employer payroll taxes	Payroll Tax Expense
	    FICA Payable
	    Federal Unemployment Tax Payable
	    State Unemployment Tax Payable

Accrue contingent liability	Loss Estimated Liability for ...
Accrue warranty expense	Warranty Expense Estimated Liability Under Warranty
Record warranty costs incurred in 2008 on sales made in 2007	Estimated Liability Under Warranty Cash, Inventory, etc.
Issue bonds at par	Cash Bonds Payable
Pay interest on bonds	Interest Expense Cash
Retire bonds at maturity	Bonds Payable Cash
Issue bond at discount	Cash Discount Bonds Payable
Pay interest, amortize discount	Interest Expense Discount
Issue interest-bearing long-term notes payable	Cash Discount on Notes Payable Notes Payable

Payment of annual interest and amortization of discount	Interest Expense
	    Discount
	    Cash

REVIEW QUESTIONS

1. *What is the appropriate level of debt for a company? How is this determined?*
The appropriate level of debt is really a personal consideration. Some individuals can tolerate significant risk, and they could live with 40%–50% or more debt/equity. Other people are risk averse and would accept no more than 15%–20% debt/equity.

One of my finance professors put it this way: You must decide whether you want to eat well or sleep well. Those who want to eat well (they have a greater income due to financial leverage on the use of debt) will go for higher levels of debt.

Those who want to sleep at night will prefer less risk and thus go for less debt.

The more debt you have relative to equity, the greater is the risk for the business.

2. *What is financial leverage and how do you measure how much leverage a company has?*

Financial leverage involves using debt to increase the return to the owners. Leverage generally refers to "lifting" a weight using a lever and a fulcrum. Financial leverage involves "lifting" or increasing the return to stockholders by borrowing money at one interest rate and investing that money in the company where it will earn more than the company is paying for the use of the money. The amount of leverage a company has is typically measured by the debt to equity ratio: total liabilities ÷ total owners' equity. A measure of how safe all this borrowing is can be evaluated by computing the times interest earned ratio: earnings before interest and taxes divided by the interest expense. This tells how many times the company earned an amount equal to the interest expense. If earnings before interest and taxes divided by interest expense equals 20, then the company's income available to pay the interest charges is 20 times the interest charge; that's safe. A number like 1 or 2 would scare me.

3. *Why are operating leases referred to as "off-balance-sheet financing?"*

Operating leases are considered a form of off-balance-sheet financing because the lessee does not record an asset or a liability as a result of signing this type of lease.

On the other hand, when a company signs a capital lease, they would record both an asset and a liability. For long-term leases, the capital lease method gives a more accurate portrayal of the economics of the transaction. However, the way the rule governing leases is written—with very specific criteria to determine whether or not a lease qualifies as a capital lease—it is relatively easy for a company to enter into a long-term lease and avoid showing either an asset or a liability by structuring the terms of the lease to avoid meeting any of the four capital lease criteria.

4. *What is the "actual or true obligation" that a company has regarding its pension plan, and why isn't this number shown on the balance sheet?*

The actual liability that a company is obligated to pay regarding their pension plan is called the "projected benefit obligation." It is the present value of all the benefits that will have to be paid to their employees under the terms of the company's pension plan. For large, established companies, this number is in the tens of millions of dollars. Because of the size of this number, the FASB determined that it would be very difficult to force companies to report this liability on their balance sheet. Thus, they came up with a compromise standard. The standard spells out how the pension expense is determined, and the projected benefit obligation, as well as a lot of additional information about the pension plan, is disclosed in a note to the financial statements.

5. *What is the minimum liability regarding a pension plan and what is the rule regarding disclosure of a minimum liability?*

The rule regarding pension cost permits companies that fully fund their annual pension expense to avoid recording any liability for pension payments. In order to require these companies to show at least *some* liability, the minimum liability was created. The minimum liability is calculated as the excess of the accumulated benefit obligation over the fair value of the pension plan assets. The minimum liability is sometimes referred to as the unfunded accumulated benefit obligation. (The accumulated benefit obligation is similar to the projected benefit obligation, but it is based on current salary levels instead of future salary levels, and it is slightly less than the projected benefit obligation.) Companies that are required to disclose a minimum liability make a journal entry debit intangible asset and credit pension obligation.

6. *What is the basic issue or problem related to reporting warranty costs?*

The accounting problem associated with warranty costs involves recording the expense in the appropriate period. Assume that the company sells televisions with a 3-year warranty covering parts and labor. We won't know the actual costs to repair the televisions covered by the warranty until the 3 years are over. However, the sales of those televisions were all recorded in the first year. Thus, to properly match revenue and expense, we need to record an expense in the first year that will reflect all the costs to be incurred in the *3* years of the warranty. We do this by making an estimate in a manner similar to the one used to estimate and record bad debt expense. Warranty costs are typically estimated as a percentage of revenue based on the company's past experiences.

7. *What are contingent liabilities and when are they reported?*

Contingent liabilities are liabilities that might become actual liabilities, depending on certain circumstances. For example, if a customer in a supermarket falls on a wet floor, breaks an arm and a leg, and then sues the store, the store has a potential or contingent liability. The requirement states that a liability should be recorded if both of these criteria are met:

a. It is probable that a liability has been created, and

b. The amount can be reasonably estimated.

In this case, the supermarket would refer this matter to their attorney, and the attorney's estimate of potential liability would be used to record this event.

8. *Why is it important to show the current portion of long-term debt as a current liability?*

When people read a company's balance sheet, they need to see a true picture of the financial position of the firm on a particular date. Readers of the balance sheet look at the company's current liabilities and compare them against the current assets to see if the company has appropriate liquidity. Since the current portion of any long-term debt must be paid in the current year, this amount should be included with the other current liabilities.

9. *If you will receive $1,000 when a bond matures, why don't all bonds just sell for $1,000?*

All bonds pay $1,000 at maturity. However, the issue price of a bond is determined by *two* components of a bond: the principal or face amount, and the interest the bond will pay. If the interest paid for the bond (we call this the stated rate of interest or coupon rate) is more or less than the market rate of interest, the bond will sell for a premium or at a discount: If the coupon rate is greater than the market rate, the bond will sell for a premium—for more than $1,000. If the coupon is less than the market rate, the bond will sell at a discount—for less than $1000.

10. *Why do increased levels of debt make a company more risky?*

When a company borrows money, it has a legal liability to pay back both principal and interest. If it doesn't earn enough money to make these payments, it could be forced into bankruptcy. In the absence of any debt, a company could have a bad year and may not be able to pay any dividends to the stockholders, but they would not be facing bankruptcy, as long as they had enough cash to pay their operating expenses.

PRACTICE MULTIPLE CHOICE QUESTIONS

1. A bond will be issued at a discount when the coupon rate of interest is

   a. less than the market rate of interest.

   b. greater than the market rate of interest.

   c. less than the stated rate of interest.

   d. greater than the stated rate of interest.

Solution: The correct answer is **a**. Choice **b** would result in the bonds selling for a premium. Choices **c** and **d** are nonsense statements because the coupon rate and the stated rate of interest refer to the same thing.

2. Which of the following is not one of the four criteria that are used to determine whether a lease qualifies as a capital lease?

   a. The lease transfers ownership.

   b. The lease contains a bargain purchase option.

   c. The term of the lease is $\geq$ 90% of the life of the asset.

   d. The present value of the minimum lease payment is $\geq$ 90% of the value of the asset at the inception of the lease.

Solution: The correct answer is **c**. Again, the question is testing whether or not you know a definition or a specific rule. The four criteria to qualify as a capital lease are often tested. In this question, choice **c** is not one of the criteria. The criterion involving the term of the lease states that the term of the lease is $\geq$ 75% of the life of the asset, not 90%. The other three criteria listed in the question are correct.

3. In order to accrue a contingent liability, the following criteria must be met:

   a. It is probable that a liability has been created.

   b. The amount can be reasonably estimated.

 c. It is reasonably possible that a liability has been created.

 d. Both a and b.

Solution: The correct answer is **d**. Here is another rule right out of the textbook. In order to accrue a contingent liability, two criteria must be met. It is probable that a liability has been created and the amount can be reasonably estimated.

 4. Discount on bonds payable is a (an)

  a. expense account.

  b. asset account.

  c. a contra-liability account.

  d. owners' equity account.

Solution: The correct answer is **c**. An account that is subtracted from another account is called a contra-account. (*Contra* means "against.") The other three choices are clearly not appropriate.

 5. Grant Corp. employs 200 office workers who each earn $500 per week and are paid each week on Friday for that week. December 31 of the current year happens to be a Thursday. What adjusting entry for salaries must be made on December 31?

a. Salaries Expense	100,000	
Salaries Payable		100,000
b. Salaries Expense	80,000	
Salaries Payable		80,000
c. Salaries Payable	80,000	
Salaries Expense		80,000
d. Salaries Expense	100,000	
Cash		100,000

Solution: The correct answer is **c**. This is a question about accruing salary expense. When the year ends, the 200 workers will have worked 4 days without having been paid. To accrue their salaries, we debit salary expense and credit salaries payable as follows:

$$200 \times 4 \times \frac{500}{5} = \$80,000.$$

CHAPTER 7

STOCKHOLDERS' EQUITY

LEARNING OBJECTIVES

After studying this chapter, you will understand

- the basic elements of the corporate form of ownership
- common stock and preferred stock
- cash dividends, stock dividends, and stock splits
- treasury stock transactions
- comprehensive income, and
- the statement of stockholders' equity

HERE IS where we are going in our study of owners' equity or stockholders' equity. We begin by looking at the three different forms of ownership: sole proprietorship, partnership, and corporation. There are numerous advantages to organizing a company as a corporation, so we will focus our attention on corporations. A major advantage is limited liability for the stockholders.

If a company is organized as a sole proprietorship or a partnership and the company is unable to pay its debts, the creditors have the right to collect this money directly from the owners. However, if the company is a corporation, the stockholders could not be called on to pay the corporations' liabilities. The owners' liability is limited, that is, they could lose their entire investment, but they would never be called on to come up with *additional* money to pay the corporation's creditors. This one simple feature is why many businesses are organized as corporations.

Corporations issue two different types of stock: common stock and preferred stock. As you can tell from those names, preferred stock has certain preferences. We will review all the features of both preferred and common stock in this chapter, as well as the appropriate journal entries. There are several different types of dividends; cash dividends are the most common. There are also property dividends and stock dividends. In addition to dividends, there are stock splits, which can have the same impact as a dividend. (For example, a 100% stock dividend has the exact same impact as a stock split on earnings per share namely, the earnings per share are cut in half. The income is unchanged and the number of shares has been doubled.) We will cover dividends and splits in this chapter. Remember, dividends are never considered as an expense; they represent a distribution of the income of the corporation to the stockholders.

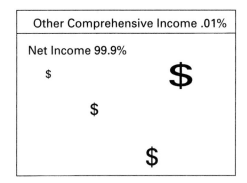

FIGURE 7-1 Comprehensive Income

Sometimes a company will simply purchase a number of shares of its own common stock. We refer to these shares as **treasury stock**. Treasury stock is a contra-owners' equity account, a subtraction from owners' equity (the word "contra" means against). Obviously, a corporation cannot "own itself," so treasury shares are not listed as assets; the cost of treasury stock is subtracted from the company's owners' equity.

The concept of **comprehensive income** is explored in this chapter. Comprehensive income consists of all changes in the net assets of an entity during a period due to transactions from nonowner sources. An easy way to get a handle on comprehensive income is to look at the diagram in figure 7-1.

As you can see, virtually all comprehensive income is made up of net income. There is a small sliver of comprehensive income that is not net income. This sliver contains three items that you may study in your accounting course:

1. Unrealized gains and losses on available-for-sale securities
2. Foreign currency translation gains and losses
3. Gains and losses associated with recording the minimum liability for a pension plan

We will review the notion of comprehensive income in this chapter.

The final topic in this chapter is the statement of owners' equity. In addition to the statement of owners' equity, companies often prepare a statement of the charges in retained earnings, which is a part of owners' equity. This statement is simply

$$\begin{array}{l} \text{Retained earnings, beginning balance} \\ \underline{+\ \text{Net income}} \\ \text{Subtotal} \\ \underline{-\ \text{Dividends}} \\ \text{Retained earnings, ending balance} \end{array}$$

The statement of owners' equity is a more comprehensive statement. It shows the changes in *every* owner's equity account. The format of the statement looks like a spreadsheet. Each owner's equity account is listed at the top of a column. The various transactions that affect the owners' equity accounts are listed on successive rows. We will look at a comprehensive statement of changes in owners' equity at the end of chapter 7.

STOCKHOLDERS' EQUITY

The accounting equation tells us that Assets = Liabilities + Owners' Equity, therefore Owners' Equity = Assets − Liabilities. This is why the owners' equity in a corporation is sometimes referred to as the **net worth** of the business, because it is equal to the total assets less the total liabilities.

Stockholders' equity represents the stockholders' interest in the company, or their claim on the assets of the firm. Since we are talking about stockholders, we must be talking about a corporation, because only corporations have stockholders.

Corporations

The corporate form of ownership is quite different from the other two forms of ownership—sole proprietorship and partnership.

The principal features of corporations are listed below:

1. Legal entity
2. Indefinite life
3. Limited liability for stockholders
4. Double taxation
5. Chartered by 1 of the 50 states
6. Governed by state corporation laws

A corporation is a legal entity. It can enter into contracts, bring a lawsuit, be sued, and so forth. Every corporation in the United States is chartered by 1 of the 50 states. We think of major corporations such as U.S. Steel, General Motors, and IBM as "national companies." They operate in all 50 states; surely their operations must be governed by an agency of the federal government. Thit is not the case.

The "reserve clause" in our constitution says that "all powers not specifically granted to the federal government are "reserved for the states." Since regulating corporations (as well as doctors, lawyers, CPA's, nurses, etc.) is not a power specifically granted to the federal government, it is therefore a state-controlled activity.

Corporations that operate in most or all of the 50 states have a choice as to where they want to file their charters. Many corporations select Delaware simply because that state's corporation laws are favorable for corporations.

Corporations have an unlimited life. If one stockholder sells all of his shares to another individual, the corporation doesn't have to be reorganized. In a partnership, if one partner leaves and another takes his or her place, the partnership has to be reorganized.

A major advantage of the corporate form of ownership is the fact that the stockholders have limited liability. This is not the case for a sole proprietor or partners in a partnership. If a group of 10 individuals pooled their resources and invested $100,000 each into a partnership, the total assets of the firm would be $1 million dollars. Assume that the partnership engaged in business transactions, borrowed money, and so forth, and then went bankrupt. If the partnership assets were not sufficient to pay off all the liabilities, the partnership's creditors could come after the individual partners to pay off these liabilities. However, if these same 10 people formed a corporation and each invested $100,000 in the corporation, and if the corporation had to file bankruptcy, the corporation's creditors *could not* come after the individual stockholders to pay the corporation's obligations. Each stockholder's liability is limited to the amount of money that he or she invested; their individual homes and bank accounts would *not* be at risk. This factor alone is the main reason for the existence of so many corporations in the United States.

There are a few drawbacks to the corporate form of ownership. One of the drawbacks is that the corporation's income is taxed twice; this is usually referred to as "double taxation." First, the corporation's income is taxed. Second, any distributions to the stockholders in the form of dividends are also taxed—hence the double taxation.

Contributed Capital

Stockholders' equity on the balance sheet is made up of two components:

1. Paid-in capital or contributed capital
2. Retained earnings

Every day, millions of shares of stock in American corporations are traded on the New York Stock Exchange. However, nearly all of these transactions have absolutely no impact on the individual corporations. Why? Answer: Because most, if not all, of these transactions involve one shareholder selling his or her shares to another investor. The corporation whose stock is being bought and sold is not a party to these transactions. Corporations typically issue stock soon after they are established. This event is referred to as an IPO—an initial public offering. The corporation is offering shares of its common stock to the public. Sometimes these events receive a great deal of publicity; do you remember hearing about Google's IPO, which took place several years ago?

The journal entry to record the issuance of 100 shares of $10 par value common stock for $25 per share is

Cash	2,500	
Common Stock		1,000
Additional Paid-in Capital		1,500

There are several things to note about this journal entry. The amount credited to common stock is the number of shares issued times the par value. Par value is a somewhat meaningless or unimportant number. It reflects the so-called legal capital of the business. Even though the par value has little impact on either the corporation or its stockholders, accountants tend to follow tradition, and this is the traditional way to record the issuance of stock. Capital stock is credited for the number of shares multiplied by the par value of the stock, and the amount paid in excess of par is credited to additional paid-in capital.

On the balance sheet, the common stock entry will show three numbers in parentheses:

1. The number of shares authorized
2. The number of shares issued
3. The number of shares outstanding

Authorized shares are the total number of shares of stock that the board of directors has given the corporation approval to issue. The shares that have been issued are those that have been purchased by stockholders. Outstanding shares are those that have been purchased by shareholders and have not been bought back by the corporation.

Retained Earnings

The retained earnings of a corporation represent exactly what the words imply, namely, all of the corporation's earnings or income that have been retained, or not paid out to the stockholders in the form of a dividend. Thus, if a corporation had earnings of $100,000, $200,000, and $300,000 in its first 3 years of existence, and paid dividends of $20,000, $40,000, and $60,000, the balance in the retained earnings account would be $600,000 − $120,000, or $480,000.

One additional factor about the retained earnings account must be mentioned at this point. The balance in retained earnings does not mean that there is an amount of cash equal to the balance in retained earnings. The retained earnings balance is simply a historical record of the earnings less the dividends. Remember that net income is not equivalent to cash flow. Net income is simply the difference between revenues and gains less expenses and losses.

If a corporation earns a positive net income, but the cash balance does not equal the net income, then where did this net income go? The answer is that the net income is reflected in all the assets less the liabilities. The company's accounts receivable could have increased; they may have purchased some land or buildings, or paid off some liabilities. Net income is not equivalent to cash flow; retained earnings is not equivalent to an amount of cash either.

One additional point: The amount of money that can legally be paid to the stockholders is limited to the balance in the retained earnings account. Remember, of course, that it is state corporation laws that govern what corporations can do.

Common and Preferred Stock

Corporations can issue either one or two different types of stock. The two different types of stock are:

1. Common stock
2. Preferred stock

Common stock (which happens to be the most common) reflects the residual owners' equity. Common stockholders' equity reflects what would be left over (the residual) after all the creditors and preferred stockholders have been paid.

Common stockholders usually have the right to vote for the members of the **board of directors**. The board of directors, which represents a group of individuals, oversees the management of the corporation. Common stockholders also have the right to receive dividends (if the board of directors declares them) and to receive payment upon liquidation of any remaining amounts.

Preferred stock represents a kind of hybrid security that is in between long-term debt and owners' equity. Preferred stock has some of the attributes of debt and some of the attributes of equity, which are summarized below:

How Preferred Stock Is Like Equity

1. It represents an ownership interest.
2. Preferred stock does not have a maturity date.
3. There are usually several specific preferences that are related to being an owner, rather than a creditor, such as preferences regarding dividends and preferences at liquidation.

How Preferred Stock Is Like Debt

1. The dividend is a stated dollar amount each year (like interest on a bond).
2. In good years or bad, the company pays the same amount of dividend.

The list below summarizes the major preferences associated with preferred stock. Let us make sure that you understand all of them.

Preferred Stock Preferences

Dividends

At liquidation

Cumulative

Participating

Convertible

Dividends on preferred stock are paid before any dividends are paid to the common shareholders. In the event of a liquidation (if the company goes out of business), the creditors are paid first, then money is paid to the preferred stockholders. The common stockholders get whatever is left after paying the creditors and the preferred stockholders.

Most preferred stock is **cumulative**. This means that if the company did not have enough cash to pay the cash dividends to the preferred shareholders, the dividend accumulates. We refer to these unpaid dividends as **dividends in arrears**. Before any dividends can be paid to the common stockholders, all the accumulated dividends in arrears must be paid to the preferred stockholders.

The **participating** feature of a preferred stock involves sharing some of the net income with the common shareholders. Assume that a company has both common and preferred stock, and during the current year, it had extremely high earnings. If the preferred stock was not participating, the preferred dividend would be exactly the same as it has been since it was issued. A 5%, $100 par value share of preferred stock would pay a dividend of $5.00 per share in both good years and bad. However, if the preferred stock was participating, here is how the dividends would be divided: Preferred stockholders are paid their normal, or routine, dividend. A dividend equal to the same percentage as that which the preferred shareholders received is paid to the common shareholders. Any additional dividends that the board of directors declares are shared by the preferred and common shareholders, usually in proportion to their total par values. This can be a very important feature if you own a participating preferred stock. If the corporation has very high net income in a given year, you certainly would like to receive a part of that income as a cash dividend.

Cash Dividends, Stock Dividends, and Stock Splits

Dividends are a *distribution* of the earnings to the stockholders. Dividends are usually paid in cash. For a cash dividend, there are three important dates:

1. The declaration date
2. The stockholder of record date
3. The payment date

The declaration date is the date that the board of directors declares the dividend, making it a legal liability of the corporation. The stockholder of record date indicates the last day someone could buy the stock and still be entitled to the dividend. The payment date is when the checks are issued and mailed to the stockholders.

Here are the two typical entries for a cash dividend—the first one is made on the declaration date and the second one is made on the payment date. For the first entry, you can debit a dividend account and then close that account to retained earnings at the end of the period, or you can just debit retained earnings directly. Assume that a cash dividend of $50,000 is declared and paid to the common stockholders. The two journal entries would look like this:

Dividends (R/E)	50,000	
Dividends Payable		50,000
Dividends Payable	50,000	
Cash		50,000

A stock dividend consists of a distribution of additional shares of the corporation's own stock instead of cash. A small stock dividend (less than 20%–25% of the total shares outstanding) is accounted for at the *market value* of the stock. A large stock dividend (more than 20%–25% of the total shares outstanding) is accounted for at the par value of the shares.

Take note of the special case of a 100% stock dividend. It has the same effect on the market price as a 2:1 stock split (which we will look at next); however, there is a difference. There is no journal entry for a split, but a stock dividend transfers money from the retained earnings account to the common stock account and (in the event of a small stock dividend) the additional paid-in capital account. When a corporation has positive net income, but does not have a lot of excess cash on hand, they might consider a stock dividend.

Assume 100,000 shares of stock are outstanding (par value $1, market value $10). A 5% stock dividend would involve 5,000 shares. This is a small stock dividend (<20%–25%). The journal entry would be

Retained Earnings	50,000 (5,000 shares × $10)
Common Stock	5,000 (5,000 × $1)
Additional Paid-in Capital	45,000 (50,000 − 45,000)

A 100% stock dividend would involve 100,000 shares (100,000 shares outstanding × 100% = 100,000 shares of stock). This is a large stock dividend (> 20%–25% of the total shares outstanding). We can break down a stock dividend into two separate transactions: First, the corporation gives the stockholders a cash dividend, and then the corporation asks the stockholders to use that cash to purchase additional shares of stock. The two journal entries would be

Retained Earnings	10,000,000	
Cash		10,000,000
Cash	10,000,000	
Common Stock		10,000,000

If you eliminate the debit and credit to cash in these entries, you have the entry for a stock dividend, namely,

Retained Earnings	10,000,000	
Common Stock		10,000,000

A stock split (typically 2 for 1) gives the stockholder two new shares for every old one. As soon as this occurs, there will be twice as many shares outstanding, and the market price of one share of common stock will immediately drop by half (the par value of the new shares will be half of the original par value).

What is the impact of a stock split? In point of fact, the stockholder is in the exact same position both before and after the split. He or she still owns the same percentage of the total shares, and the total market value of his or her shares is the same. The stockholder simply has twice as many shares; each new share is now worth half of what the old shares were worth before the split. (Remember that the impact of a 2:1 split on the market price of the stock is exactly the same as for a 100% stock dividend, namely, the market price drops by half.)

Most stockholders welcome a split because shares of stock seem to gravitate to a certain value. If the stock is selling for $30 per share and there is a 2:1 split, the new shares will be worth $15, but there is a good chance that over time, the market price will climb to $30 again. Companies will split the shares to reduce the price of the stock to get it into (what they believe) is an optimal price range. They do this to keep the stock at an attractive price for investors. When a stock's price is too high, many investors will not want to buy it.

People who invest in the stock market often have a goal; some may want to double their money in a year. It's a lot easier to double your money with a stock that costs $5; it has to go up only 5 points during the year. A $50 stock would have to go up 50 points in that same period to make the same percentage return.

Treasury Stock

Every now and then, a corporation purchases shares of its own common stock from a local stockbroker. You may well ask, Why would they buy shares of their own stock when they could simply print up new shares? Here is the answer: From time to time, corporations need to have shares of their own stock to fulfill stock option and stock purchase plan transaction *and* these shares must be registered with the SEC. Since the shares that they would buy from a stockbroker are already registered (and since the registration process is quite costly), it is cost-effective to buy shares that are outstanding and already registered, instead of printing new shares that would have to be registered.

We refer to these shares as "treasury stock." The term comes from the fact that when the company purchases these shares, it places them in the corporation's treasury. There are actually two different methods for accounting for treasury stock: the cost method and the par value method. We will illustrate and use the cost method.

There are two typical journal entries associated with treasury stock:

1. The purchase of treasury stock
2. The sale of treasury stock

When treasury stock is purchased (using the cost method), we debit treasury stock and credit cash. The treasury stock is a contra-owners' equity account. The amount in the account is subtracted from total owners' equity.

When treasury shares are sold, there is usually a difference between the cost and the selling price of the shares. This difference yields a gain or a loss. However, it does not make any sense for a corporation to have a gain or loss by buying and selling itself. Therefore, the difference between the cost and the selling price is credited to additional paid-in capital if there is a gain. If there is a loss, additional paid-in capital is debited (if there were any previously recognized gains). If there were no additional amounts of paid-in capital arising from previous treasury stock transactions, the retained earnings account is debited.

EXAMPLE:

IBM buys 100 shares of IBM common stock for $50 per share.

Treasury Stock	5,000	
Cash		5,000

IBM sells 10 shares of treasury stock for $70 per share.

Cash	700	
Treasury Stock		500
Additional Paid-in Capital		200

IBM sells 10 shares of treasury stock for $40 per share.

Cash	400	
APIC	100	
Treasury Stock		500

The balance in the treasury stock account is subtracted from total owners' equity on the balance sheet. Furthermore, cash dividends are not paid to shares being held in the treasury (to whom would you pay the dividend?). ■

Other Comprehensive Income

The concept of **comprehensive income** was developed by the FASB as part of its conceptual framework project. Comprehensive income includes *all* changes in the net assets of a business from transactions and events involving nonowners. It includes all changes in the equity of a business (assets less liabilities) except investments by owners and dividends paid to owners.

If we draw a picture of comprehensive income, it would look like figure 7-2.

The overwhelming majority of comprehensive income is made up of net income. In fact, there are only a few specific items that make up other comprehensive income. Here are three such items:

1. Unrealized gains and losses on available-for-sale securities
2. Foreign currency translation adjustments
3. Adjustments in computing the minimum liability related to a company's pension plan

Accumulated other comprehensive income is shown on the balance sheet as part of owners' equity.

Other Comprehensive Income .01%
Net Income 99.9%

FIGURE 7-2 Diagram of Comprehensive Income

Statement of Stockholders' Equity

When the financial statements are prepared, along with the income statement, balance sheet, and statement of cash flows, the company also prepares a statement of owners' equity. This statement is usually presented in the form of a grid, or spreadsheet. Across the top of the statement, there are column headings representing each component of owners' equity:

Common Stock

Additional Paid-in Capital

Retained Earnings

Treasury Stock

Accumulated Other Comprehensive Income

Along the side of the page are row headings representing the beginning balance, the ending balance, and every transaction that had a direct impact on the balance of one of the components of owners' equity, such as net income, issuance of common stock, and so forth.

Figure 7-3 below shows a typical statement of owners' equity.

	Common Stock	APIC	Retained Earnings	Other Accumulated Comprehensive Income	Treasury Stock	Total Owners' Equity
Company Name Statement of Owners' Equity for the year ending 12/31/08						
Beginning Balance	$2,000	$500	$800	$600	<100>	$3,800
Net Income			500			500
Foreign Currency Translation Adjustment				100		100
Purchase Treasury Stock					<200>	<200>
Issue Common Stock	350	100				450
Pay Cash Dividend			<200>			<200>
Ending Balance	$2,350	$600	$1,100	$700	<$300>	$4,400

FIGURE 7-3 Statement of Stockholders' Equity

Balance Sheet Presentation

On the balance sheet, owners' equity is made up of four basic elements, or components:

1. Paid-in capital
2. Retained earnings
3. Accumulated other comprehensive income
4. Treasury stock

A typical owners' equity section of the balance sheet might look like this:

Owners' Equity

Paid-in Capital

Common Stock, par $1.00 (5,000,000 shares authorized, 500,000 issued and outstanding)	$500,000
Additional Paid-in Capital	2,000,000
Retained Earnings	3,000,000
Accumulated Other Comprehensive Income	100,000
Less Treasury Stock	<200,000>
Total Owners' equity	$5,900,000

DEMONSTRATION PROBLEM   *Comprehensive Owners' Equity Problem*

Geraldine Lauro, Inc. had the following balances on January 1, 2007:

Common stock ($10 par)	$100,000 (authorized 500,000 shares, issued and outstanding 100,000)
Additional paid-in capital	$50,000
Retained earnings	$750,000

The following transactions took place during 2006:

June 1 Declared and paid a 5% stock dividend to the common shareholders when the market price of the stock was $20

July 1 Declared and paid a $2 per share cash dividend to the common shareholders

August 1 Declared a 2:1 stock split

September 1 Purchased 1,000 shares of its own common stock for $18.00 per share

October 1 Reissued 500 of the 1,000 shares purchased on September 1 for $20 per share

Required: Prepare journal entries for the transactions above and show how the stockholders' equity section of the balance sheet would look on December 31, 2006.

6/1	Retained Earnings	100,000	
	Common Stock		50,000 (5,000 shares × $10 par value)
	Additional Paid-in Capital		50,000

(A 5% stock dividend is considered a small stock dividend, which is accounted for at the market value of the shares; thus, 5% of 100,000 shares = 5,000 dividend shares × market price of $20 = $100,000 debited to retained earnings. The credit to common stock is the number of shares multiplied by the par value (5,000 × $10 = $50,000) and the excess goes to additional paid-in capital.)

| 7/1 | Retained Earnings | 210,000 | |
| | Cash | | 210,000 |

Cash dividends are paid on the outstanding shares. In this problem, we started with 100,000 shares of common stock outstanding, but the first journal entry involved the issuance of 5,000 additional shares. Thus, the cash dividend is 105,000 shares × 20, or $210,000.

8/1 There is no journal entry for a stock split. What will happen is that the number of shares will double and the par value will drop by half. Thus, after the split, there will be 105,000 × 2, or 210,000 par $5 shares outstanding.

9/1	Treasury Stock	18,000	
	Cash		18,000
10/1	Cash	10,000	
	Treasury Stock		9,000
	Additional Paid-in Capital		1,000

(Treasury stock is accounted for at cost. The shares go on the books at cost and they go off the books at cost. Any gains go to additional paid-in capital; any losses go first as a debit to additional paid-in capital to reduce any previously recognized gains, then they are debited to retained earnings. Gains and losses on treasury stock are not a part of net income.)

Owners' Equity   The owners' equity section of the balance sheet would look like:

Common Stock ($5.00 par value, 1,000,000 shares authorized, 209,500 shares issued and outstanding)	$150,000
Additional Paid-in Capital	101,000
Retained Earnings	440,000
Less Treasury Stock (500 shares)	<9,000>
Total Stockholders' Equity	$682,000

Note: On the balance sheet for common stock, you must show the par value, as well as the number of shares authorized, issued, and outstanding. The shares in the treasury have been issued, but are not outstanding. The additional paid-in capital is made up of the original balance of $50,000, plus another $50,000 when the stock dividend was declared, and $1,000 from the sale of the treasury shares. The balance in retained earnings equals the beginning balance of $750,000 less $100,000 for the stock dividend and less $210,000 for the cash dividend. This is a somewhat simplified problem. If there were more transactions, you might want to set up

T-accounts to help you accumulate the totals for the balance sheet. Just for the record, here is what your retained earnings T-account would look like:

Retained Earnings

$100,000	$750,000
210,000	

$440,000   ■

SUMMARY OF JOURNAL ENTRIES

One technique that I find to be very useful is to take this list of transactions and journal entries, cover the right-hand side of the page with a blank sheet of paper so that you can just see the description of the transaction, and then write out each journal entry. After writing out each entry, just slide the paper down a bit and check to see that you made the correct entry. Do this before your exams to test your understanding of the material.

Transaction	Journal Entry
Issue common stock at par	Cash
	Common Stock
Issue common stock above par	Cash
	Common Stock
	Additional Paid-in Capital
Declare a cash dividend	Retained Earnings
	Dividends Payable
Pay cash dividend	Dividends Payable
	Cash
Declare and pay a cash dividend	Retained Earnings
	Cash
Declare and pay a small stock dividend (recorded at the market price of the stock)	Retained Earnings
	Common Stock
	Additional Paid-in Capital
Declare and pay a large stock dividend (recorded at the par value of the stock)	Retained Earnings
	Common Stock
Stock split (No account balances change when a stock split occurs.)	There is no journal entry for a stock split.
Purchase treasury stock	Treasury Stock
	Cash
Reissue treasury stock at a gain	Cash
	Treasury Stock
	Additional Paid-in Capital
Reissue treasury stock at a loss	Cash
	Retained Earnings
	Treasury Stock

REVIEW QUESTIONS

1. *Does the retained earnings account represent an amount of cash that is available to pay dividends to the stockholders?*

The balance in the retained earnings account at any point reflects the total income that the company has earned since it was organized, less any dividends paid. The balance in the retained earnings is totally independent of the balance in cash (or any other asset). The retained earnings balance is like the running total in a ball game; it is the score. Retained earnings represent all the income that the company has earned less any distributions in the form of dividends.

2. *What is the significance of par value? What exactly does par value mean?*

Par value has minimal significance. It represents the legal capital of the firm, which is a measure of the firm's permanent capital. From an operational viewpoint, it is the amount that must be paid for a share of stock for the stockholder to have limited liability. Beyond this, it has no meaning, yet accountants traditionally record the issuance of common stock this way: The amount of cash paid is debited to cash. The number of shares of stock issued, multiplied by the par value, is credited to common stock and the excess is credited to additional paid-in capital. In some states, companies may pay dividends if there is a positive balance in additional paid-in capital; we refer to these dividends as liquidating dividends.

3. *What is a stock dividend and what is a stock split? How are these two items similar and how do they differ?*

A stock dividend is just like a cash dividend, but the stockholder receives shares of the company's stock instead of cash. There is a journal entry to record stock dividends. Retained earnings is debited, and common stock is credited. Small stock dividends are recorded at the market price of the stock. Large stock dividends are recorded at the par value of the common stock.

In a stock split (typically, 2:1), the stockholder is given two new shares of common stock for each old share. Note that a 100% stock dividend would have exactly the same impact on the market price as a 2:1 stock split. The market price would drop by half. That's the similarity. The major difference is that there is a journal entry for a stock dividend, but no entry for a stock split. Thus, only a stock dividend results in reducing retained earnings. A stock split has no effect on the balance in retained earnings.

4. *What are earnings per share, and what is meant by basic earnings per share and diluted earnings per share?*

Earnings per share are essentially what the words indicate—the earnings (net income) of the company on a per share basis. We compute the earnings per share by taking the net income less any preferred dividends, and divide that amount by the number of shares of common stock outstanding. This tells the stockholders what each share of common stock earned. The earnings per share must be disclosed in two ways:

basic earnings per share and diluted earnings per share. The basic earnings per share reflect the actual earnings per share. The diluted earnings per share reflect a "what if" calculation.

To compute **diluted earnings per share**, we examine every **potentially dilutive security** (that's a security that isn't common stock now, such as convertible preferred stock or convertible bonds, but that could become common stock through exercise by the owner of the security) and assume that each potentially dilutive security is exercised, or converted, into common stock at the earliest possible date. Then we calculate what the earnings per share would be. The diluted earnings per share figure is disclosed to alert the shareholders about what could happen to earnings per share *if* everyone who owned a potentially dilutive security decided to exercise their option to acquire shares of common stock.

5. *What is the difference between owning preferred stock versus common stock?*

Preferred stock has a number of preferences associated with it. The preferred dividend is a fixed dollar amount. Preferred stockholders receive the same dividends every year regardless of whether the company earned a large or small net income. Other stock preferences (which may or may not be included) are convertible, cumulative, and participating. Convertible preferred stock can be converted into common stock. With cumulative preferred stock, if the company cannot pay the dividend in a given year, the dividend that is "skipped" (i.e., not distributed) accumulates and must be paid to the preferred stockholders before any dividends can be paid to the common stockholders. With a participating preferred stockholders, after the preferred stockholders get their regular dividend and the common stockholders receive their dividends, if any money remains that the company wants to distribute as a dividend, the preferred stockholder "participates" and thus receives an additional dividend. Typically, only common stockholders vote for the board of directors; preferred stockholders do not get to vote. In addition to voting for the directors, common shareholders are entitled to receive dividends if they are declared by the board of directors.

6. *What is convertible preferred stock?*

Convertible preferred stock allows the preferred stockholders to convert, or exchange, his or her shares of preferred stock and receive a stated number of shares of common stock, based on a predetermined formula.

7. *What is treasury stock? Why do companies buy back their own stock when they could simply print new shares?*

Treasury stock represents shares of the company's own common stock that the company has purchased on the general market (and put in their treasury—hence the name treasury stock). The most common reason for a company to buy back its own common stock is to be able to fund employees' stock purchase plans and stock option plans. You may wonder why the company does not simply print additional shares. The reason is that the shares that they issue under stock purchase plans and stock option plans must be *registered* with the SEC. This is a very costly process; thus, it is simply cheaper to buy shares on the open market that have already been registered.

8. *Why don't all corporations pay cash dividends?*

Some companies that are very profitable assume that their stockholders could not earn as high a return if they were given a share of the corporation's earnings in the form of a cash dividend. So, the company simply keeps the money and reinvests it in the company where it may be earning as much as 15%−20%. Individual stockholders would be hard pressed to find ways to invest their dividends and earn 15%−20%. Microsoft Corp. had not paid a dividend until very recently, based on this same logic.

9. *From a stockholders perspective, which would be preferable—a stock dividend or a stock split?*

A stockholder would most likely prefer a stock split, since this gives him or her more shares of stock, which hopefully will increase in value and does not reduce retained earnings the way that a stock dividend would. Since dividends are limited by the balance in retained earnings, stockholders want retained earnings to be as large as possible.

10. *What are the main advantages of organizing a business as a corporation?*

The major advantage of the corporate form of ownership is limited liability for stockholders. If the corporation becomes bankrupt, the creditors cannot come after the stockholders to pay the corporation's debts. This is not true of a sole proprietorship or a partnership.

PRACTICE MULTIPLE CHOICE QUESTIONS

1. The following information must be shown on the balance sheet for each class of stock:

   a. The number of shares authorized

   b. The number of shares issued

   c. The number of shares outstanding

   d. All of the above

Solution: The correct answer is **d**. We have seen several questions like this one already; there are three items and then choice **d** is all of the above. Remember, if any two seem correct, then there is a very good chance that all of the above is the right answer.

2. The journal entry for a small stock dividend would be

   a. Retained Earnings
       Common Stock
       Additional Paid-in Capital

   b. Retained Earnings
       Common Stock

   c. Additional Paid-in Capital
       Common Stock

   d. Dividends Payable
       Common Stock
       Additional Paid-in Capital

Solution: The correct answer is **b**. A small stock dividend is recorded at the market value of the stock. Therefore, there must be two accounts credited—common stock for the number of shares multiplied by the par value, and additional paid-in capital for the excess above par. Choice **a** would be the correct answer for a large stock dividend. Choices **c** and **d** are not standard journal entries.

3. The journal entry to record a 2:1 stock split is

    a. Retained Earnings
           Common Stock

    b. Common Stock
           Additional Paid-in capital

    c. Common Stock
           Cash

    d. There is no journal entry for a stock split.

Solution: The correct answer is **d**. This is almost a trick question. The rule is simple: There is no journal entry for a stock split because none of the balances in any owners' equity account is affected by a stock split. Choice **a** would be the correct answer for a large stock dividend. Choices **b** and **c** make no sense in the context of this question.

4. Which of the following items is included in other comprehensive income?

    a. Extraordinary items

    b. Contingent liabilities

    c. Unrealized gains and losses on available-for-sale securities

    d. Foreign currency transaction gains and losses

Solution: The correct answer is **c**. Choices **a** and **b** have nothing to do with comprehensive income. Choice **d** is a tricky one. As it turns out, foreign currency translation gains and losses are part of comprehensive income, but foreign currency transaction gains and losses are not.

5. When a company buys treasury stock and then sells it for more than they paid for the shares, the excess goes to

    a. other gains and losses.

    b. retained earnings.

    c. additional paid-in capital.

    d. common stock.

Solution: The correct answer is **c**. The so-called gains and losses on treasury stock transactions do not go to the income statement (you cannot show a profit by buying and selling your own stock). Instead, the gains are credited to additional paid-in capital. Losses are first debited to additional paid-in capital to reduce any previously recorded gains, then they are debited to retained earnings. Choice **b** would be a correct answer for losses on treasury stock transactions. Choice **a** is an income statement caption, and these gains and losses do not go to the income statement. Choice **d** is simply wrong.

CHAPTER 8

THE STATEMENT
OF CASH FLOWS

LEARNING OBJECTIVES

After studying this chapter, you will understand:

- the three major sources of cash flows
- the direct approach and the indirect approach to preparing a statement of cash flows
- converting operating revenues and expenses on the accrual basis to the cash basis
- determining the cash flows from operating activity by making additions to and subtractions from net income, and
- a six-step approach to preparing a statement of cash flows

HERE IS where we are going in our study of the statement of cash flows. There are three principal financial statements: the income statement, the balance sheet, and the statement of cash flows. We have looked at the income statement and the balance sheet in some detail, now we will focus our attention on the statement of cash flows.

The income statement shows the amount of profit that the company earned during the period. The balance sheet shows the financial position of the company on a given date. Both of these statements are important. However, if we want to know how much cash the business is generating, we need to look at the statement of cash flows. This statement is very important, since without an adequate amount of cash, the business will not survive.

The format of the statement of cash flows always looks the same. The cash flows are divided into three categories:

1. Cash from operating activities

2. Cash from investing activities

3. Cash from financing activities

The sum of the cash flows from these three sources equals the change in cash for the period. This is exactly equal to the difference between the beginning balance of cash on the balance sheet and the ending balance of cash.

The three categories of cash flows are easy to understand. Cash from operating activities reflects the cash receipts and disbursements that are part of the *core business activities* of the firm. Cash from investing activities involves buying and selling noncurrent assets. The final category is cash from financing activities. The transactions reflected here include issuing stocks and bonds, borrowing (or repaying) money, purchasing (or reselling) treasury stock, and paying dividends.

The sum of the cash flows from these three categories equals the change in cash. If you add the change in cash to the beginning balance of cash, the total would equal the ending balance in cash.

In addition to the cash flows listed above, the statement of cash flows often has a schedule appended to it—the schedule of noncash investing and financing activities. This schedule is used to report investing and financing activities that did not involve cash.

As we shall see in this chapter, there are two different approaches to calculating cash from operating activities—the **direct approach** and the **indirect approach**. The direct approach involves adding all the cash receipts from the basic operations of the business and subtracting all the cash disbursements. Since most businesses keep track of revenues and expenses using the accrual basis, if we use the direct method on the statement of cash flows, we must convert all the accrual numbers to the cash basis—this could be a lot of work. Using the indirect approach is a bit easier, all we have to do is begin with net income and eliminate any items that are included in net income but did not involve cash. The result is cash from operating activities.

Here's another "commercial announcement" from your author. If I were asked to make up a final exam for an introductory financial accounting class and were told that the exam must consist of a single problem, the problem that I would use would be the preparation of a statement of cash flows. Why? The answer is that preparing a statement of cash flows involves issues and transactions from virtually every chapter in this book.

Study this chapter very carefully, and review the demonstration problems (several times, perhaps). You might also ask your instructor to give you the solution to several statement of cash flows problems from your textbook. You want to be able to "do these problems in your sleep."

OBJECTIVES OF THE STATEMENT OF CASH FLOWS

The statement of cash flows is one of the three major financial statements, along with the income statement and the balance sheet. Remember that all three of these statements articulate; that is, they are linked. The change in the cash balance on the balance sheet from the beginning of the period to the end of the period is the bottom line on the statement of cash flows.

The statement of cash flows has two objectives:

1. To explain the change in cash from the beginning of the year to the end of the year

2. To show the results of three different types of activities:
   a. Operating activities
   b. Investing activities
   c. Financing activities

FORMAT OF THE STATEMENT OF CASH FLOWS

Based on the objectives listed above, the basic outline of the statement of cash flows looks like this:

Company Name

Statement of Cash Flows

for the year ending 12/31/07

Cash from Operating Activities

Cash from Investing Activities

Cash from Financing Transactions

Change in Cash

Schedule of Noncash Investment and Financing Activities

The cash flows from *operating activities* are essentially the cash flows from the basic operations of the business. For example, for The Gap, cash from operating activities would come primarily from selling clothing.

The cash flows from *investing activities* come from buying and selling assets. The cash flows from *financing activities* involve issuing stocks and bonds, long-term liabilities transactions, treasury stock transactions, and paying cash dividends.

The schedule of noncash investing and financing transactions appears on the bottom of the page, below the line that shows the change in cash. This schedule is very important. Every now and then, a company enters into a transaction that affects long-term assets and owners' equity, but does not involve cash. For example, assume that a company acquired land by issuing shares of stock. This is certainly an investing transaction (acquiring land) and it is also a financing activity (issuing common stock), but it clearly had nothing to do with cash. Under current GAAP, transactions such as the one above (acquiring land for cash) must be disclosed in the schedule of noncash investing and financing activities.

Several years ago, a transaction like the one described in the previous paragraph was reported on the statement of cash flows as follows:

In the investing activity section:

Acquire Land (by issuing common stock)

In the financing section:

Issue Common Stock (to acquire land)

The problem with this disclosure was that it was confusing. People saw these items and were convinced that all of these items were either a source or a use of cash. Under the current rules, showing this transaction in the schedule leaves no doubt that this transaction, while an investing event and a financing event, did not have anything to do with cash.

There are two different approaches to preparing a statement of cash flows:

1. The direct approach
2. The indirect approach

The two approaches compute cash flows from operating activities in a completely different manner. Otherwise, everything else on the statement is exactly the same.

Using the direct approach, cash from operating activities is calculated by taking all the cash receipts from operations and subtracting all the cash disbursements from operations. This would not be problematical, except for the fact that we generally record transactions using the accrual basis, not the cash basis. Thus, to get the cash receipts and cash disbursements for the direct method, we have to convert virtually everything from the accrual basis to the cash basis. You can do this, but you have to think about it, and it can be difficult.

The indirect approach is different. Under this approach, we begin with a number that is quite close to the number we are looking for. The number we begin with is net income. Net income is pretty much equal to cash flows from operating activities, *except* that it includes a few items that do not affect cash. So, all we have to do is eliminate those items that do not affect cash but are included in calculating net income, and what we are left with is *cash flows from operating activities.*

When I explain the indirect approach in class, I usually tell this story. A sculptor is asked, How do you carve an elephant from a large block of granite? Here is his answer: You just take the block of granite and chip away everything that does not look like an elephant. This is how we apply the indirect method. We start with net income and chip away everything that did not involve cash.

Let us look at a simple example. Assume that revenues were $1,000 (all cash) and expenses were $800 (all cash except for $100 of depreciation expense). To compute the cash flows from operating activities, begin with the net income. Revenue of $1,000 less expenses of $800 equals an income of $200. Take the net income of $200 and eliminate the depreciation expense. Do this by adding $100 to the net income. (Depreciation expense was subtracted from revenue, but did not use up cash; therefore, eliminate a minus $100 by adding $100.) Thus, the cash flow from operating activity is $300—net income of $200 plus the depreciation expense of $100. Another way to prove that the cash flow is really $300 would be to take all the cash revenues and subtract cash expense. The expenses were $800 and $100 of the expenses were not cash; thus, the cash expenses were $800 − $100, or $700. Now take the cash revenue of $1,000 less the cash expenses of $700, and the result is the same $300.

As it turns out, there are truly just a handful of transactions (like depreciation expense) that must be added to or subtracted from net income to generate cash from operating activities using the indirect method. We will review all of these items in the chapter, and I will present an all-inclusive list of virtually all possible adjustments to net income to determine the cash from operating activities.

In addition to items such as depreciation expense (which must be *added* to net income), there are other items, such as a gain on the sale of an asset (which must be subtracted). The logic is simple. We added back the depreciation expense because it was subtracted from revenue originally in determining net income, but it didn't use up any cash. Similarly, we subtract the gain on the sale of an asset because it was originally added to revenues to determine net income, but it didn't represent cash inflows (the cash that came in when the asset was sold is the selling price)—that number is shown in the cash from investing activities section of the statement.

We will review the calculations for cash flows from operating activities using both the direct and the indirect method in chapter. Furthermore, there are several rather comprehensive demonstration problems in the chapter that I will walk you through. In the real world, most corporations report to their stockholders using the indirect approach. In this chapter, I will introduce you to a step-by-step process for preparing a statement of cash flows using the indirect method.

Figures 8-1 and 8-2 illustrate the statement of cash flows prepared using the indirect approach and the direct approach.

A STEP-BY-STEP APPROACH TO SOLVING STATEMENT OF CASH FLOWS PROBLEMS

Here are six simple steps:

1. Read the problem carefully. Determine which approach is being used. Become familiar with the accounts; note any unusual transactions or statement elements.

2. Outline the solution on your paper—no numbers yet.

3. Calculate the change in cash from the balance sheet and enter the resulting number on the bottom of the statement of cash flows. (Do not change this number as you work through the problem.)

4. Evaluate the additional information, using T-accounts to analyze the changes in each account and to determine whether any numbers from your analysis of a particular account belong on the statement of cash flows. Check off on the balance sheet each account that you have analyzed.

5. Now go down the balance sheet and analyze every account that has not been checked off.

6. Edit your solution.

Now we will look at how to prepare a statement of cash flows using both approaches. We will walk through two demonstration problems. Just to let you know, at the end of the chapter there is another, more comprehensive problem, with solutions, using both the direct and indirect approaches.

Cash from Operating Activities		Cash Received from Customers	
Net Income		Interest received	+
Adjustments to Net Income		Dividends received	+
Depreciation Expense	+	Less Payments to Employees	< >
Amortization Expense	+	Less Payments to Suppliers	< >
Loss on Sale of Building	+	Less Payments of Interest	< >
Less Gain on Sale of	< >	Less Payments of Income Tax	< >
Investment			
Less Increase in Inventory	< >		
Increase in A/P	+		
Cash from Investing Activities		Cash from Investing Activities	
Purchase Building	< >	Purchase Building	< >
Proceeds from Sale of Land	+	Proceeds from Sale of Land	+
Purchase Investments	< >	Purchase Investments	< >
Cash from Financing Activities		Cash from Financing Activities	
Issue Common Stock	+	Issue Common Stock	+
Retire Bonds	< >	Retire Bonds	< >
Pay Cash Dividends	< >	Pay Cash Dividends	< >
Change in Cash			

Schedule of Noncash Investing & Financing Transactions	**Schedule of Noncash Investing & Financing Transactions**
Acquire building by issuing common stock	Acquire building by issuing common stock
Acquire land by issuing note payable	Acquire land by issuing note payable

Note: The two approaches produce statements of cash flows that are identical with regard to cash from investing and cash from financing activities. The amount of cash from operating activities will be exactly the same, but the method for computing the number is very different.

FIGURE 8-1 Statement of Cash Flows— Indirect Approach

FIGURE 8-2 Statement of Cash Flows— Direct Approach

Preparing the Statement of Cash Flows (Direct Approach)

The critical step in preparing a statement of cash flows using the direct approach is determining the cash from operating activities. We need to come up with the cash receipts and cash disbursements for operating events or transactions. We begin with collections from customers. If all sales were for cash, this would be simple, but most companies make both cash and credit sales. To convert sales to the cash basis, we take the total sales figure and adjust that number for the change in accounts receivable. Thus, if total sales were $100,000 and accounts receivable decreased by $10,000, cash from customers must have been $110,000 ($100,000 in sales, *plus* we collected $10,000 of accounts receivable on top of that).

Computing payments to suppliers (for purchases of merchandise inventory) involves two adjustments—one for changes in the level of inventory and one for the changes in accounts payable. The total calculation would be as follows:

Payments to suppliers = Cost of goods sold + increase in inventory or
− decrease in inventory
+ decrease in accounts payable, or
− increase in accounts payable

Payments to employees is quite simple:

Payments to employees = Salary expense + decrease in salaries payable, or
− increase in salaries payable

The chart below summarizes most of the basic calculations that you might need to make:

Calculating Cash from Operating Activities Using the Direct Approach

Receipts from customers = Sales + decrease in accounts receivable, or − increase in accounts receivable

Receipts of interest = Interest revenue + decrease in interest receivable, or − increase in interest receivable

Payments to suppliers = Cost of goods sold + increase in inventory, or − decrease in inventory + decrease in accounts payable, or − increase in accounts payable

Payments of operating expenses = Operating expense + increase in prepaid expenses, or − decrease in prepaid expenses + decrease in accrued liabilities, or − increase in accrued liabilities

Payment to employees = Salary expense + decrease in salaries payable, or − increase in salaries payable

Payment of interest = interest expense + decrease in interest payable, or − increase in interest payable

Payment of income tax = Income tax expense + decrease in taxes payable, or − increase in taxes payable

The cash flows from investing activities consist of buying and selling non-current assets. There are two things to remember about the sale of a depreciable asset: First, it's the proceeds from the sale that gets into the investing section; second, the gain or loss on the sale is included as an adjustment to net income in the operating activities section.

The cash flows from financing activities include issuing stock and bonds, borrowing money from the bank, treasury stock transactions, and the payment of cash dividends. Making up T-accounts will really help you with your analysis in this area.

DEMONSTRATION PROBLEM 1 *Statement of Cash Flows (Direct Approach)*

The comparative balance sheet for B. Browdy Inc. as of December 31, 2006 and 2007, as well as the income statement for the year ended on December 31, 2007, are presented in Figure 8-3 below.

Balance Sheet
B. Browdy Inc.
for the year ending 12/31/08

Assets	2008	2007	Liabilities	2008	2007
Cash	$118,000	$10,000	Accounts Payable	$35,000	$25,000
Accounts Receivable	85,000	15,000	Salaries Payable	0	5,000
Supplies	12,000	20,000	Notes Payable	250,000	50,000
Inventory	20,000	25,000	Total Liabilities	305,000	80,000
Prepaid Rent	22,000	30,000	Owners' Equity		
Total Current Assets	257,000	100,000	Common Stock	100,000	100,000
Land	140,000	40,000	Retained Earnings	119,000	110,000
Buildings	50,000	50,000	Total Owners' Equity	219,000	210,000
Less Accumulated Depreciation	<15,000>	<10,000>			
Equipment	50,000	60,000	Total Liabilities		
Less Accumulated Depreciation	<21,000>	<20,000>	+ Owners' Equity	$524,000	$290,000
Patent	63,000	70,000			
Total non-current assets	267,000	190,000			
Total Assets	$524,000	$290,000			

Income Statement
B. Browdy Inc.
for the year ending 12/31/08

Sales Revenue	$250,000
Less Cost of Goods Sold	155,000
Gross Profit	95,000
Less Operating Expenses:	
Salaries	3,000
Rent	12,000
Depreciation Expense	11,000
Amortization of Patent	7,000
Supplies	18,000
Interest	20,000
Total Expenses	71,000
Income from Operations	24,000
Gain on Sale of Equipment	10,000
Net Income	$34,000

FIGURE 8-3 Preparing a Statement of Cash Flows: Direct Approach

Additional Information: A piece of equipment that cost $10,000 and was 50% depreciated was sold for $15,000.

Required: Prepare a statement of cash flows using the direct approach.

Solution:

1. The first step is to read the problem carefully.

2. Put an outline of the statement on paper—just the main captions. It should look like this:

> Statement of Cash Flows
> B. Browdy Inc.
> for the year ending 12/31/08
> Cash from Operating Activities
> Cash from Investing Activities
> Cash from Financing Activities
> Change in Cash

3. The third step is to compute the change in cash and put that number on the bottom line of the statement of cash flows. In this problem, the change in cash is $118,000 − $10,000, or $108,000. No matter what numbers I come up with in the body of the statement, I am not going to change that $108 figure; that's definitely the right number.

4. Now begin your analysis. Start with the cash flows from operating activities. Using the direct method, take the numbers from the income statement, which are based on accrual accounting, and convert them to cash.

Let's start with collections from customers. Sales were $250,000 and accounts receivable increased by $70. That means that the company did not collect the full $250,000 in cash, but received only $180,000 ($250,000 − $70,000). Now enter the first line in the cash flows from operating activities section: Collections from Customers $180,000.

Now let us work on the expenses, starting with cost of goods sold. The cash flow related to this expense item is the cash paid to suppliers for inventory that the company purchased from vendors. In this case, it is the cost of goods sold [$155,000 less the decrease in inventory ($5), less the increase in accounts payable ($10,000)] for a total cash disbursement of $140,000. Enter that number on the statement.

Payments to employees are equal to salary expense plus the decrease in salaries payable. That would be $3,000 + $5,000, or $8,000.

Payments for supplies would be equal to the supplies expense on the income statement less the decrease in supplies (18,000 − 8,000 = 10,000). (Using some of the supplies that the company already had on hand meant that there was that much less that the company had to go out and use cash to buy.)

Payment for rent would be equal to the rent expense on the income statement of $12,000 less the decrease in prepaid rent of $8, or $4.

The only other cash flow item in the income statement is the gain on the sale of equipment. Make a quick calculation:

Cost of Equipment	$10,000
Accumulated Depreciation	$5,000
Book Value	$5,000
Selling Price	$15,000
Gain on Sale	$10,000

The proceeds from this transaction, $15,000, belong in the investing section.

That completes our review of the income statement items, now let us turn to the balance sheet. We are looking for any items that could result in cash flows. Look at the land account; it increased from $40,000 to $140,000, indicating that the company purchased land for $100,000. Enter that number in the investing section. Notes payable increased by $200. That looks like the company borrowed $200,000 from the bank and signed a note. For that item, add "Borrow Cash from Bank, Sign Note Payable, $200,000." This item goes in the financing section of the statement. Always make up a T-account to analyze retained earnings. Here we go:

Retained Earnings

	110,000
25,000	34,000

119

What this analysis tells us is that B. Browdy Inc. must have paid a dividend of $25; that item goes in the financing section.

Believe it or not, you are finished. Your statement of cash flows now looks like this:

Statement of Cash Flows
B. Browdy Inc.
for the year ending 12/31/08

Cash from Operating Activities:

Collections from Customers	$180,000
Payments to Suppliers	<140,000>
Payments to Employees, Salaries	<8,000>
Payments for Supplies	<10,000>
Payments for Rent	<4,000>
Net Cash Flows from Operating Activities	18,000

Cash from Investing Activities:

Purchase Land	<100,000>
Proceeds, sale of equipment	15,000
Net Cash Flows from Investing	<85,000>

Cash Flows from Financing Activities:

Borrow Money from Bank, sign note	200,000
Pay Cash Dividends to Stockholders	<25,000>
Net Cash from Financing Activities	175,000
Change in Cash ($18,000 − $85,000 + $175,000)	$108,000

That's all there is to it. After you do a few problems like this one, you should have no trouble at all with a major statement of cash flows problem. At the end of this chapter, there is a comprehensive problem that you can do using either the direct approach or the indirect approach. Solutions for both approaches are presented. ∎

Preparing the Statement of Cash Flows (Indirect Approach)

The indirect approach is by far the more popular approach, and this is the approach that you will most likely encounter on exams. Remember that we are going to compute *cash from operating activities* by starting with net income and adjusting or eliminating items that are included in net income, but did not bring in or use up cash. To make things a little easier, I have prepared a list of the most common adjustments to net income in order to generate the number for cash from operating activities (see figure 8-4 below).

Note that items 2 through 6 are pairs of related items that have the opposite impact on net income in determining cash flows from operating activities. For example, in no. 2, we add to net income the loss on the sale of assets and we subtract from net income the gain on the sale of assets.

Just a quick note about the last two items on each side of figure 8-4. There is a simple rule that you can memorize: **Changes in current assets have the opposite direction effect; changes in current liabilities have the same direction effect**. For example, if a current asset increased during the year, we would subtract the amount of the increase. If a current liability increased during the year, we would add the amount of the increase to the net income. A long explanation of why this rule works isn't really necessary. Just remember the rule.

If you want a quick explanation, here it is. What we are doing here is simply adjusting from the accrual basis to the cash basis. Look back at page 184. To determine collections from customers, for example, we took the sales plus the decrease in accounts receivable or minus the increase in accounts receivable. Note that we added the decrease and subtracted the increase in accounts receivable. In other words, the changes in a current asset have the *opposite direction effect*. Now let us solve the problem by using our six-step approach.

Solving the Problem

First, you need to be familiar with what the problem will look like. Typically, you will have a comparative balance sheet for 2 years (possibly the income statement)

Add to Net Income	Subtract from Net Income
1. Depreciation and amortization expense	—
2. Loss on the sale of noncurrent asset	2. Gain on sale of noncurrent asset
3. Loss from subsidiary using the equity method	3. Income from subsidiary using the equity method
4. Amortization of bond discount	4. Amortization of bond premium
5. Decrease in current asset	5. Increase in current asset
6. Increase in current liability	6. Decrease in current liability

FIGURE 8-4 Adjustments to Net Income: Indirect Approach

and usually a list of specific transactions that took place during the year labeled as "Additional Information."

Now let us go through the *six* steps for solving this problem:

1. Read the problem carefully. Determine whether the direct or indirect method is being used. Read the problem data carefully and highlight or underline the key transactions, amounts, dates, and so forth.

2. Put a blank statement of cash flows on your paper. You will just have the heading, the three sections, and the change in cash (the bottom line—double underlined—and below that a schedule of noncash investing and financing transactions). In the operating section, you will just have a line labeled "Net Income," and below that, the word "Adjustments." Now that you have the complete format of the statement on your paper, all that remains is filling in the blanks.

   This is what your paper should look like at this point:

   Statement Heading (Name of Statement, Name of Company, and Date)

   Cash from Operating Activities

      Net Income

      Adjustments

   Cash from Investing Activities

   Cash from Financing Activities

   Change in Cash

   Schedule of Noncash Investing and Financing Activities

3. Calculate the change in cash from the balance sheet and put that number on the bottom line of your solution.

EXAM TIP

Do not change this number, even if you get a different total when you add up all the items on the statement. This number—the change in cash—is a very easy number to calculate; Make sure you get it right.

---

4. Now it gets to be a bit more of a challenge. Work through the additional information one item at a time. Make up one or more T-accounts, entering the beginning and ending balances and any transaction data. Then ask yourself this question: Are there any numbers that are part of my analysis that belong in the statement of cash flows, either as an adjustment to net income or as an investing or financing item? You may have more than one number from a given transaction. Let me give you an example:

   Let's say that the first transaction was the sale of a building for $300,000 cash. The cost of the building was $500,000, and it was 25% depreciated. The beginning and ending balances for the building account and the accumulated depreciation building account are as follows:

Building—Beginning balance	$2,000,000
Ending balance	1,600,000
Accumulated Depreciation—Building Beginning balance	200,000
Ending balance	$100,000

The first thing to do is to make up two T-accounts and enter the beginning and ending balances (use check marks to indicate the beginning, and ending balances). Along side these T-accounts, make the calculation for the sale of the building (and enter the number in the T-account).

Building		Accumulated Depreciation: Building		Building:	
2,000,000	500,000	125,000	200,000		
100,000			25,000	Cost	$500,000
1,600,000			100,000	Less Accumulated Depreciation	<125,000>
				Book value	375,000
				Selling price	300,000
				Loss	<$75,000>

Assume that this is all the information you have about the building.

This analysis identifies two numbers that belong on the statement of cash flows. The $300,000 proceeds from the sale of the building is an investing activity item. The loss on sale is part of net income, but did not use up cash; therefore, it must be added back to net income.

Now, look at the two T-accounts. They don't balance, so we are going to make some assumptions. The building has net debits of $1,500,000, yet the ending balance is $1,600,000. What happened? Answer: They must have purchased a building for $100,000. That would be an investing activity item. The accumulated depreciation account doesn't balance either. It has net credits of $75,000, yet the balance in the account at the end of the period is $100,000. The missing number must be the depreciation expense for the current year. The journal entry to record depreciation is

Depreciation Expense
    Accumulated Depreciation—Asset

Thus, add a $25,000 credit to the accumulated depreciation account, and add back the $25,000 to net income in the operating activity section of the statement. Note that this analysis generated four entries on the statement of cash flows:

a. Proceeds from the sale of a building (+ $300,000 investing activities)
b. Add back the loss to net income (+ $75,000 operating activities)
c. Purchase building (<$100,000> investing activities)
d. Add back $25,000 of depreciation expense to net income (+ $25,000 operating activities)

After you have completed the analysis of these transactions, you will have completely explained the changes in two accounts—building and accumulated depreciation—building. On your problem page, place a check mark next to those two accounts. Do this, because the next step after analyzing all of the additional information is to go down the balance sheet and attempt to analyze every account other than cash. If any account has a check mark next to it, that means that the account has already been analyzed and therefore you can skip it.

What if you read a transaction like this:

"Acquire building by issuing common stock." Could this transaction explain the change in cash during the year? NO! However, it does represent both an investing and a financing transaction, but it didn't involve any cash. These transactions are listed in the schedule of noncash investing and financing transactions that you put on the bottom of your statement of cash flows.

EXAM TIP

There are two common mistakes students tend to make when doing these problems on exams:

1. They analyze the transaction properly, but they omit one or more items that belong on the statement of cash flows.

2. They enter all the numbers, but they add instead of subtracting, or vice versa. You can avoid these two mistakes simply by being careful. Being aware of these typical errors should help you avoid them.

---

5. Now go down the balance sheet and analyze every account that has not been checked. Remember the simple rule about changes in current assets (other than cash) and current liabilities. If a current asset increases, we subtract that amount from net income. If a current asset has decreased, we add that amount to net income. In other words, *changes in current assets have the opposite direction effect*. Increases are subtracted, decreases are added. For current liabilities, it's the other way around. Increases in current liabilities are added to net income, decreases are subtracted from net income. In other words, *changes in current liabilities have the same direction effect*.

If a number is missing, make the single most logical assumption. For example, if land began the year with a balance of $50,000 and ended with

$80,000, the logical assumption is that the company purchased land for $30,000. This would represent a cash outflow in the investing activities section of the statement of cash flows.

If bonds payable began the year with a balance of $100,000 and ended the year with a balance of $150,000, the logical assumption is that the company issued $50,000 of bonds. This would represent a cash inflow in the financing activities section of the statement.

The retained earnings account is one account that you certainly want to analyze with a T-account. Sometimes, the only way you can determine the net income is by analyzing the retained earnings T-account.

6. Edit your work. Check your calculations. Do the numbers add up? Do the numbers on the statement of cash flows have the right sign?

I spend a lot of time going over the statement of cash flows in class for several reasons:

- It is an important statement.

- The statement of cash flows covers virtually all the chapters in our text. So, if a professor was able to ask only one question on an exam in a financial accounting course, he or she just might select a comprehensive statement of cash flows problem, which would essentially test your knowledge of the entire course.

DEMONSTRATION PROBLEM 2 *Statement of Cash Flows (Indirect Method)*

Adele Inc.'s comparative balance sheet for 2007 and 2008 is shown below:

	2008	**2007**		**2008**	**2007**
Assets			**Liabilities**		
Cash	$130,000	$350,000	Accounts Payable	$55,000	$35,000
Marketable Securities	20,000	100,000	Taxes Payable	50,000	40,000
Accounts Receivable	75,000	55,000	Notes Payable	100,000	100,000
Inventory	80,000	50,000	Salaries Payable	20,000	50,000
Total Current Assets	305,000	555,000	Total Current Liabilities	225,000	225,000
Land	180,000	80,000	Bonds Payable	100,000	0
Building	800,000	50,000	Total Liabilities	325,000	225,000
Accumulated Depreciation— Building	<100,000>	<25,000>	Common Stock	450,000	350,000
Equipment	90,000	100,000	Additional Paid-in Capital	300,000	200,000

Accumulated			Retained Earnings	220,000	25,000
Depreciation—			Total Owners'	970,000	575,000
Equipment	<60,000>	<50,000>	Equity		
Patent	80,000	90,000			
Total non-current					
assets	990	245			
Total Assets	$1,295,000	$800,000	Total Liabilities +	$1,295,000	$800,000
			Owners' Equity		

Additional Information Transactions for 2008:

1. Equipment with a cost of $50,000 (accumulated depreciation of $20,000) was sold for $75,000 cash.

2. Marketable securities were sold for $50,000. There were no other transactions in this account.

3. Net income was $295,000.

4. Land was acquired by issuing bonds payable of $100,000.

Required: From the information above, prepare a statement of cash flows using the indirect method.

Solution: This problem calls for a statement of cash flows using the indirect method. We are going to solve this problem using the six-step approach. The first step is to read the problem carefully. The second step is to put the format of the statement on paper—just an outline with no numbers. It should look like this:

Statement of Cash Flows
for the year ending 12/31/08

Cash from Operating Activities:
 Net Income
 Adjustments:
Cash from Investing Activities
Cash from Financing Activities
Change in Cash
Schedule of Noncash Investing and Financing Activities

The third step is to calculate the change in cash from the balance sheet and put that number on the bottom line of the statement of cash flows. The fourth step is to work through the additional information, using T-accounts if necessary, to determine the impact on the statement of cash flows of the items listed here. If a T-account needs a debit or a credit entry to balance the account, make the most logical assumption regarding that number. For example, if you need a debit of $250,000 to balance the buildings account, the logical assumption is that the company acquired a building for $250,000 cash. As you complete your analysis of each balance sheet account, place a check mark next to that account on the balance sheet. The fifth step is to go down the balance sheet and analyze every account that has not been checked off.

Let us look at the four additional information items:

1. The equipment account had a beginning balance of $100,000 and an ending balance of $90,000, and the equipment that was sold cost $50,000. The missing number is a debit of $40,000 that must have been a purchase of equipment for cash, which is an investing activity.

   Since the selling price of the equipment was $75,000 and the book value was $30,000 ($50,000 − $20,000 = $30,000), there was a gain on the sale of $45,000. This must be subtracted from net income in the cash from operating activities section of the statement. The accumulated depreciation account had a $50,000 beginning balance and a $60,000 ending balance. When the company sold the equipment for $75,000, they wrote off $20,000 from the accumulated depreciation account ($50,000 − $20,000 = $30,000). If the ending balance in the accumulated depreciation account is $60,000, the company must have taken an additional $30,000 of depreciation this year. Analyzing these two accounts generated four entries on the statement of cash flows:

   a. Proceeds from the sale of equipment, + $75,000 (investing activities)
   b. Purchase equipment for cash <40,000> (investing activities)
   c. Depreciation expense on equipment for the year, + $30,000 (operating activities)
   d. Gain on the sale of equipment, subtracted from net income <45,000>, (operating activities)
   (See the T-accounts below.)

Equipment

Beginning balance	100,000	50,000	Cost of equipment sold
The missing number must be a purchase.			
	40,000		
Ending balance	90,000		

Accumulated Depreciation—Equipment

		50,000	Beginning balance
Accumulated depreciation on the equipment that was sold 20,000			
		30,000	Depreciation for the year
		60,000	Ending balance

2. Marketable securities had a beginning balance of $100,000 and an ending balance of $20,000. Securities were sold for $50,000. These securities must have cost $80,000 ($100,000 − $20,000), therefore the transaction generated a loss of $30,000. This loss did not use up cash, but was reported as part of income, therefore we must add $30,000 to net income in the cash from operating activities section of the statement

of cash flows. In addition, the proceeds from the sale ($50,000) must be added in the cash from investing section of the statement (see T-account below).

Marketable Securities

100,000	
	80,000
20,000	

3. The net income was $295,000. This increases the retained earnings account. Retained earnings had a beginning balance of $25,000 and an ending balance of $220,000 ($25,000 + $295,000 = $320,000). Since we know that the ending balance is $220,000, the missing number must be a cash dividend of $100,000. The net income will be the first number in the cash from operating activities section, and the cash dividends will be subtracted in the cash from financing activities section (see T-account below).

Retained Earnings

| The missing number must be cash dividends of 100,000. | 25,000 beginning balance |
| | 295,000 |

220,000 ending balance

4. The final piece of additional information was that land was acquired by issuing bonds of $100,000. We really don't need any T-accounts to complete this analysis. This is a noncash investing and financing transaction and should be reported in the schedule below the statement of cash flows.

The only other items that affect cash from operating activities are the changes in two current asset accounts—accounts receivable and inventory. Both accounts increased, so we subtracted the increase from net income. (Our rule is that changes in current assets have the opposite direction impact; changes in current liabilities have the same direction impact.) We also must add back depreciation and amortization expense.

We have covered most of the items in the investing and financing sections. The building account increased by $750,000, therefore we entered a cash disbursement of $750,000 in the investing activities section (purchase of building). In the financing activities section, both the common stock and additional paid-in capital accounts increased by $100,000. Therefore, the company must have issued common stock for $200,000, which would explain why both of those accounts increased by 100,000.

At this point, you are finished. Now sit back and admire your work. Your statement of cash flows should look like this:

Adele Inc.
Statement of Cash Flows
for the year ending 12/31/08

Cash from Operating Activities	
Net Income	$295,000
Less Gain on Sale of Equipment	<45,000>
Plus Loss on Sale of Marketable Securities	30,000
Less Increase in Accounts Receivable	<20,000>
Less Increase in Inventory	<30,000>
Plus Depreciation Expense ($30,000 + $75,000)	105,000
Plus Amortization of Patent	10,000
Net Cash from Operating Activities	345,000
Cash from Investing Activities	
Proceeds, sale of equipment	75,000
Proceeds, sale of marketable securities	50,000
Purchase of Building	<750,000>
Purchase of Equipment	<40,000>
Net Cash from Investing Activities	<665,000>
Cash from Financing Activities	
Issue Common Stock Above Par ($100,000 + $100,000)	200,000
Pay cash dividends	<100,000>
Net Cash from Financing Activities	100,000
Change in Cash (345,000 − 665,000 +100,000)	$220,000

Problem-Solving Takeaways

1. Once you calculate the change in cash by comparing the beginning and ending balances of cash, enter it on the bottom line of the statement of cash flows. If your statement doesn't balance, don't change that number.

2. Use T-accounts to analyze the accounts and to determine the proper transactions that should appear in the statement of cash flows.

3. Be sure to prepare a T-account analysis of the retained earnings account. Sometimes, the only way you can determine the net income is by analyzing the retained earnings account.

4. Remember this rule when adjusting net income to determine cash flows from operating activities: Changes in current assets have the opposite direction effect; changes in current liabilities have the same direction effect. If accounts receivable increase during the year, the amount of the increase is subtracted from net income. If accounts payable increase during the year, we add the amount of the increase to net income. ∎

Comprehensive Illustration

DEMONSTRATION PROBLEMS 3 AND 4   *Preparation of the Statement of Cash Flows—Direct and Indirect Methods*

Susan Inc.
Comparative Balance Sheet
for the year ending 12/31/08

	2008	2007
Assets		
Current Assets:		
Cash	$6,000	$100
Accounts Receivable	2,500	1,300
Inventory	500	400
Supplies	200	1,000
Prepaid Rent	300	0
Total Current Assets	9,500	2,800
Long-term Investments		
Marketable Securities	100	200
Property, Plant, and Equipment		
Land	300	500
Buildings	3,600	1,600
Accumulated Depreciation—Building	<300>	<100>
Equipment	700	700
Accumulated Depreciation—Equipment	<300>	<200>
Patents	5,000	0
Total non-current assets	9,100	2,700
Total Assets	$18,600	$5,500
Liabilities		
Current Liabilities:		
Accounts Payable	1,000	200
Taxes Payable	1,300	300
Salaries Payable	1,500	500
Total Current Liabilities	3,800	1,000
Long-term Liabilities		
Bonds Payable	5,000	2,000
Total Liabilities	8,800	3,000
Owners' Equity		
Common Stock	5,300	2,000
Retained Earnings	4,500	500
Total Owners' Equity	9,800	2,500
Total Liabilities + Owners' Equity	$18,600	$5,500

Susan Inc.
Income Statement
for the year ending 12/31/08

Sales		$20,000
Less Cost of Goods Sold		<6,000>
Gross Profit		14,000
Operating Expenses:		
Salaries Expense	$5,000	
Rent Expense	2,000	
Supplies Expense	1,500	
Depreciation Expense	300	
Amortization of Patent	500	
Tax Expense	2,000	
Total Operating Expenses		11,300
Income from Operations		2,700
Gain on Sale of Securities		500
Gain on Sale of Land		800
Net Income		$4,000

Preparing the Statement of Cash Flows—Direct Approach

The key here is to be able to convert from the accrual basis to the cash basis. It really isn't that hard; you just have to think about what you are doing. Let us begin. The first section is cash from operating activities; this is simply restating the income statement (which is on the accrual basis) to the cash basis. The first number is collection from customers. This is calculated by looking at the sales and the change in accounts receivable. Sales were $20,000 and accounts receivable increased by $1,200. This means that $1,200 in sales were not collected in cash. So, we simply take the $20,000 in sales and subtract the increase in accounts receivable of $1,200 to get $18,800.

We analyze the expenses in the same way. Rent expense was $2,000 on the income statement, and the company increased the prepaid rent by $300; thus, the cash payment for rent must be $2,000 + $300, or $2,300. The payment for inventory involves three elements: the cost of goods sold, the balance in the inventory account, and the balance in accounts payable. We begin with the cost of goods sold, which was $6,000. Since the inventory increased, we add $100 to the $6,000. Since accounts payable went up by $800, we subtract $800 from the $6,100 and get $5,300. (The increase in accounts payable of $800 represents $800 that the company didn't pay in cash. They charged the purchase of $800 of inventory. Therefore, we subtract $800 from the cost of goods sold.)

The payments for salaries and taxes follow the same pattern. The cash disbursement is equal to the expense on the income statement plus the decrease in the related payable, or minus the increase in the related payables. The payment for supplies is the expense on the income statement, plus the increase in supplies or minus the decrease in supplies.

The payment for salaries is therefore $5,000 (the expense on the income statement) less the increase in the salaries payable on the balance sheet, or $4,000. The payment for taxes is $2,000 (the expense on the income statement) less the increase in taxes payable on the balance sheet. The payment for supplies is $1,500 (the expense) less the decrease in supplies on the balance sheet. (Because the company used $800 of supplies that they already had, they didn't have to lay out $800 cash to buy them.)

The cash flows from investing activities are much more straightforward. The building went up by $2,000. Therefore, the company must have purchased a building for $2,000; that's a cash outflow of $2,000. The patent account went up from zero to $5,000, and there was $500 of patent amortization. Therefore, the company must have purchased a patent for $5,000 ($5,500 − $500 = $5,000). So, the cash disbursement for patents is $5,500. Land was sold at a gain of $800, and the land account on the balance sheet decreased by $200. To sell land that cost $200 and generate an $800 gain would require a company to sell the land for $1,000 ($1,000 − $200 = $800). Thus, the proceeds from the sale of the land must have been $1,000. Using the same logic, we see that the company must have sold the securities for $600 ($600 − $100 = $500).

The cash flows from financing activities are even easier. The common stock account increased by $3,300. The company must have issued $3,300 worth of common stock; that's a cash inflow. Bonds payable also increased by $3,000; that is a $3,000 cash inflow. At this point, we are finished. When doing a problem like this on an exam, compare your results to the change in cash that you calculated earlier. If there is a difference, don't change the change in cash amount; that should be correct. Instead, look at the individual items on your statement for a mistake.

The completed statement of cash flows appears below as follows:

Susan Inc. Statement of Cash Flows for the Year Ending 12/31/08 (Direct Method)

Cash from Operating Activities:

Collections from Customers	$18,800
Payment for Rent	<2,300>
Payment for Merchandise Inventory	<5,300>
Payment for Salaries	<4,000>
Payment for Taxes	<1,000>
Payment for Supplies	<700>
Net Cash from Operating Activities	5,500

Investing Activities:

Purchase Patent	<5,500>
Purchase Building	<2,000>
Proceeds, sale of land	1,000
Proceeds, sale of securities	600
Net Cash from Investing Activities	<5,900>

Financing Activities:

Issue Common Stock	3,300
Issue Bonds	3,000
Net Cash from Financing Activities	6,300
Increase in Cash (5500 − 5900 + 6300)	**$5,900**

Preparation of the Statement of Cash Flows—Indirect Approach

Using this approach, we don't have to work through all the conversions from the accrual to the cash basis. Cash from operating activities is going to be the net income plus or minus adjustments. These adjustments eliminate from the net income all the items that did not involve cash, thus permitting us to determine the *cash from operating activities*. In our problem, the net income is $4,000. Now for the adjustments. Depreciation and amortization are typical adjustments; they are expenses that are reported on the income statement, but they do not involve cash; therefore, we add these numbers back. Depreciation expense on the income statement was $300 (we add that back) and amortization of the patent was $500 (we add that back). The gains on the sale of land and securities were included in net income, but these gains did not involve cash. The cash in these transactions was the selling price of the assets, and that will go in the investing activities section of the statement of cash flows. These gains are not cash, so they need to be eliminated. Therefore, we subtract the $800 gain on the sale of the land and the $500 gain on the sale of the securities.

All the other adjustments reflect changes in either current assets or current liabilities. There is a simple rule for these adjustments:

Changes in current assets have the opposite direction effect; changes in current liabilities have the same direction effect.

You don't have to actually know why this rule works; you just have to know the rule. Consider anti-lock brakes in a car. Do you have these in your car? Do you know how they work? Probably not. All you have to know is the rule: If you step on the brake pedal, the car comes to a stop. It's the same thing with changes in current assets and current liabilities. A change in a current asset has the opposite direction effect. That is, if a current asset increases, we subtract that amount from net income. If a current asset decreases, we add that amount to net income. Take accounts receivable as an example. If sales were $10,000 and accounts receivable increased by $2,000, how much cash did the company get? Well, it's the $10,000 in sales less the increase in accounts receivable. The company collected $8,000 in cash and accounts receivable went up by $2,000. If sales were $10,000 and accounts receivable went down by $2,000, then the company would have collected $12,000 ($10,000 of this period's sales, plus the company also collected $2,000 from accounts receivable (which came from the prior year's sales).

Let's do a few of the adjustments in our problem. Accounts receivable **increased** by $1,200; therefore, we **subtract** $1,200 from net income. Inventory **increased** by $100; therefore, we **subtract** $100 from net income. Accounts payable **increased** by $800; therefore, we **add** $800 to net income. Just remember the rule: Changes in current assets have the *opposite direction effect* (increases are subtracted, decreases are added); changes in current liabilities have the *same direction effect* (increases are added, decreases are subtracted).

Remember that no matter which approach you use—direct or indirect—the cash flows from investing activities and the cash flows from financing activities are exactly the same. The only difference between the two methods is how the cash flows from operating activities are computed; the dollar amount of the cash flows from operating activities will be exactly the same.

The completed statement of cash flows appears below:

Susan Inc. Statement of Cash Flows for the Year Ending 12/31/08 (Indirect Method)

Operating Activities:

Net Income	$4,000
Gain on Sale of Securities	<500>
Gain on Sale of Land	<800>
Amortization of Patent	500
Depreciation Expense	300
Increase in Accounts Receivable	<1,200>
Increase in Inventory	<100>
Decrease in Supplies	800
Increase in Prepaid Rent	<300>
Increase in Accounts Payable	800
Increase in Taxes Payable	1,000
Increase Salaries Payable	1,000
Net Cash from Operating Activities	5,500

Investing Activities:

Purchase Patent	<5,500>
Purchase Building	<2,000>
Proceeds, sale of land	1,000
Proceeds, sale of securities	600
Net Cash from Investing Activities	<5,900>

Financing Activities:

Issue Common Stock	3,300
Issue Bonds	3,000
Net Cash from Financing Activities	6,300
Increase in Cash (5500 − 5900 + 6300)	**$5,900**

REVIEW QUESTIONS

1. *What is the difference between the direct approach and the indirect approach to preparing a statement of cash flows?*

The only difference between the two approaches is the manner in which cash from operating activities is computed. With the direct approach, cash from operating activities is equal to cash receipts from operating activities less cash disbursements from operating activities. This is essentially done by converting the results of operations on an accrual basis to a cash basis. With the indirect approach, cash flows from operating activities are determined by starting with net income and eliminating any items that did not involve cash, such as depreciation expense, which is an operating expense but does not use up cash.

2. *What is the purpose of the schedule of noncash investing and financing activities?*

There are two objectives associated with the statement of cash flows:

a. To explain the change in cash from the beginning of the year to the end of the year

b. To disclose the results of operating, investing, and financing transactions. Some of these transactions affect cash and they are disclosed in the body of the statement. However, there are some investing and financing transactions that do not involve cash. Examples of these transactions include

- issue common stock to acquire land,
- retire a note payable by issuing a bond, and
- acquire equipment by issuing preferred stock.

Since these transactions do not affect cash, they would not play a role in explaining how the balance in cash changed, hence they are not included in the statement of cash flows. However, they do represent significant investing and financing transactions that would be of interest to readers of the statement of cash flows. Therefore, they are included in a separate schedule, below the statement of cash flows.

3. *Why is the statement of cash flows so important?*

The statement of cash flows is critical because although it is important to earn a profit, if the company is going to survive in the long run, it must generate positive cash flows from its core business activity. Therefore, when the income statement and balance sheet are reviewed to determine profitability and financial position, there is also great interest in the statement of cash flows, which indicates the cash flows from operating, investing, and financing activities, and thus explains the change in cash from the beginning to the end of the period.

4. *What are the typical adjustments to net income to generate cash from operating activities?*

When preparing a statement of cash flows using the indirect method, cash from operating activities is determined by starting with net income and eliminating any items that did not involve cash. The typical adjustments to net income are

a. depreciation and amortization expense,

b. income or loss from investments carried on the books using the equity method,

c. gains and losses of the sale of long-term assets, and

d. changes in current assets and current liabilities.

5. *What are the typical transactions in the investing and financing sections of the statement of cash flows?*

The typical investing and financing transactions that involve cash are as follows:

Investing	Financing
Proceeds from the sale of assets	Issue new shares of stock
Cost of assets acquired	Issue or retire bonds
	Issue or retire stock
	Purchase or sale of treasury stock
	Pay cash dividends

6. *Why is the amount of cash from operating activities so important?*

The cash flows from the core business activity of the company represent the major ongoing source of money for the company. Yes, you can obtain cash by selling an asset or borrowing from a bank, but these transactions are just temporary fixes. To continue to be a thriving business entity, the company must generate a significant amount of positive cash flows from operating activities.

PRACTICE MULTIPLE CHOICE QUESTIONS

1. Which of the following is not a separate section of the statement of cash flows?

   a. Operating activities
   b. Financing activities
   c. Budgeting activities
   d. Investing activities

Solution: The correct answer is **c**. The three sections of the statement of cash flows are operating, investing, and financing. Budgeting is an accounting activity, but it does not appear on the statement of cash flows

2. During the year, Best Beth Co. acquired a building by issuing 5,000 shares of Best Beth common stock. Where on the statement of cash flows would this transaction appear?

   a. Investing activities

   b. Financing activities

   c. Budgeting activities

   d. Separate schedule of noncash investing and financing activities

Solution: The correct answer is **d**. The bottom line on the statement of cash flows is the change in cash from the beginning of the period to the end of the period. A transaction involving shares of common stock and a building clearly has nothing to do with the change in cash; hence, this transaction is reported on a separate schedule.

3. In computing cash from operating activities using the indirect method, which of the following would be added to net income?

   a. Gain on sale of equipment

   b. Amortization of patent

   c. Increase in accounts receivable

   d. Decrease in accounts payable

Solution: The correct answer is **b**. Choice **a** is a gain that would be subtracted from net income. Increases in current assets have the opposite direction effect; thus, an increase in accounts receivable would be subtracted. Hence, choice **c** is wrong. Choice **d** is also wrong, because changes in current liabilities have the same direction effect. Thus, a decrease in accounts payable would be subtracted from net income as well.

4. Grant Corp. sells a building with a book value of $3 million for $5 million. How would this transaction be reported on the statement of cash flows?

   a. The gain of $2,000,000 would be subtracted from net income in the operating activities section.

   b. The $5,000,000 proceeds would be added in the investing activities section.

   c. The $2,000,000 should be added in the investing activities section.

   d. Both **a** and **b**

Solution: The correct answer is **d**. The proceeds from the sale should be added in the investing activities section and the gain on the sale should be subtracted from net income. Choice **c** is wrong because the gain does not belong in the investing activities section of the statement of cash flows.

5. Paying a cash dividend to the common stockholders is reported in the statement of cash flows as

   a. a subtraction in the operating activities section.

   b. a subtraction in the investing activities section.

   c. a subtraction in the financing activities section.

   d. a subtraction in the budgeting activities section.

Solution: The correct answer is **c**. This is basically a definition that you have to know. In the financing activities section, the typical entries are issue and redeem stock, issue and redeem bonds, and the payment of a cash dividend. Note that simple a declaration of a cash dividend would not be entered on the statement of cash flows.

CHAPTER *9*

REVIEW OF FINANCIAL STATEMENTS AND FINANCIAL STATEMENT ANALYSIS

LEARNING OBJECTIVES

After studying this chapter, you will understand

- horizontal and vertical analysis
- common-size income statements and common-size balance sheets
- financial ratio analysis
- DuPont analysis computing ROI and dividing it into its two components, and
- liquidity, activity, leverage, and profitability ratios

HERE IS where we have come from and here's where we are going in our study of accounting. In the first few chapters, you were introduced to the three basic financial statements:

1. The income statement
2. The balance sheet
3. The statement of cash flows

The income statement shows the results of operations for a period of time. The balance sheet shows the financial position at a point in time. The statement of cash flows explains the change in cash from the beginning to the end of the year. In the middle chapters, we focused on how the numbers that are reported in the financial statements are generated. We covered such topics as estimating bad debt expense in conjunction with accounting for receivables, calculating the cost of goods sold using different flow assumptions, and computing depreciation expense using a variety of methods.

In this final chapter, we are going to focus on evaluating a company's performance and financial position using the data contained in these financial statements. We will begin with **horizontal and vertical analysis**, and then cover a technique developed many years ago by the accountants at DuPont.

That brings us to the concept of **financial ratio analysis**. A financial ratio is simply one number divided by another number, where a meaningful relationship exists between the two numbers. For example, we are usually interested to see if the company is able to pay its current obligations as they come due. Generally, the company will pay these obligations using assets that are listed on the balance sheet as current assets. Thus, there is a relationship between current assets and current liabilities—current assets will be used to pay current liabilities. Current assets divided by current liabilities is called the current ratio.

Many financial ratios can be calculated, but we will look at four groups of ratios that focus on the following four aspects of a company's financial situation:

1. Liquidity
2. Activity
3. Solvency/Leverage
4. Profitability

Liquidity refers to a firm's ability to pay its current obligations as they come due. Activity ratios look at operating efficiency. Solvency ratios focus on the firm's use of financial leverage. You can probably guess what profitability ratios deal with.

Finally, two comprehensive demonstration problems are presented and solved. One problem deals with the income statement and one deals with the balance sheet. Both problems call on specific problem-solving skills that will also be useful on your exams. We will review these skills and strategies in detail as we solve these two problems.

Now that we have reviewed the basic financial statements, as well as the rules for recording the transactions that make their way to the statements, we should devote some time to analyzing these financial statements. If we are looking at the financial statements of a real company, what conclusions about that company can we reach on the basis of an analysis of these statements? What techniques or tools can we utilize in preparing this analysis?

HORIZONTAL AND VERTICAL ANALYSIS

One of the most basic analytical tools is horizontal, or trend, analysis. We calculate values for some of the basic financial statement numbers and look at the trend over time. For example, refer to figure 9-1, which highlights some key income statement numbers.

Here we are looking at the data horizontally, or over a period of time. Another way of looking at the numbers would be to take the income statement or the balance sheet for a specific period and look at the numbers vertically, from top to bottom. However, instead of the numbers being stated in dollars, we will convert them to percentages. For the income statement, we will convert each dollar figure to a percentage

Variable	2007	2006	2005	2004	2003
Gross revenue	$200,000	$150,000	$130,000	$120,000	$100,000
Cost of goods sold	110,000	80,000	65,000	55,000	40,000
Gross profit	90,000	70,000	65,000	65,000	60,000
Income from operations	40,000	25,000	25,000	30,000	30,000
Net income	30,000	15,000	15,000	20,000	20,000

FIGURE 9-1 Horizontal Analysis

of total revenue. Thus, total revenue will become 100%, and every other number will be expressed as a percentage of total revenue. For the balance sheet, we convert every dollar figure to percentage of total assets. We refer to these "percentage statements" as "common-size" financial statements.

A common-size financial statement helps us analyze the company's financial position and performance. When we look at a financial statement expressed in dollars, it is sometimes difficult to determine how a specific number has changed, for example, over a 2-year period, if total revenue has also changed. Let me use a simple example.

Assume that telephone expense was $10 million in 2004 and $14 million in 2005. Is this a positive or a negative change? Is this good or bad? Well, if total revenue stayed the same for both years at $200,000,000, then telephone expense increased from 10/200, or 5% of total revenue to 14/200, or 7% of total revenue. Since we would expect the telephone bill to be proportional to the level of business activity, this increase from 5% to 7% is bad. Expenses should increase in proportion to activity. However, if total revenue had increased from $200,000,000 to $300,000,000, then telephone expense as a percentage of total revenue would have decreased to 14/300,000, or about 5%. By converting all the numbers to percentages, we get a much better understanding of the behavior of the numbers, because we have a common frame of reference—either total revenue for the income statement or total assets for the balance sheet.

DUPONT METHOD

One of the most significant *metrics*, or numbers, that we can use to analyze a company is the return on investment, or ROI.

By way of introduction, let me pose a question. Assume that I have a company which produced a net income of $20,000,000. How do you evaluate the firm's profitability? That's not a simple question. For example, if the $20 million net income was earned by your campus bookstore, that was probably a good year, since most college bookstores are relatively small operations, with minimal capital invested. However, it the company was IBM, or Microsoft, or the Ford Motor Company, the $20 million net income would be indicative of a very poor performance, because these companies represent on enormous investment of capital.

To really understand a number reported on the financial statements, you have to compare it to something else, to have a frame of reference. Using the DuPont method (an analytical technique developed by the accountants at DuPont many years ago), we calculate ROI as follows:

$$ROI = \frac{\text{Net income}}{\text{Average total assets}}$$

Now we can evaluate the net income because we know how big the company is, since we are comparing the net income to the total dollars invested in the business. However, the next step illustrates the beauty or the power of the DuPont Method.

We divide the ROI calculation into two subcalculations:

$$ROI = \text{Margin} \times \text{Turnover}$$

$$\frac{\text{Net income}}{\text{Average total asset}} = \frac{\text{Net income}}{\text{Sales}} \times \frac{\text{Sales}}{\text{Average total assets}}$$

What does this tell us? Answer: How ROI is generated and what we can do to improve ROI. There are two components of ROI: margin and turnover. Margin tells us the amount of profit per dollar of sales. To improve this number, most companies would attempt to reduce operating expenses or increase selling prices, thus increaseing net income. Turnover measures the ability of the company to use their assets to generate sales. One way to improve turnover is to reduce investment in certain assets—to streamline the company—to get "lean and mean." Obviously, if we take the second equation from above,

$$\frac{\text{Net income}}{\text{Sales}} \times \frac{\text{Sales}}{\text{Average total assets}},$$

and cancel out the sales in both the margin's denominator and the turnover's numerator, we are left with

$$\frac{\text{Net income}}{\text{Average total assets}},$$

which is ROI, so what have we gained? We have gained an insight into the components of ROI. If we wanted to improve ROI, we know what to do, namely, increase margin or increase turnover.

The DuPont approach is simple and elegant. You can tell a great deal about the company with very little effort.

FINANCIAL RATIO ANALYSIS

With in the DuPont method, we made use of three separate calculations. Each of these three calculations consisted of a *ratio*—one number divided by another number. We could take every financial statement number and divide it by every other financial statement number, and we would get mostly garbage. The key is to take two numbers that are related in some way and compute a meaningful ratio. As it turns out, there are a number of standard, or typical, ratios that are used all the time in analyzing a set of financial statements. These ratios are usually divided into several different groups of related ratios. We will focus on four groups of ratios:

1. Liquidity
2. Activity
3. Solvency
4. Profitability

Liquidity Measures

Liquidity refers to the company's ability to pay their obligations as they come due. How do we evaluate the company's ability to pay its bills? One place to start would be by comparing all the cash plus the items that could be converted to cash to the bills currently due. We do this by computing

$$\frac{\text{Current assets}}{\text{Current liabilities}}$$

We refer to this calculation as the **current ratio**. As a general rule of thumb, the current ratio is considered good if it is at least 2:1.

Remember that current assets typically consists of five items:

1. Cash
2. Marketable securities
3. Accounts receivable
4. Inventory
5. Prepaid expenses

If we have bills that must be paid and we run out of cash, we can always sell our investment in marketable securities, and we can sell, factor, or borrow on our accounts receivable. The other two current assets—inventories and prepaid expenses—are not as liquid. For example, if most of our inventory is work-in-process, how much money could you get for half a computer or two thirds of a car? So, there is another ratio we use to measure liquidity—the **quick ratio**, or the **acid test**:

$$\text{Quick ratio} = \frac{\text{Cash, Marketable securities, and Accounts receivable}}{\text{Current liabilities}}$$

We refer to the numerator of this ratio as the quick assets. The general rule of thumb for a quick ratio is that it be greater than 1:1.

Another way to measure liquidity is to subtract current liabilities from current assets instead of dividing. We refer to this as **working capital** or **net working capital**:

$$\text{Working capital} = \text{Current asset} - \text{Current liabilities}$$

Here, the larger the number, the better (up to a point). Too much money sitting in a checking account in a bank isn't very productive.

Activity Measures

There are several ratios that are used to evaluate activity. One of these ratios is a component of the DuPont method—total asset turnover:

$$\frac{\text{Net income}}{\text{Average total assets}}$$

This ratio tells us about the company's ability to use their assets to generate sales. A variant of total asset turnover is Property, Plant, and Equipment turnover, calculated as

$$\frac{\text{Net income}}{\text{Average property, plant, and equipment}}$$

Inventory turnover is calculated by dividing cost of goods sold by the average inventory. This tells us how often the inventory came in (was purchased) and went out (was sold). We call this inventory turnover. Note that since inventory is reported at cost, the numerator must also be stated at cost; thus, we use cost of goods sold in the numerator instead of sales.

When looking at inventory turnover, consider this: Which company would have a greater turnover, a grocery store like Safeway or a jewelry store like Tiffany's? Clearly, the inventory in a grocery store turns over a great deal more often than that in a high-priced jewelry store. This points out the need to compare the ratios you compute to some standard or norm, and these norms should be industry specific. This would take into account the differences between a grocery store and a jeweler.

Another ratio involving inventory is called **days sales in inventory**, calculated as

$$\text{Days sales in inventory} = \frac{\text{Average inventory}}{\text{Daily cost of goods sold}}$$

Like the **inventory turnover ratio**, since inventory is recorded at cost in the accounting records, sales must be stated in terms of cost of goods sold:

$$\text{Daily cost of goods sold} = \frac{\text{Total cost of goods sold}}{365}$$

Most companies try to minimize their investment in inventory. This ratio is one way to see if they have been successful.

We evaluate the receivables by calculating days sales outstanding, that is,

$$\text{Days sales outstanding} = \frac{\text{Average accounts receivable}}{\text{Credit sales per day}},$$

where

$$\text{Credit sales per day} = \frac{\text{Total credit sales}}{365}.$$

Let's say you compute this ratio and get 45. Is that good or bad? Well, you would want to compare the number calculated to the company's credit terms. If the company's credit terms are 2/10, n/30, we should expect the balance in accounts receivable at any one time to be equal to about 30 days' worth of sales. If we compute 45 days, something is wrong. The ratio doesn't tell you *what* is wrong; it simply alerts you that there may be a problem. You have to look at the situation and find out what is causing the problem. The company may not be sending out their bills in a timely manner, they may be extending credit to the "wrong" companies, and so forth.

Solvency/Leverage

The ratios in this group focus on the extent to which the company is using borrowed funds (OPM, or other people's money) to boost up (leverage) the earnings to the stockholders. If the company's ROI is 17% and the company can borrow at 10%, then they should be able to take the borrowed funds, invest the money in the company, and earn a 17% return after they pay the 10% cost of the money; the extra earnings go to the stockholders.

To measure the *amount* of debt financing, we calculate the **debt ratio** or the **debt-to-equity ratio**:

$$\text{Debt ratio} = \frac{\text{Total liabilities}}{\text{Total liabilities} + \text{Stockholders'equity}}$$

$$\text{Debt to equity} = \frac{\text{Total liabilities}}{\text{Total stockholders'equity}}$$

Finally, we can get some impression about the company's ability to pay the interest by calculating the times interest earned ratio:

$$\text{Times interest earned} = \frac{\text{Earnings before interest and taxes (EBIT)}}{\text{Interest expense}}$$

Profitability

There are a number of ways to measure profitability. We have already seen ROI:

$$\text{ROI} = \frac{\text{Net income}}{\text{Average total assets}}$$

Another measure of profitability is **return on equity**:

$$\text{Return on equity} = \frac{\text{Net income} - \text{Preferred dividends}}{\text{Average stockholders'equity}}$$

Earnings per share is the income per share of common stock:

$$\text{EPS} = \frac{\text{Net income} - \text{Preferred dividends}}{\text{Weighted average number of shares of common stock outstanding}}$$

Two other ratios let us know about the dividends being paid to the stockholders. One ratio measures the rate of return on an investment in common stock, based on the

Category	Ratio	Computation
Liquidity	Current ratio	Current assets ÷ Current liabilities
Liquidity	Quick ratio	Cash, marketable securities, and accounts receivable ÷ Current liabilities
Liquidity	Net working capital	Current assets less Current liabilities
Activity	Total asset turnover	Net income ÷ Average total assets
Activity	Day's sales in inventory	Average inventory ÷ Daily cost of goods sold
Activity	Day's sales outstanding	Average accounts receivable ÷ Credit sales per day
Leverage	Debt ratio	Total liabilities ÷ (Total liabilities + Owners' equity)
Leverage	Debt to equity	Totall iabilities ÷ Total owners' equity
Profitability	Return on investment	Net income ÷ Average total assets
Profitability	Return on equity	Net income less preferred dividends ÷ Average owners' equity
Profitability	Earnings per share	Net income less preferred dividends ÷ Average number of shares of common stock outstanding
Profitability	Dividend yield	Annual dividend ÷ Market price of a share of common stock
Profitability	Dividend payout	Annual dividend ÷ Annual net income

FIGURE 9-2 Financial Ratio Summary

dividend (**dividend yield**). A second ratio indicates how much of the annual income is paid to the stockholders in the form of a dividend (dividend payout).

$$\text{Dividend yield} = \frac{\text{Amount of dividend}}{\text{Average market price of share of common stock}}$$

$$\text{Dividend payout} = \frac{\text{Annual dividend}}{\text{Annual net income}}$$

Summary

The ratios we looked at in this chapter are summarized in figure 9-2 above:

DEMONSTRATION PROBLEM 1 *Preparation of Partial Income Statement*

Alfred Inc. reported income from continuing operations of $750,000 *before taxes* for the year ending December 31, 2008. The following transactions took place in 2008, but were not included in the calculation of either income from continuing operations before taxes or net income:

1. There was a fire in one of the warehouses that completely destroyed the building and its contents. The loss, which was not covered by insurance, amounted to $150,000.

2. The company discontinued the operation of its photo division and sustained a loss of $200,000.

3. Marketable securities classified as available-for-sale securities were sold and a gain of $125,000 was realized.

4. A piece of equipment costing $250,000 (10-year estimated useful life, $30,000 estimated salvage value) was erroneously charged to expense when acquired on January 1 of the current year. All plant assets are depreciated using the sum of the year's digits method.

5. The ending inventory was overstated by $50,000.

Required: Prepare an income statement for 2008, starting with income from continuing operations before taxes. Include appropriate per-share amounts. There were 50,000 shares of common stock outstanding throughout the year, and the tax rate on all items was 35%.

Solution: The first step is to set up a schedule to determine the correct income from continuing operations. Call it Schedule A. It should look like this:

Income from continuing operations, as originally reported $750,000

Adjustments
-
-
-

Income from continuing operations, as corrected   _____

The second step is to evaluate all data given in the problem, to determine where on the income statement each item should go. Remember that income tax expense is shown on the income statement on the basis of the income from continuing operations. Any income or loss on the income statement after income from continuing operations must be shown with the tax effect calculated separately for each individual item. (We call that *showing the item net of tax.*)

Here is the evaluation of the five items from the data given in problem:

1. The fire loss is considered an extraordinary item and is shown on the income statement after discontinued operations.

2. The loss on the discontinued operations is shown on the income statement after income from continuing operations (and tax expense).

3. The gain on the sale of marketable securities is part of income from continuing operations, so $120,000 is added on schedule A.

4. The equipment that was purchased and expensed should have been capitalized and depreciated. Thus, expenses were overstated by $250,000. However $40,000, of depreciation that should have been recorded was not. (The depreciation calculation is $250,000 less $30,000 = $220,000 × 10/55 = $40,000.) Thus, the net effect on net income is $250,000 − 40,000 = $210,000. We must add $210,000 to net income on schedule A.

5. We can determine the impact of the inventory error by using the cost of goods sold model, which we covered in Chapter 4.

Put a plus or a minus sign next to each item that is affected by the error. In this case, the understatement of ending inventory results in an understatement of gross profit and hence an understatement of net income. Thus, we must add $50,000 to schedule A.

Beginning inventory	ok	Sales	ok
+ Purchases	ok	− cost of goods sold	+
= goods available for sale	ok	= gross profit	−
− ending inventory	−	:	
= Cost of goods sold	+	= Net income	−

You can now complete Schedule A

Schedule A

Income from continuing operations, before taxes as originally reported	$750,000
Adjustments:	
Gain on sale of marketable securities	125,000
Error in recording equipment and depreciation	210,000
Error in computing ending inventory	50,000
Income from continuing operations, before taxes as corrected	$1,135,000

Now prepare the complete income statement:

Income Statement
Alfred Inc.
year ended 12/31/08

Income from Continuing Operations before taxes		$1,135,000
Income Tax Expense (1,135,000 × .35)		397,250
Income from Continuing Operations		737,750
Discontinued Operations:		
Loss on Disposal of Photo Division	<$200,000>	
Less Applicable Tax	70,000	<130,000>
Income Before Extraordinary Item		607,750
Extraordinary Item:		
Uninsured Fire Loss	<150,000>	
Less Applicable Tax	52,500	<97,500>
Net income		$510,250
Earnings per Share Disclosure:		
Income from Continuing Operations		$14.76
Discontinued Operations		<2.60>
Income Before Extraordinary Item		12.16
Extraordinary Item		<1.95>
Net Income		$10.21 ∎

Problem-Solving Takeaways

1. Whenever you have a problem that requires a financial statement that begins with a specific line item, such as an income statement that begins with income from continuing operations before taxes, and the number that you are given is incorrect (because of certain omissions or errors), you should set up a schedule to recompute that number. (Most students fail to do this. They begin the problem with income from continuing operations before taxes as $750,000, which is clearly wrong, and then they have difficulty with the problem because they don't know where to put the adjustments.)

2. Whenever you have an inventory error, simply prepare a brief worksheet with the cost of goods sold computation and the gross profit computation. Enter pluses or minuses next to the items that have the error or errors. You should be able to see the impact on the various variables. Remember, many inventory errors are counterbalancing, so the balance in retained earnings will be correct after 2 years. Note that in this problem, the retained earnings account was overstated; however, that information was not a required element of this problem.

DEMONSTRATION PROBLEM 2 *Preparation of a Balance Sheet*

The controller of Esther Inc. prepared the following balance sheet as of 12/31/08:

Assets		Liabilities	
Cash	$200,000	Short-term Notes Payable	$100,000
Accounts Receivable	150,000	Long-term Liabilities	200,000
Inventory	300,000	Owners' Equity	
Equipment, net	400,000	Common Stock ($10 par)	500,000
Patent	150,000	Retained Earnings	400,000
Total Assets	1,200,000	Total Liabilities and Owners' Equity	1,200,000

The following information is available:

1. $50,000 of the cash balance has been set aside to retire a bond that will mature in 2008.

2. The accounts receivable total of $150,000 is made up of an accounts receivable gross of $180,000 less a $30,000 allowance for uncollectibles. Based on an aging of the receivables, it has been determined that the balance in the allowance account should be $45,000.

3. Inventory purchased in December, costing $50,000 FOB Shipping Point, was in transit on December 31 and was not included in the ending inventory figure.

4. The equipment has a cost of $500,000 less $100,000 of accumulated depreciation. Depreciation on one piece of equipment (cost $100,000, 5-year life, $20,000 estimated salvage value) was not recorded in 2006. Amortization of the patent in 2006 was $10,000.

5. The long-term liability is made up of a 10-year bond that was issued at par.

6. Cash dividends of $2 per share were declared on December 24. No journal entry was made to record the declaration of the dividend.

Required: Prepare a classified balance sheet as of December 31, 2008, from the information presented above.

Solution: After reading this problem, it is clear that the balance sheet provided in the problem has the correct line items (with one or two exceptions), but the numbers need to be adjusted. Therefore, you could start this problem by making up a balance sheet with the line items that are given in the problem. Then compute the correct balances, given the problem data. Note that some of the errors will affect net income, thus we will have to adjust the retained earnings account. Always make up a T-account for retained earnings.

The corrected balance sheet would look like this:

Balance Sheet
Esther Inc.
as of 12/31/08

Assets

Current Assets

Cash ($200,000 − $50,000)		$150,000
Accounts Receivable	180,000	
Less Allowance for Uncollectibles ($45,000 per aging)	<45,000>	135,000
Inventory ($300,000 + $50,000)		350,000
Total Current Assets:		635,000
Long-term Investments:		
Bond Sinking Fund		50,000
Property, Plant, and Equipment		
Equipment	$500,000	
Less Accumulated Depreciation	<116,000>	384,000
Intangible Assets:		
Patent		140,000
Total non-current assets		574,000
Total Assets		**1,209,000**
Liabilities		
Short-term Notes Payable		100,000
Dividends Payable		100,000
Total Current Liabilities		**200,000**
Long-term Liabilities:		
Bonds Payable		200,000
Total Liabilities		**400,000**
Owners' Equity		
Common Stock		500,000
Retained Earnings		309,000
Total owners' equity		809,000
Total Liabilities and Owners' Equity		**1,209,000**

Retained Earnings

		400,000	
Additional bad debt expense	15,000	50,000	Impact of inventory error
Additional depreciation	16,000		
Additional amortization	10,000		
Declaration of cash dividend	100,000		

309,000 Adjusted balance ∎

Impact of Inventory Error: Use the cost of goods sold model and the gross profit calculation. Enter pluses and minuses next to each item that is wrong, and you should see the impact of a particular error.

Beginning Inventory	Sales
+ Purchases	− Cost of goods sold +
Goods available	Gross profit −
− Ending Inventory −	
Cost of goods sold +	

In this problem, the ending inventory was understated, causing cost of goods sold to be overstated; thus gross profit and net income were both understated. The missing depreciation is calculated as follows:

$$\$100,000 - \$20,000 = \$80,000/5 = \$16,000$$

Problem-Solving Takeaways

1. When you are preparing a financial statement and you have most, if not all, of the accounts or line items, it is a good idea to start by preparing the statement in blank; indicate the line items with no numbers. Then just make the computations and fill in the numbers.

2. When preparing a balance sheet, if there are a number of errors that affect net income, you should make up a T-account for retained earnings to accumulate all of the items that affected net income, which will also impact the balance in retained earnings.

REVIEW QUESTIONS

1. *What is the single most important ratio?*

That's a difficult question to answer. It depends on several factors, such as your relationship to the business (stockholder or creditor), the company's past performance, what is happening in the company's industry and the economy overall, and so forth. However, that being said, a good overall measure of performance is ROI (return on investment), calculated by dividing net income by average total assets. This ratio compares the income of the business with the amount of money invested in the business. It does not tell you everything. For example, it doesn't give you a clue about the firm's liquidity or their use of leverage, but it certainly is a good place to start.

2. *What is the DuPont method and how is it useful?*

DuPont analysis explains or breaks down ROI into two component ratios—margin and turnover. In equation format, it looks like this:

$$\text{Return on investment} = \text{Margin} \times \text{Turnover}$$

$$\frac{\text{Net income}}{\text{Average total assets}} = \frac{\text{Net income}}{\text{Sales}} \times \frac{\text{Sales}}{\text{Average total assets}}$$

Thus, if a company wants to improve their ROI, they can do one (or both) of the following: Improve the profit margin by generating more profit per dollar of sales, or increase turnover by generating more sales per dollar of investment in assets.

3. *What is leverage and how do you assess a firm's use of financial leverage?*

Leverage is simply OPM—using other people's money. If the firm has an ROI of 18% and they can borrow money at 10%, they increase the return to the stockholders by borrowing at 10% and investing the money in the business, where it earns 18%. Pay back 10% to the bank, and the excess increases the rate of return to the stockholders.

There are really only two questions concerning a firm's use of leverage: how much and how safe. The "how much" is usually indicated by one of these two ratios: the debt ratio or debt-to-equity ratio. This tells us what proportion of the company is financed by debt. The "how safe" is usually measured by the times interest earned ratio, which is EBIT/Interest expense (EBIT is earnings before interest and taxes; that's the money that is available to pay the interest). From a safety standpoint, we would prefer a low percentage of debt relative to equity and a high number for times interest earned.

4. *What are common-size financial statements and why are they useful?*

Common-size statements are prepared by converting the dollar amounts in the statement to a percentage. On a common-size income statement, total revenue is 100% and every other number is a percentage of total revenue. On a common-size balance sheet, total assets are 100% and every other number is presented as a percentage of total assets.

PRACTICE MULTIPLE CHOICE QUESTIONS

1. The accounts receivable turnover ratio is computed by dividing

   a. net sales by ending receivables

   b. net credit sales by average net accounts receivable.

   c. total sales by ending receivables.

   d. total sales by average receivables.

Solution: The correct answer is **b**. Ideally, this ratio is computed by dividing net credit sales by average net accounts receivable. The other choices are not correct.

2. The inventory turnover ratio is computed by dividing

   a. sales by average inventory.

   b. sales by ending inventory.

   c. cost of goods sold by ending inventory.

   d. cost of goods sold by average inventory.

Solution: The correct answer is **d**. When computing ratios, balance sheet items such as inventory or accounts receivable are usually incorporated in ratios as an average. Thus, the inventory turnover ratio is properly computed by dividing cost of goods sold by average inventory. Since inventory is stated at cost, you must compare it to cost of goods sold, not sales.

3. The asset turnover ratio is computed by dividing

   a. net income by average total sales.

   b. net income by ending total sales.

   c. net sales by average total assets.

   d. net sales by ending total assets.

Solution: The correct answer is **c**. The comment in the previous question applies here as well. Balance sheet items such as total assets are incorporated as averages in calculating ratios. Thus, the proper calculation of the asset turnover ratio is net sales/Average total assets.

4. What is the formula for the current ratio?

   a. Current assets/Current liabilities

   b. Current liabilities/Current assets

   c. Current revenue/Current expenses

   d. None of the above

Solution: The correct answer is **a**. The current ratio is computed by dividing current assets by current liabilities. The other answers are wrong.

5. What are the components of inventory turnover?

   a. Sales and cost of goods sold

   b. Sales and inventory

   c. Inventory and assets

   d. Cost of goods sold and average inventory

Solution: The correct answer is **d**. This is essentially the same as question 3. The two values used in computing inventory turnover are cost of goods sold and average inventory. Inventory is stated at cost in the accounting records. Therefore, we compare inventory with cost of goods sold instead of with sales, which are stated at the retail, or selling, price.

BASIC COLLEGE SKILLS

LEARNING OBJECTIVES

After studying appendix A, you will understand how to

- prepare for class effectively
- read your textbook to get the most out of it
- do your homework in the most efficient manner
- get the most out of each class meeting
- use a study group effectively
- answer multiple choice questions, solve long problems, and respond to essay questions
- prepare for exams and
- take an exam and earn a high grade

ONE OBJECTIVE of this book is to make sure that you have all the necessary skills to earn a good grade in your accounting course, plus all the other courses that you will take while you are in college. As indicated in the preface, I have noticed that most students are not fully prepared for what they will encounter in college. All students need to acquire a set of study skills to do well in college. This appendix introduces a great many of the techniques that I have learned or developed myself in more than 40 years of studying and teaching accounting. Many of these tips and techniques can be applied in your other courses. Most of these tips are accounting specific—they will help you earn high grades on your accounting exams.

COLLEGE SKILLS

Most students arrive at college with virtually no training in such areas as

- how to study,
- how to do homework,
- how to prepare for different types of exams, and
- how to take an exam.

As it turns out, these are very important skills that are quite simple to master and apply. They can help you learn more, get higher grades, and actually enjoy the process.

Preparing for Class

Your professor probably gave you a course outline or syllabus on the first day of class. This document lays out the structure of the course. It may indicate exactly what will be covered at each class meeting (e.g., pages to read in the text, homework problems to complete, group activities, etc.).

Most professors spend a lot of time preparing for class, and you should, too. I find that the more time I spend preparing for class, the better the class goes and the more I enjoy it. I think you will find the same thing. If you come to class well prepared, you will learn more, and the class will be much more enjoyable.

Some students think that if they ask a lot of questions, the professor will think that they are stupid and won't like them; hence, they don't ask questions. Actually, the reverse is true. Professors generally like the students who ask questions; it shows that they are interested in the subject and really want to learn.

Here's an important tip: *Never* leave the classroom if something happened in class that you did not understand without resolving the matter. This goes for the lecture, examples or calculations on the board, homework problems, anything. If you don't understand something in class, *ask a question right at that moment.* Do not let the class end before you have had a chance to ask your question.

Homework problems are a part of every accounting course. In a sense, this is a test of whether you have learned the material. Can you actually do accounting? I am a firm believer in testing yourself. You want to be as sure as you can be as to whether you have really learned the material.

Preparing for class involves several different activities. I had a professor in my undergraduate accounting program who did not speak English very well, but he told us something in class one day that has remained with me for more than 40 years. He said, "Must read book, must do problems." That was his message. To be successful in the class and get a high grade, you had to do **both** of these activities: read the textbook and spend time solving the homework problems. These two activities are very important. At this point, let us focus on reading your textbook.

Reading the Textbook

You probably know how to read your textbook. However, I want to help you read it in the most thorough way, in a way that will make sure that you understand the material and learn how to use that understanding to actually do accounting.

One of your most useful tools is a yellow highlighter. This simple device can really help you learn. It will also come in handy when you are doing homework and taking exams.

The key to reading the book is to "make the book yours." By this, I mean making marks in the book to make it useful to you in learning accounting. After you finish reading your textbook my way, it will be so useful to you that you won't even think of selling it back to the bookstore at the end of the semester.

As you read the book, I recommend that you underline or highlight everything you read that you consider especially important. The items that you underline will most likely consist of the following:

- Basic accounting concepts
- Journal entries
- Calculations
- Formats for solving problems
- FASB standards

In addition to highlighting or underlining the key material in the text, I also recommend that you write in the margins. Now, you probably know how to underline a textbook as you read it, but you may not be used to writing in the margins. Putting notes in the margins really makes it *your book*. The more you underline and write in your book, the more useful the book will become. What kinds of things should you write in the margins? Things like this:

- This is really important!
- I don't understand this, so I will definitely ask the professor about it in the next class (you could simply put a big "?" in the margin).

   (Some students who are reluctant to ask a question in class will come up to the professor after class and ask their question. Most professors do not like this. First of all, they are probably on their way to another class, office hours, a meeting, or lunch. But more important, they want you to ask the question in class, so they can give you an answer that the entire class will hear. If you have a question, it is likely that a number of other students have the same question. So don't be afraid to ask questions in class; you will be doing yourself and your professor a favor, and of course, the professor's answers should help you understand the material.)

- Write down the equation or formula for computing something, such as Assets = Liabilities + Owners' Equity. Asset accounts increase on the left and decrease on the right.

- Tips or tricks for remembering something, such as the balance sheet must always balance, the assets must equal the liabilities + owners' equity, the current ratio = current assets divided by current liabilities.

- Problem-solving aids, such as "Be sure to close the income summary account to retained earnings."

The more you write in the margins, the more you will remember. The very act of writing it helps you learn and retain the concept, even if you never look at it again. However, you will look at it again, and *you will remember it* because *you* thought it was important and *you* wrote it in the margin. I suggest that you prepare an outline of the key points in the chapter. Guess what, that process will be very simple if you have identified the key items by underlining and writing in the margins.

All of the ideas that are presented in this book will help you get an A, and it all starts with reading the textbook. Textbooks are used in almost all college courses, but not every course is "textbook driven." Accounting I (Financial Accounting) is a textbook-driven course. The textbook defines the course, and the goal of every student is to learn the material in the textbook. (If you are an accounting major, this course becomes especially important because next year you will most likely take Intermediate Accounting I and II, which cover, in much greater depth, the material in Accounting I. If you are not an accounting major, be glad that you are not required to take Intermediate Accounting, which can be a very challenging course.)

I want to really stress the idea of making the textbook your personal tool. As you highlight or underline key concepts and write ideas in the margins, you are customizing your book. When you want to "look something up," the marks you made and the ideas you put in the margins will help you. In my 12 years as a college student, I took a number of economics courses, and whenever I had a problem understanding something, I went back to my first economics text that I had underlined and marked up. Usually, I knew just where to look in the book to find the answer to my question. Make the textbook yours and it will be a terrific tool and a resource to you throughout your undergraduate career.

One other thing that I have pointed out before: It is often said that "accounting is the language of business." There is a great deal of truth to this statement. Therefore, whether or not you are an accounting major, whether or not you will ever take another course in financial accounting, in this course you will be learning the language of business. Since most students in the course are business majors, the terminology and concepts you learn here will be applicable in virtually all your business courses. Doing well in this course will help you in almost all of your other business courses.

Doing Homework

Let us assume that your homework assignment is to read chapter 5 and do exercise 5-5 and problem 5–12, and let us also assume that you have read the chapter as I have suggested, highlighting or underlining the key concepts and writing notes to yourself in the margins. Now you need to find out if (1) you just read the chapter (as you would read a novel) or (2) you read it like a chapter in an accounting textbook and learned how to do some accounting tasks or how to solve certain accounting problems. Doing the homework problems will let you know whether you have achieved either 1 or 2 above.

Before we get into using the homework as a test of your reading, let's talk about how to solve a homework problem, which is essentially the same skill set you will use to solve problems on your midterm(s) and final.

The first thing we need to cover is, how do you begin doing an accounting problem? Most students simply start reading the problem from top to bottom, just as it appears in the textbook. This seems obvious, but there is a better approach. In fact, you should begin the problem at the bottom by reading the requirements first, which tells you what you have to do with the problem information. After you read the requirements, *then* you read the problem information, beginning at the top. Why do it this way? I'll explain with a story.

Let's say I'm your accounting professor and one day I walk into class and read for 45 minutes from a chapter in your textbook. Then, I ask a single question based on what I just read to you for 45 minutes. How many people do you think will get the right answer? Probably a very small percentage. What if I asked the question first, and then read for 45 minutes? What percentage of the class would get the right answer? Everyone, because they knew what the question was and they would be listening for the answer as I read from the textbook.

Reading the requirements of a problem first is like knowing the question before the professor reads for 45 minutes. If you read the requirements first, you know what you have to do. Now you can read the problem information with the requirements in mind. You know what information is relevant to the solution, and you know what information is irrelevant. (If you read the problem information first, how can you tell the relevant information from the irrelevant? You can't.)

Therefore, we begin the problem by reading the requirements, so we know what we have to do with all this information, and we can tell which information is relevant. When reading the problem information, I strongly suggest using a highlighter to highlight the key bits of information (interest rates, dollar amounts, dates, etc.). Reading the problem is a critical part of solving a problem. (By the way, the CPA exam has been given for so many years that there have been numerous studies done regarding performance on the exam. Based on these studies, the number one reason for failure on the CPA exam *is not reading the questions carefully.*)

Reading a problem with a highlighter makes you a more careful reader, you will be paying attention to what is written, and since you know what the problem requirements are, you will be looking for the key bits of information to highlight.

Once you have read the requirements and the problem information, the next step is to visualize what your solution should look like, and to put an outline of the solution on your paper. This outline should have a proper heading, and if you need supporting schedules, they should be labeled and cross-referenced to the solution outline. The solutions to many accounting problems have a standard format. They may involve financial statements such as an income statement or a balance sheet, the computation of cost of goods sold, a bank reconciliation, and so forth. In this book, I have covered many of the typical accounting problems—quite a few of which have a standard format. Your job is to know the format for a given problem and to be able to make all the computations to arrive at the solution.

Let me tell you another story to emphasize why it is important to begin with an outline of your solution. Let's say your professor walks into class one day and asks everyone to draw a picture of the Statue of Liberty. What would this work of art look like? It would probably not be very artistic. However, what if the professor handed out a piece of paper with an outline of the Statue of Liberty on it and a set of colored pencils and asked you to fill in the outline. Don't you think that these results would look a lot better? It's much easier to fill in an outline than to begin with a blank page.

So, after you have read the requirements and the problem information, put an outline of your solution on your paper—no numbers yet, just the format of the solution with blank spaces where the numbers would go. If any of the numbers in your outline need to be calculated, make up a separate supporting schedule—just the outline without any numbers. Now, start completing the supporting schedules and fill in the numbers for your solution. Cross reference the supporting computations. Let's do a very simple example to give you the idea.

Illustrative Problem Data

The following data pertain to Gisell, Inc. for the year 2008:

Beginning inventory	$500
Purchases	400
Equipment (purchased in 2007)	
Cost	2,500
Estimated salvage value	500
Estimated life	10 years
(Depreciation calculated using Straight-line)	
Salary expense	100
Rent expense	50
Ending inventory	600

Required Prepare an income statement for Gisell, Inc. for 2008.

The requirements ask you to make up an income statement. Then there is some information. After reading the requirements and the problem information, I put the following outline on my paper:

Income Statement
Gisell, Inc.
Year Ended 12/31/2008

Revenue	$
Less Cost of goods sold (from schedule A)	_____
Gross profit	
Less Operating expenses:	
Salary expense	
Rent expense	
Depreciation expense (from schedule B)	
Total operating expenses	_____
Net income	═══════

Schedule A   Computation of cost of goods sold (This was covered in chapter 4.) (The cost-of-goods-sold figure will go on the income statement.)

Schedule B   Computation of depreciation expense (This was covered in chapter 5.)

Straight-line depreciation

$$(Cost - Salvage\ value)/Life\ in\ years$$

(The depreciation expense will go on the income statement.)

Now make the computations and fill in the outline. Students sometimes get lost doing a problem, but if they can visualize what the solution will look like (perhaps because they have seen similar problems before), it's a lot easier to fill in an outline than to deal with a blank sheet of paper.

Begin by completing schedule A and schedule B:

Schedule A   Computation of cost of goods sold

$$Cost\ of\ goods\ sold = \$500 + \$400 = \$900 - \$600 = \$300$$

(to income statement)
Then

Schedule B   Straight-line depreciation:

$$(Cost - Salvage\ value)/Life\ in\ years$$
$$\$2,500 - \$500/10 = \$200$$

(to income statement)

Now I fill in the income statement outline:

Income Statement

XYZ Company

Year Ended 12/31/07

Revenue		$800
Less Cost of Goods Sold (from Schedule A)		<300>
Gross profit		500
Less Operating expenses:		
Salary expense	$100	
Rent Expense	50	
Depreciation Expense (From Schedule B)	200	
Total Operating Expenses		350
Net Income		150

The supporting schedules are very important. Let us assume that you made a mistake in computing cost of goods sold. You didn't subtract properly and did the following:

$$\$500 + \$400 = \$900 - \$600 = \$200$$

You made a mistake subtracting $600 from $900; otherwise the schedule is correct. If you did this calculation in your head or on your calculator, but didn't write any of the numbers down, and just entered the $200 figure into your income statement, it would be wrong, you would get no credit for computing the cost of goods sold, and your final answer would also be wrong and might get some partial credit or not, depending on the grader. However, by having the supporting schedule on your paper, the grader can see that you know how to calculate cost of goods sold, but you simply made a subtraction error; you will definitely receive partial credit for computing cost of goods sold and will probably also get partial credit for the net income.

The key point here is this: You want to maximize your chances for partial credit. Therefore, show all your supporting calculations.

By cross-referencing your supporting calculations, your work looks organized and professional; the grader can see where all your numbers came from, and you should get the maximum partial credit.

Refer to figure A-1 for a summary of my general problem-solving method.

What to Do in Class

First of all, if it is possible, select a seat in the very front of the classroom, right in front of the professor. Believe it or not, there is a correlation between sitting in the front row of a classroom and getting a high grade. I have personally observed this relationship over a very long period of time. That is not to say that a person who sits in the back of the room cannot get an A in the course. However, I firmly believe that

1. Read the instructions for the problem first.
2. Read the problem data, highlighting or underlining key bits of information.
3. Visualize what the solution should look like.
4. Put an outline of the solution on paper, including supporting schedules needed to calculate numbers that will be part of the solution.
5. Complete the supporting schedules and put the numbers in the solution (be sure to cross-reference these numbers to the appropriate supporting schedule).
6. Complete the solution.
7. Edit your work. (This last step is very important. At this point, you want to ask yourself one of these questions: Does my answer make sense? Am I "in the ballpark"?

FIGURE A-1 A General Problem-Solving Method

you have a much better chance of learning accounting and getting a high grade if you sit in the front of the class. (A lot that goes on in the very back of the classroom, such as taking a nap or chatting with a classmate, simply does not happen in the first row.) In addition, when you sit in the front, you tend to pay more attention to the professor, and you will certainly be engaged in what goes on.

Come to Class Prepared

If you want to get the most out of each class, it is essential that you come to class prepared. That means that you have read the assigned pages in the textbook, and that you have prepared a complete solution to each homework problem. (You may not be able to complete every problem; the important thing is to make an honest effort on each problem.) Another element in preparing for class is to make up a list of questions for the professor, based on reading the chapter and trying to do the homework. You will probably find that most of the students in your classes will not ask questions at all, that means that you will have plenty of opportunity to ask your questions.

As a professor, I encourage my students to ask questions. If one student is having trouble with a particular concept, the chances are that several other students have the same question. By having a student actually ask the question during class, I have another opportunity to explain the concept. Hopefully, after hearing my response, the entire class will have a better understanding of the concept.

Correcting Your Homework

In my accounting classes, I go over every single homework problem and put the complete solution on the blackboard. My belief is that students are capable of reading the textbook and learning generally accepted accounting principles. What they have difficulty with, and what I can offer in the way of help, is how to apply what they have learned from reading the textbook, and how to solve accounting problems.

Your professor is probably a CPA. He or she has been out there in the business world actually doing what accountants do. This is where most students need help. You read the textbook, you know what GAAP is, but you are still unable to do the homework problems and get the right answer. What you need to learn are problem-solving strategies, how to approach a problem, a systematic way of looking at the problem, and preparing a solution to the problem.

Forming a Study Group

Accounting is a challenging course. Most college students have never studied this subject in high school, or anywhere else. There is an enormous amount of new terminology, new concepts, and new types of problems to be solved. In other words, there is a lot of work to be done to do well in this course. If you can get together with several other students in your class and form a study group, you can share the workload. You can help each other with homework and exam preparation, and maybe make the course more enjoyable.

How to Select the Study Group Members

- Select good students who have earned high grades.
- Select students who live near you or have the same schedule. That will permit all the group members to meet on a regular basis.
- Select students who you know, and who you feel comfortable working with.

Activities for the Study Group Assign individual group members to become the group expert for specific chapters in the textbook. All group members should give this person a copy of their class notes for their particular chapter. The student who is responsible for chapter 3, for example, would take all the group's class notes for chapter 3, plus his or her own notes, and create a complete outline of chapter 3. This outline would include

- basic concepts;
- vocabulary/terminology;
- a list of all the journal entries in the chapter;
- a list of the basic problems in the chapter, together with step-by-step solutions;
- multiple choice questions on the topics of the chapter; and
- predictions for which problems the professor is most likely to put on the exams.

Now, that's a lot of work. But if you have three or four group members, and your textbook has 14 chapters, then each group member only has to be the group expert for 4 or 5 chapters maximum. And, each group member winds up with 14 very complete chapter outlines, which you can use to help you study, learn the material, and prepare for the exams in the class.

At the end of the course, you will have these 14 chapter outlines, which will be very helpful in studying for the final, as well as serving as a reference for your other business courses. Accounting issues come up in virtually all business courses, whether the subject is finance, marketing, international business, and so forth.

Get together regularly with your study group and go over each chapter:

1. Do you have any questions after reading the chapter? Maybe someone in the group can answer the question. Otherwise, be sure to ask the professor in the next class.

2. Do you have any questions after hearing the lecture? Same idea. Perhaps someone in the group can answer the question, if not, ask the professor in the next class.

3. Work on homework problems together.

4. Make up practice midterm and final exam questions. Everyone in the group should try to solve each of these problems. The more different types of problems you practice, the less likely you will have any unpleasant surprises on the exams. (i.e., encountering a problem that you are unprepared for).

5. Make sure that you know how to solve all of the different problem types.

Practicing What You Have Learned and Testing Yourself

There are at least two different types of understanding or learning that takes place when you are taking a college course:

1. An understanding of, or a familiarity with, a basic concept. You have read about a given topic, you understood what you read, but you are not really sure how to apply this understanding to be able to answer a multiple choice question on this topic, or to be able to solve a problem using this knowledge or understanding.

2. A second and very different type of learning takes place when you can *use your understanding* of a concept to be able to *apply this knowledge* and use it to solve a problem.

One of the goals of this book is to move you from the first type of learning to the second type of learning—which is what you want to attain.

The job of an accounting professor is to move the class from a vague understanding of the basic concepts to an operational understanding of the basic concepts so that the students can *apply* what they have learned and be able to *do accounting* and *solve accounting problems.*

What you are aiming for is an operational understanding of the subject matter. You understand the basic concepts and you can apply that understanding to actually do accounting.

One way to know if you have reached this operational level of understanding is to test yourself. There are many ways to test yourself:

1. Do additional homework problems from your textbook. Your professor should be able to give you the answers to these problems.

2. Have a member of your study group make up problems for you to solve.

3. Go to the study guide for your textbook. Here you will find a variety of multiple choice and long problems to test yourself.

4. Go online to the Web site for your textbook where there should be a number of different types of questions and problems for you to solve.

5. Look at the multiple choice questions in this book.

You want to work these problems without looking back in your textbook or notes. What you want to determine is this: Can I *apply* what I have learned and solve various accounting problems.

Preparing for Exams

Let me tell you a true story about an undergraduate student athlete at my university. He was one of the top five high school basketball players in the country. After being recruited by a huge number of colleges, he decided to accept a full scholarship and enroll at our school. When he accepted his scholarship, he told the university that he wanted to have a room in the gym, instead of the dormitory. Of course, students can't live in the gym, and he was told this. He then had a counteroffer. He would live in the dorm if he was given a key to the gym. Both parties agreed, and he lived in the dorm but he could let himself into the gym whenever he wanted.

What was his reason for all this? Very simple—he wanted to practice playing basketball all the time, and he did. He was an outstanding college basketball player. He scored about 25 points a game and was a first-round NBA draft choice after his junior year.

Why have I told you this story? The point should be pretty obvious. The key to success in any field is *practice*. Repetition—doing the same thing over and over again—is what makes somebody really good at a particular task. Take a successful concert pianist, or figure skater, or basketball player, and I will show you someone who practices or rehearses hour after hour, day after day. My suggestion to you is to practice or rehearse as much as you can in preparation for your exams.

Studying can sometimes be a passive activity; you simply reread some chapters in your textbook. This will not help you very much on the exam; the exam doesn't test your ability to read a textbook. The exams test your ability to answer questions, solve accounting problems, and perhaps write an essay. The way you prepare for an exam is to actually do what is required on the exam. This means doing lots of multiple choice questions, solving lots of accounting problems, and writing lots of essays.

In his book *What Smart Students Know*, Adam Robinson makes this point very clearly. He simply says, "You are rehearsing for a performance. Most of the time students spend studying for exams in the traditional way is wasted because they aren't practicing what they'll have to do on the test. Rereading underlined passages in the textbook and classroom notes are not skills tested on exams, and will not improve your ability to answer questions on your exams. To rehearse for a test means practicing what you'll be doing on a test."[1]

If your exams will consist of multiple choice questions and accounting problems (which is typical), then you must rehearse by doing lots and lots of multiple choice questions and accounting problems.

One problem you may have is deciding what topics to concentrate on. I can make some suggestions here. Generally, your instructor will be making up your exams. This is the same person who gave the lectures and selected the homework problems. So pay attention. He or she selected the topics for the lectures and the homework because he or she thought they were important. Therefore, check your lecture notes and check the homework assignments, and you should have some clues about what the exam questions might look like.

Most accounting textbook publishers provide a computerized test bank for the instructor. This permits your instructor to create midterm and final exams on his or her computer. All one does is select from a list of questions and problems. Generally, the questions in the test bank were written by the same person or people who wrote the homework problems in the text. In fact, many of the test bank questions and problems are designed to be similar to the homework problems. Therefore, if your instructor selected particular homework questions, there is a good chance that he or she will select exam questions that are similar to the ones that were assigned for homework.

The message here is simple: When you are preparing for an exam, be sure to practice the homework problems. In fact, I would do each homework problem several times until you can practically do the problem in your sleep. When you take the exam and you encounter problems very much like the homework, you will certainly be ready.

When preparing for an exam, you want to be engaged; you want to be actively doing something, such as answering questions and solving problems. So, you will need lots of questions and problems to practice on. Where will you find them? Let me suggest several sources:

- The Web site for your textbook
- The study guide for your textbook
- Practice multiple choice questions in this book
- Review books containing just accounting questions and problems

Have you ever taken an exam and then received your graded exam in the next class, earned a poor grade, and said to yourself, "I really thought that I knew that stuff?" What happened? You thought you knew the material, but in reality you did not. Question: How do you go from "I *thought* I knew the stuff" to "I *know* I know the stuff?" Answer: By testing yourself. This is the only way to really find out if you

---

[1] Adam Robinson, *What Smart Students Know* (New York: Crown Publishers, 1993), 177.

understand the material and can actually use that understanding to answer questions and solve problems.

Let me tell you another story. I had a student who had been in several of my accounting classes and was also enrolled in a CPA review course that I was teaching. He passed all four parts of the exam on his first sitting (at that time, only about 10% of the candidates passed all four parts on their first attempt). To make matters even more challenging for him, English was not his native language. After the exam, I asked him if he thought he had passed, and he told me he was certain that he had passed. Naturally, I asked him how he *knew* that he had passed. This is what he said: "Every time we did multiple choice questions in class, I got about 85% correct. Sixty percent of the exam is multiple choice, and I was averaging about 85% when tested in class, plus I usually was able to do quite well when we practiced on long problems. Thus, I was pretty sure that I would pass."

The moral of the story is quite simple: If you make an honest effort to test yourself with exam-type questions and problems, and you do well when you test yourself, then you should know that you are going to do well on the exam.

Here is another true story that is right on point. I had a student in my Intermediate Accounting class who got a score like 52 or 53 on the first midterm. She came to see me after the exam and told me that she was very shocked at her grade. In the course of our discussion, I asked her if she did a number of multiple choice questions as she prepared for the exam. She said that she did. When I asked her how she did on these practice questions, she told me that she got about half of them right. Well, if you are doing about 50% in practice, you shouldn't be surprised when you get a grade like 52 or 53.

My recommendation: Do a lot of multiple choice questions. Do 10 at a time and give yourself a grade on each set of 10. Keep doing questions until you are happy with the scores you are getting. People who average about 80% in practice tend to get high grades on their exams; people who get about half right in practice tend to get grades in the 50's.

Here's another tip related to testing yourself. As you practice multiple choice questions, when you are determining your score on each set of 10 questions, make a list of "what I learned" from attempting each question. Add this list to your outline of the chapter.

Taking Exams

General Exam Strategies   You want to get a good night's sleep before you take an exam; cramming the night before an exam is usually counterproductive. If you have been following my advice, you would have been studying for the exam throughout the course, and therefore there would be no need for cramming.

When you come to the exam, what do you bring? I have watched thousands of students take accounting exams, and it always amazes me to see how many students take the exam with a pen. You really don't want to use a pen. Pencils and large erasers are what you want to use. Generally, you will be permitted to bring a calculator to the exam, and given how inexpensive they are, you may want to have a backup calculator in your backpack, just in case.

Which Questions to Answer First

When you walk into a classroom to take an exam, the first decision you must make is this: Which question do I do first? Most students never even realize that there is a decision to be made here. They simply answer the questions in the order that they are presented on the exam. However, if the exam consists of different types of questions, there may be an optimal order for you to do the questions, and it might be quite different from the order in which they appear on the exam.

Consider an exam such as the old paper-and-pencil CPA exam. Several parts of this exam consisted of multiple choice questions and essays. Even though the multiple choice questions came first, clever students started with the essays. Here's what they did. They read the four essays and prepared an outline of their answer. Then they put aside their four outlines and did the 60 multiple choice questions. Then they wrote the four essays.

How can this tactic help you? The answer is simple. After spending about an hour thinking about the four essays and making up an outline of your essay, the topics of the four essay questions are fresh in your mind. When you do the 60 multiple choice questions, you will most certainly find ideas within the multiple choice questions that you can add to your essay outlines. You will be looking for these items and you will find them. In a sense, the exam itself is providing you with partial answers to the essay questions; you just have to be alert. You simply add the material from the multiple choice questions to your essay outlines, and then you write the four essays.

You can use this same strategy on any exam that has a combination of multiple choice questions and essays. Remember to leave lots of room in your outlines for the "free essay answers" that you will pick up as you do the multiple choice questions. (If you did the multiple choice questions first, you wouldn't know what the essay topics were, and hence you wouldn't recognize the material in the multiple choice questions that you could have used to answer the essay questions.)

If the exam consists of problems and multiple choice questions, you may want to look over the problems to see what the topics are, then do the multiple choice questions, keeping in mind the problem topics and marking any multiple choice questions that may have information that can help you with the problems. Then, after you have completed all the multiple choice questions, tackle the problems. Do the easiest one first. The easiest one for you might not be the easiest one for someone else—just take care of yourself. Doing the easiest one first gets you going. If you did the hardest one first because it was the first one presented on the exam, and you didn't know how to do it, you risk putting yourself in "panic mode," and then you will not even be able to do the easy questions.

Tips for Answering Multiple Choice Questions

Multiple choice questions are very common on accounting exams; they permit your instructor to cover a lot of different material. You should expect to see a lot of multiple choice questions on your exams. In fact, on the new CPA exam, there are only two types of questions: multiple choice and simulations.

The fist critical skill in answering any type of question is to read the question carefully. If you see a lengthy multiple choice question, it is usually advantageous to let your eyes move down to the last sentence in the question—this is where the actual question is asked. Now that you know what the question is, you can read the question from the top, looking for the information you need to answer the question. As you read the question, be sure to look for these words:

Always

Never

Sometimes

Usually

Not

Either

I tell my students that it is usually a good idea to read the questions with a highlighter in your hand, this way you can highlight those key words, plus other key terms in the problem, such as dates, interest rates, and so forth.

Reading with a highlighter in your hand will slow you down a bit, but I think that this is a positive factor. By reading more slowly, you are less likely to miss something important in the question. You become a more careful reader, and this is what you want.

If you come upon a question that you simply cannot answer, try to eliminate one or more of the choices. If you only can eliminate one or two of the choices, that's OK. Now, with the remaining choices, make an educated guess. If you were able to eliminate two of the four choices, you have a 50–50 chance of getting the right answer. You may also want to put a question mark next to this question, so that if you have some time at the end of the exam, you can revisit these questions. (I can't tell you how many exams I have seen where a student leaves a multiple choice question blank, even though there is no penalty for guessing. A wrong answer and no answer receive the same grade!) *You must answer every question*!

After you come up with your answer, ask yourself these questions: Is my answer "in the ballpark?" Does this answer make sense? Then compare your answer to the four or five choices and select your answer. Always keep on the lookout for information contained in one question that might help you on another question.

Tips for Solving Accounting Problems   We have covered some of this material in the section on doing homework in this appendix, but the message bears repeating: There is a "best way" to solve an accounting problem on an exam.

First, read the instructions. This tells you what the question or problem is asking, and what your solution must contain (journal entries, a balance sheet or income statement, some computation, etc.). You need to read this before you read the problem data.

Now that you know what you must do with this information, read the body of the question, using your highlighter to identify key numbers, dates, terms, and so forth.

The next step is to visualize your solution, and put this solution on paper in outline form. If any of the numbers in your solution need to be calculated, prepare a separate schedule to calculate this number, and cross-reference the schedule to your solution.

Let's say that the problem asks you to prepare an income statement—so at some point you put an outline of an income statement on your paper. The first three lines of this statement are

Revenue (Sales)

Less Cost of Goods Sold

Gross Profit

If you must compute revenue from three or four other numbers, make up a separate schedule, labeled computation of revenue, and cross-reference it to the first line of your income statement, which is revenue. Therefore, the person who grades your paper can tell where your number for revenue came from, and if you made an error in computing that number, you would still get partial credit for the revenue figure.

Always keep asking yourself these questions:

- Have I seen a question like this before, as a homework assignment or a question that I looked at in reviewing for the exam?
- Are there some basic relationships that I know that relate to this topic? If so, I am going to write them on my exam paper as a guide.
- Is my answer "in the ballpark"? Does my answer make sense? (For example, there is a standard question that asks you to calculate the price that a bond will be issued for. You will learn, if you don't already know this, that a bond can sell for par, a discount (less than par), or a premium (more than par). Let's say that you determine, by reference to the coupon rate of the bond and the market rate of interest, that the bond in your exam question will sell for a premium. It is a $500,000 bond, and you calculate the issue price to be $495,000. Well, that can't be correct, since you have already determined that the bond will sell for a premium—therefore, the correct answer must be greater than $500,000. Most students just go into a "calculation mode" on exams and never consider whether their answer makes sense or not. This is a key point. You want to make sure that all your answers make sense.

Tips for Writing Essays   Fist of all, just like any other type of exam question, it is very important to read the question very carefully. I have already pointed out that the other questions on the exam might contain information that you can use in preparing your answer to a particular essay question. Make sure that you keep alert for this information as you work your way through the exam.

Preparing an outline of your answer helps you organize your thoughts, and it also helps you insert information that you picked up from the other questions on the exam.

An important part of answering essay questions is to incorporate everything you know about the topic, as long as it is relevant in some way. If you are unsure about the relevancy of a certain point, include it.

Tips for Maximizing Partial Credit   Making sure that you get the maximum partial credit is an important issue. When you do an accounting problem on an exam, and you do not get the complete correct answer, how can you make sure that at least you get the most partial credit? The answer is that you must show the person grading your paper that you do have an understanding of the concepts involved and you know how to do some of the problem.

One thing that I have noticed over many years of teaching and grading accounting exams is that some students essentially give up on a problem if they cannot prepare a complete solution to the problem, even if they do know how to do one or more parts of the problem. If you find yourself in this situation, *do all the parts that you are capable of doing*, and explain how you would go about doing the parts that you simply cannot complete. This should give you some partial credit for the parts that you did complete correctly, and you might even get some credit for your explanations of how you would do the parts you did not complete. The key point here is that you want to get credit for every thing that you know, even if it is only a small part of a question or problem. All the partial credit adds up, and it might be the difference between an A and a B on an exam.

For numerical calculations, be sure to show all your computations. Students working with a calculator might be tempted to use the calculator to make the computation and then just write down the result of the computation, without showing on the exam paper how they reached the final figure. Accounting exams are loaded with computations and it's a good general rule to show the complete calculation on your paper; this will guarantee that you get the maximum credit for knowing how to make the calculation, even if one or more of your numbers are incorrect.

I have just provided you with a number of study skills, strategies, and techniques. Use them in all your courses and you will be very successful in college.

THE TIME VALUE OF MONEY

LEARNING OBJECTIVES

After studying appendix B, you will understand

- one equation for present and future value problems
- how to use standard present value and future value interest tables
- ordinary annuities and annuities due
- how to convert interest factors for an ordinary annuity into interest factors for an annuity due
- how to draw cash-flow time diagrams
- how to make present value and future value calculations and
- how to calculate the issue price of a bond

INTRODUCTION

The time of value of money is a topic that you will probably encounter in several of your business classes. It is an important topic in accounting. Interest computations made using the techniques illustrated here are used in conjunction with accounting for property, plant, and equipment; liabilities (bonds and notes payable); leases and pensions to name just a few.

It would be a good idea to have a firm grasp of this topic. Learn it once, and you can use these techniques over and over again.

BASIC CONCEPTS

Money has a time value. In other words, a dollar received today is worth more than a dollar to be received a year from now. Why? Because the dollar that is received today can be put in the bank and earn a year's amount of interest, making it worth more than the dollar received at the end of the year. There are really only three critical things that you have to know to apply the concepts related to present value:

1. One equation
2. Four basic tables
3. How to draw a time diagram

1. The equation that we use to make a present value (and future value) computation is

$$\boxed{\text{Amount} \times \text{Interest factor} = \text{Answer}}$$

2. There are four basic tables which contain the interest factors that we need to substitute in the equation:
   a. Future value of a sum
   b. Present value of a sum
   c. Future value of an ordinary annuity
   d. Present value of an ordinary annuity

   A sum is simply an amount of money. An annuity is a stream of equal dollar amounts. If the first payment in an annuity comes at the end of the first period, we refer to it as an ordinary annuity. If the first payment comes at the beginning of the first period, we refer to it as an annuity due. (Ordinary annuities are much more common. We will focus on them first. At the end of this appendix, we will cover annuities due.)

3. A critical step in making these calculations is to be able to draw a time diagram. I will show you how to make a time diagram for each of the four basic tables. You will want to remember how they look, so you can feel comfortable using these diagrams to solve problems.

Future Value of a Sum

If you put $100 in the bank today, how much will it be worth at the end of 1 year or at the end of 5 years? This is a question about the future value of a sum. The time diagram associated with this computation is

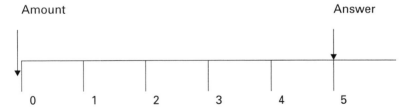

Note that the present is indicated by a zero. The 1 on the diagram refers to the end of the first period (0 is the *beginning* of the first period, or today). This diagram has an amount (the sum) at present, and we want to know how much that amount will be worth (the answer) at the end of the fifth period.

Note that time in these calculations is referred to as "periods." The period actually refers to how often the interest is compounded. Typical compounding is either

- Annually,
- Semi-annually, or
- Quarterly.

If the interest is compounded annually, then the periods in the table refer to years, and you use the *annual* interest rate. If the interest is compounded semi-annually, each compounding period is 6 months. To find the number of compounding periods in a problem, multiply the years involved by the number of compounding periods. Thus, if we want to know the future value of a sum at the end of 5 years and the interest is 12% compounded annually, we simply look in the table for period 5 in the 12% column. If we want the future value of a sum at the end of 5 years, and the interest is 12% per year compounded semi-annually, we multiply $5 \times 2 = 10$ compounding periods and divide the annual interest rate by 2 to get 6% per compounding period. Then we look in the table in the column for 6% interest and look at the value in the table at row 10 (for 10 periods).

Let's make the two calculations for the question raised earlier. What is the future value of $100 at the end of 1 year and at the end of 5 years if the interest rate is 12% compounded annually?

The equation is

$$\text{Amount} \times \text{Interest factor} = \text{Answer}$$

For 1 year, we look at the table for the future value of a sum for one period at 12%. (Table B-1) The interest factor is 1.12000. Thus,

$$\$100 \times 1.120000 = \$112.00$$

For 5 years, we look at the table for five periods at 12%; the interest factor is 1.76234; thus,

$$\text{Amount} \times \text{Interest factor} = \text{Answer}$$
$$\$100 \times 1.76234 = \$176.23$$

In the 5-year problem, if the interest is compounded semi-annually, we just multiply $5 \times 2 = 10$ periods and look in the $12/2 = 6\%$ column for 10 periods:

$$\text{Amount} \times \text{Interest factor} = \text{Answer}$$
$$\$100 \times 1.79085 = \$179.09$$

Once you know how to use one table, you know how to use them all. Let's move to present value.

Present Value of a Sum

In this case, we have an amont of money to be received in the future and we want to know its present value. An easy way to understand the meaning of present value is to ask this: How much money would I have to put in the bank today to have that much money at the end of x periods?

Using the same example as before, we ask this question: What is the present value of $100 to be received at the end of 5 years, assuming interest at 12% compounded annually?

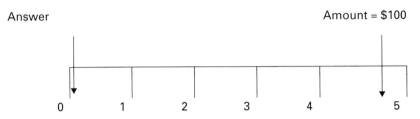

Step 1:   Write the equation.

$$\text{Amount} \times \text{Interest factor} = \text{Answer}$$

Step 2:   Substitute a value for the amount ($100) and the interest factor from the table for present value of a sum. (See table B-2)

$$\text{Amount} \times \text{Interest factor} = \text{Answer}$$
$$\$100 \times .56743 = \$56.74$$

If the interest in this problem had been 12% compounded semi-annually, multiply the number of years by 2 (5 × 2 = 10 periods), divide the annual interest rate by 2 (12/2 = 6), and look up the interest factor in table B-2 under the 6% column at row 10 (10 compounding periods).

$$\text{Amount} \times \text{Interest factor} = \text{Answer}$$
$$\$100 \times .55839 = \$55.84$$

Question: What is the impact on the present value of a sum if the interest rate increases?

Answer: The present value decreases. Why? An easy way to see this is to say, If the bank is paying a *higher* rate of interest, to reach my stated goal of having $100 in my account at the end of 5 years, I can put *less* in the bank today because the money will be earning more interest.

Future Value of an Ordinary Annuity

An annuity is a stream of equal payments. An ordinary annuity is a stream of equal payments where the first payment comes at the *end* of the first period. An ordinary annuity of $100 payments each year for 5 years would look like this:

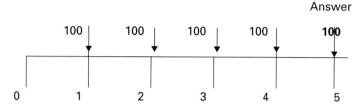

If we want to know how much these five payments will be worth at the end of the fifth period, we use the same formula,

$$\text{Amount} \times \text{Interest factor} = \text{Answer},$$

and look up the interest factor for the future value of a 5-year ordinary annuity at 12% interest in table B-3.

The future value is

$$\$100 \times 6.35285 = \$635.29$$

Present Value of an Ordinary Annuity

The time diagram for the present value of an ordinary annuity looks just like the diagram for the future value of an annuity, except that we want the answer at the present—at the beginning of the first period. The time diagram looks like this:

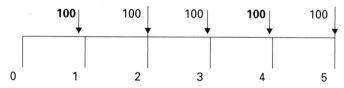

We look up the interest factor for the present value of an ordinary annuity for 5 years at 12% in table B-4. The answer is

$$\text{Amount} \times \text{Interest factor} = \text{Answer}$$
$$\$100 \times 3.60478 = \$360.48$$

Future Value of an Annuity Due

An annuity due is similar to an ordinary annuity. It is a stream of equal payments. In this case, the first payment comes at the *beginning* of the first period. If you are given a table with interest factors for an annuity due, simply use them. However, you rarely get such a table. If you only have ordinary annuity tables, you can convert the ordinary annuity interest factors into annuity due interest factors. Just multiply the ordinary annuity factor by 1 plus the interest rate.

Continuing with our basic example, the following time diagram illustrates a 5-year annuity due:

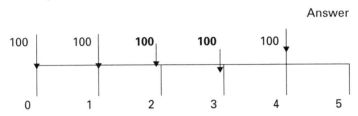

To solve for the future value, use the same basic equation;

$$\text{Amount} \times \text{Interest factor} = \text{Answer}$$

Assuming that you do not have an annuity due table, look up the interest factor for the future value of an ordinary annuity for 5 years at 12% (6.35285) and multiply it by $(1 + .12)$, or $6.35285 \times 1.12 = 7.11519$, then substitute in your equation as follows:

$$\text{Amount} \times \text{Interest factor} = \text{Answer}$$
$$\$100 \times 7.11519 = \$711.52$$

Present Value of an Annuity Due

Computing the present value of an annuity due is just like making the calculation for an ordinary annuity, but with a different interest factor. First, draw the time diagram for a 5-year $100 annuity due:

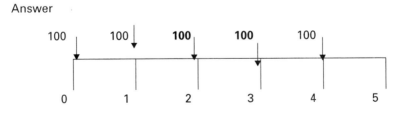

To get the interest factor, go to the table for the present value of an ordinary annuity for 5 years at 12%. The interest factor is 3.60478. Multiply that by $(1 + .12)$, or 1.12000, to get 4.03735. Substitute in the equation to determine the present value of the annuity due:

$$\text{Amount} \times \text{Interest factor} = \text{Answer}$$
$$\$100 \times 4.03735 = \$403.735$$

MAKING PRESENT VALUE AND FUTURE VALUE CALCULATIONS: A SUMMARY

To make present value and future value calculations, we use a single equation and interest factors from four interest tables. Here is the equation one more time:

$$\text{Amount} \times \text{Interest factor} = \text{Answer}$$

There are four basic interest tables that correspond to the four time diagrams shown next:

TABLE B-1   Future Value of a Sum

TABLE B-2   Present Value of a Sum

TABLE B-3   Future Value of an Ordinary Annuity

TABLE B-4   Present Value of an Ordinary Annuity

Note that the equation contains three elements, but there are really four different variables involved because the interest factor is a function of two values:

1. The interest rate
2. The number of periods

If you know the value of any three of the variables, you can use the equation to calculate the fourth value. These problems are very easy. For example, consider the following information: The company has $20,000 today, and they want to know how much this amount will be worth at the end of 3 years, assuming interest at 8%. First, we draw a time diagram:

The time diagram helps you identify the appropriate interest table. In this case, we need table B-1, the future value of a sum. The interest factor for 3 years at 8% is 1.25971. Substitute the values in the equation and determine the answer:

$$\text{Amount} \times \text{Interest factor} = \text{Answer}$$
$$\$20,000 \times 1.25971 = \$25,194$$

If the problem provided the present value and the future value, and asked you to calculate the interest, begin by drawing the time diagram:

To solve this problem, we could use either the future value of a sum table or the present value of a sum table. (We will look at both approaches.)

If you use the future value table, you would write the equation and substitute the two values you know as follows:

$$\text{Amount} \times \text{Interest factor} = \text{Answer}$$

$20,000 $\times$ Interest factor = $25,194, and solve for the interest factor:

$$\text{Interest factor} = \$25,194/\$20,000 = 1.2597$$

Then go to table B-1, the future value of a sum, and go to the row labeled $n = 3$; run your finger along the row until you come to the value 1.2597. Look at the top of the column and you will find that the interest rate is 8%.

If you use the present value table, substitute the values in the equation and solve for the interest factor:

$$\text{Amount} \times \text{Interest factor} = \text{Answer}$$

$25,194 \times$ Interest factor $= \$20,000$, and solve for the interest factor:

$$\text{Interest factor} = \$20,000/\$25,194 = .79383$$

Then go to table B-2, the present value of a sum, and go to the row labeled $n = 3$; run your finger along the row until you come to the value .79383. Look at the top of the column and you will find that the interest rate is 8%.

You may also be given the interest rate and be asked to calculate the number of periods. You would do it the same way: Substitute the values you know in the equation, solve for the interest factor, and then go to the table and read the number of periods.

For our problem, let us use the table for the present value of a sum. Our equation would look like this:

$$\$25,194 \times \text{Interest factor} = \$20,000,$$
$$\text{Interest factor} = \$20,000/\$25,194,$$
$$\text{Interest factor} = .79383$$

Now go to the table, look in the 8% column, run your finger down the column until you find the value .79383, look to the left, and you will find that the number of periods is 3.

To summarize, whenever you are doing present value or future value calculations, there are four critical things you must do:

1. Draw a time diagram of the cash flows involved. Remember that the present time is indicated by a **zero; 1** indicates the end of the first period. Here is a time diagram for a deferred annuity, which we are about to cover:

| 0 | 1 | 2 | 3 | 4 | 5 | 6 | 7 | 8 | 9 | 10 |

2. Determine which table contains the interest factor you need to solve the problem. Just looking at the time diagram should help you determine which table is involved. In this appendix, and hopefully in your notes, you have a time diagram that corresponds to each of the four tables. Make sure that you know how to draw the time diagram that corresponds to each of the four tables.

In addition, you should know how to convert interest factors for an ordinary annuity into interest factors for an annuity due. (You take the interest factor for the ordinary annuity and multiply it by 1 + the interest rate.)

3. Write the basic equation on your paper, substitute the values for the various variables, and calculate your answer. Remember, if interest is compounded more than once a year, the number of compounding periods will be greater than the number of years and the interest rate per compounding period will be less than the annual interest rate.

4. Edit your work. Don't just multiply and divide. Think! ask yourself this question: Does my answer make sense? For example, if you are calculating the issue price of a $10 million bond, which you are told was issued at a discount, your answer must be less than $10 million.

Deferred Annuities

An annuity is a series of payments in equal amounts. There are two basic types of annuities: ordinary annuities and annuities due. The first payment in an ordinary annuity comes at the *end* of the first period. The first payment in an annuity due comes at the *beginning* of the first period. Another type of annuity is a deferred annuity, where the first payment comes several periods after the first period.

Look back at the time diagram for a deferred annuity. In this case, it is a 5-year annuity, where the first payment comes at the end of the sixth period. How do we calculate the present value of this annuity? If we look up the interest factor for a 5-year ordinary annuity in table A-4, and multiply this interest factor times the amount of each payment, we will get the present value of the annuity at the beginning of the sixth period. However, the number we want is the present value of the annuity at present, not 6 years later. There are actually several different ways to approach this calculation using the equation and the interest tables.

First Approach: You could take the present value of each of the payments on an individual basis, using interest factors from table B-2, the present value of a sum, and then add up the five resulting values. Assume that each payment is for $1,000, beginning at the end of year 6, with an interest rate of 10%. Here are the computations:

Payment 1	$1,000 × .56447 = $564.47
Payment 2	$1,000 × .51316 = $513.16
Payment 3	$1,000 × .46651 = $466.51
Payment 4	$1,000 × .42410 = $424.10
Payment 5	$1,000 × .38554 = $385.54
Total present value	**$2,353.78**

Second Approach: You could take the present value of the 5-year annuity using the interest factors in table B-4 (the present value of an ordinary annuity), which would give you a value at the end of year 5. Then you could use the interest factors in table B-2 to get the present value of the sum that we just calculated. Thus, we solve the problem in two stages. Here are the computations:

$$1,000 \times 3.79079 = 3,790.79$$
$$3,790.79 \times .62092 = \textbf{\$2,353.78}$$

Third Approach: We could create an interest factor for this specific problem, namely, the present value of a 5-year deferred annuity, with the first payment coming at the end of the sixth period. The interest factor is computed by taking the interest factor for a 10-year annuity and subtracting from that number the present value of a 5-year annuity. The difference would be the present value of a 5-year deferred annuity. Here are the computations:

Present value of a 10-year ordinary annuity	6.14457
Less the present value of a 5-year ordinary annuity	<3.79079>
Present value of the deferred annuity for our problem	2,353.78

Now just multiply the amount of each payment times the deferred annuity interest factor:

$$\$1,000 \times 2.35378 = \$2,353.78$$

Obviously, the third approach is the quickest and also the most elegant, but as you can see, all three approaches give you the same answer.

One Final Problem

How about one more problem, just for the fun of it (and also to make a point)? Let's say you get married on January 1, 2009, and have a baby born exactly 1 year later on January 1, 2010. Assume that you and your spouse want to send this child to college for 4 years, and we anticipate that tuition at that time will be $50,000 per year. If the child will begin college in 2028, paying tuition on December 31 of each year, beginning in year 2028, how much money will you have to deposit on the day he or she is born if you want to accumulate enough money to pay the tuition for all 4 years, assuming that the bank is paying 10% interest?

First, draw a time diagram of this situation:

						50K	50K	50K	50K
1	2	3	4	5	...	18	19	20	21

Note: Before we make the actual computations, I would like you to make a guess as to how much money you will have to put in the bank on the day the baby is born, to be able to pay the tuition beginning in 18 years. We will check out your guess in a few minutes.

What we have here is a deferred annuity, so let us compute the interest factor for that deferred annuity:

The present value factor for a 22-year annuity beginning on December 31, 2028, at 10% per year, is 8.77154.

Next, subtract the present value of an 18-year ordinary annuity. The present value of an 18-year ordinary annuity is 8.20141.

Finally, calculate the interest factor for this deferred annuity:

Present value of a 22-year annuity at 10%	8.77154
Less the present value of an 18-year annuity at 10%	<8.20141>
The interest factor for our deferred annuity is	.57013

Now, we use the interest factor for the deferred annuity to find the present value:

The present value is $50,000 × .57013 = $28,506.

If the bank is paying 10% interest, if you deposited $28,506 on the day that the baby was born, when he or she begins college in 18 years, you would have enough money to pay $50,000 of tuition for 4 years.

How did you do with your guess to the question posed on the previovs page? Most people are very surprised to learn how little money you have to place in the bank to be able to withdraw $50,000 four times—That's a total of $200,000. Most people guess much higher.

This little exercise was more than just for fun. It is very important for you to have an appreciation of the impact of compound interest. The calculation you just made should help.

Computing the Issue Price of a Bond

This is a problem that comes up all the time on exams, and you should certainly know how to do this. When a bond is issued, the person buying the bond is essentially buying two streams of payments: the principal which will be received at maturity, plus the interest, which will be a stream of payments, typically one interest payment per year.

Let us assume the following facts:

Grant Inc. issues $500,000, in 8%, 10-year term bonds when the market rate of interest was 9%. What will Grant receive for the bonds?

Solution: We need to calculate the present value of the principal, plus the present value of the interest, all discounted at the market rate of interest. The formula is

Amount × Interest factor = Answer

PV of principal = $500,000 PV of a sum at 9% for 10 years

PV of principal = $500,000 × .42241 = $211,205

PV of principal = $500,000 × .42241 = $211,205

PV of interest = $500,000 × .08 = $40,000 × PV of an ordinary annuity at 9% for 10 years

PV of interest = $40,000 × 6.41766 = $256,706

Present value of principal	$211,205
Present value of interest payments	256,706
Total issue price	$467,911

TABLE B-1   Future Value of 1 (Future Value of a Single Sum)

(n) Periods	2%	$2^1/_2$%	$FVF_{n,i} = (1 + I)^n$ 3%	4%	5%	6%
1	1.02000	1.02500	1.03000	1.04000	1.05000	1.06000
2	1.04040	1.05063	1.06090	1.08160	1.10250	1.12360
3	1.06121	1.07689	1.09273	1.12486	1.15763	1.19102
4	1.08243	1.10381	1.12551	1.16986	1.21551	1.26248
5	1.10408	1.13141	1.15927	1.21665	1.27628	1.33823
6	1.12616	1.15969	1.19405	1.26532	1.34010	1.41852
7	1.14869	1.18869	1.22987	1.31593	1.40710	1.50363
8	1.17166	1.21840	126677	1.36857	1.47746	1.59385
9	1.19509	1.24886	1.30477	1.42331	1.55133	1.68948
10	1.21899	1.28008	1.34392	1.48024	1.62889	1.79085
11	1.24337	1.31209	1.38423	1.53945	1.71034	1.89830
12	1.26824	1.34489	1.42576	1.60103	1.79586	2.01220
13	1.29361	1.37851	1.46853	1.66507	1.88565	2.13293
14	1 31948	1.41297	1.51259	1.73168	1.97993	2.26090
15	1.34587	1.44830	1.55797	1.80094	2.07893	2.39656
16	1.37279	1.48451	1.60471	1.87298	2.18287	2.54035
17	1.40024	1.52162	1.65285	1.94790	2.29202	2.69277
18	1.42825	1.55966	1.70243	2.02582	2.40662	2.85434
19	1.45681	1.59865	1.75351	2.10685	2.52695	3.02560
20	1.48595	1.63862	1.80611	2.19112	2.65330	3.20714
21	1.51567	1.67958	1.86029	2.27877	2.78596	3.39956
22	1.54598	1.72157	1,91610	2.36992	2.92526	3.60354
23	1.57690	1.76461	1.97359	2.46472	3.07152	3.81975
24	1.60844	1.80873	2.03279	2.56330	3.22510	4.04893
25	1.64061	1.85394	2.09378	2.66584	3.38635	4.29187
26	1.67342	1.90029	2.15659	2.77247	3.55567	4.54938
27	1.70689	1.94780	2.22129	2.88337	3.73346	4.82235
28	1.74102	1.99650	2.28793	2.99870	3.92013	5.11169
29	1.77584	2.04641	2.35657	3.11865	4.11614	5.41839
30	1.31136	2.09757	2.42726	3.24340	4.32194	5.74349
31	1.84759	215001	2.50008	3.37313	4.53804	6.08810
32	1.88454	2.20376	2.57508	3.50806	4.76494	6.45339
33	1.92223	2.25885	2.65234	3.64838	5.00319	6.84059
34	1.96068	2.31532	2.73191	3.79432	5.25335	7.25103
35	1.99989	2.37321	2.81386	3.94609	5.51602	7.68609
36	2.03989	2.43254	2.89828	4.10393	5.79182	8.14725
37	2.08069	2.49335	2.98523	4.26809	6.08141	8.63609
38	2.12230	2.55568	3.07478	4.43881	6.38548	9.15425
39	2.16474	2.61957	3.16703	4.61637	6.70475	9.70351
40	2.20804	2.68506	3.26204	4.80102	7.03999	10.28572

TABLE B-1 Future Value of 1

8%	9%	10%	11%	12%	15%	(n) Periods
1.08000	1.09000	1.10000	1.11000	1.12000	1.15000	1
1.16640	1.18810	1.21000	1.23210	1.25440	1.32250	2
1.25971	1.29503	1.33100	1.36763	1.40493	1.52088	3
1.36049	1.41158	1.46410	1.51807	1.57352	1.74901	4
1.46933	1.53862	1.61051	1.68506	1.76234	2.01136	5
1.58687	1.67710	1.77156	1.87041	1.97382	2.31306	6
1.71382	1.82804	1.94872	2.07616	2.21068	2.66002	7
1.85093	1.99256	2.14359	2.30454	2.47596	3.05902	8
1.99900	2.17189	2.35795	2.55803	2.77308	3.51788	9
2.15892	2.36736	2.59374	2.83942	3.10585	4.04556	10
2.33164	2.58043	2.85312	3.15176	3.47855	4.65239	11
2.51817	2.81267	3.13843	3.49845	3.89598	5.35025	12
2.71962	3.06581	3.45227	3.88328	4.36349	8.15279	13
2.93719	3.34173	3.79750	4.31044	4.88711	7.07571	14
3.17217	3.64248	4.17725	4.78459	5.47357	8.13706	15
3.42594	3.97031	4.59497	5.31089	6.13039	9.35762	16
3.70002	4.32763	5.05447	5.89509	6.86604	10.76126	17
3.99602	4.71712	5.55992	5.54355	7.68997	12.37545	18
4.31570	5.14166	6.11591	7.26334	8.61276	14.23177	19
4.66096	5.60441	6.72750	8.06231	9.64629	16.36654	20
5.03383	6.10881	7.40025	8.94917	10.80385	18.82152	21
5.43654	6.65860	8.14028	9.93357	12.10031	21.64475	22
5.87146	7.25787	8.95430	11.02627	13.55235	24.89146	23
6.34118	7.91108	9.84973	12.23916	15.17863	28.62518	24
6.84847	8.62308	10.83471	13.58546	17.00000	32.91895	25
7.39635	9.39916	11.91818	15.07986	19.04007	37.85680	26
7.98806	10.24508	13.10999	16.73865	21.32488	43.53532	27
3.62711	11.16714	14.42099	18.57990	23.88387	50.06561	28
9.31727	12.17218	15.86309	20.62369	26.74993	57.57545	29
10.06266	13.26768	17.44940	22.89230	28.95992	56.21177	30
10.86767	14.46177	19.19434	25.41045	33.55511	76.14354	31
11.73708	15.76333	21.11378	28.20560	37.58173	87.56507	32
12.67605	17.18203	23.22515	31.30821	42.09153	100.69983	33
13.69013	18.72841	25.54767	34.75212	47.14252	115.80480	34
14.78534	20.41397	28.10244	38.57485	52.79962	133.17552	35
15.96817	22.25123	30.91268	42.81808	59.13557	153.15185	36
17.24563	24.25384	34.00395	47.52807	66.23184	176.12463	37
18.62528	26.43668	37.40434	52.75616	74.17966	202.54332	38
20.11530	28.81598	41.14479	58.55934	83.08122	232.92482	39
21.72452	31.40942	45.25926	65.00087	93.05097	267.86355	40

TABLE B-2   Present Value of 1 (Present Value of a Single Sum)

(n) Periods	2%	$2\frac{1}{2}$%	3%	4%	5%	6%
		$\mathbf{PVF}_{n,i} = \frac{1}{(1+I)^n} = (1+i)^{-n}$				
1	.98039	.97561	.97087	.96154	.95238	.94340
2	.96117	.95181	.94260	.92456	.90703	.89000
3	.94232	.92860	.91514	.88900	.86384	.83962
4	.92385	.90595	.88849	.85480	.82270	.79209
5	.90573	.88385	.86261	.82193	.78353	.74726
6	.88797	.86230	.83748	.79031	.74622	.70496
7	.87056	.84127	.81309	.75992	.71068	.66506
8	.85349	.82075	.78941	.73069	.67684	.62741
9	.83676	.80073	.76642	.70259	.64461	.59190
10	.82035	.78120	.74409	.67556	.61391	.55839
11	.80426	.76214	.72242	.64958	.56468	.52679
12	.78849	.74356	.70138	.62460	.55684	.49697
13	.77303	.72542	.68095	.60057	.53032	.46884
14	.75788	.70773	.66112	.57748	.50507	.44230
15	.74301	.69047	.64186	.55526	.48102	.41727
16	.72845	.67362	.62317	.53391	.45811	.39365
17	.71416	.65720	.60502	.51337	.43630	.37136
18	.70016	.64117	.58739	.49363	.41552	.35034
19	.68643	.62553	.57029	.47464	.39573	.33051
20	.67297	.61027	.55368	.45639	.37689	.31180
21	.65978	.59539	.53755	.43883	.35894	.29416
22	.64684	.58086	.52189	.42196	.34185	.22751
23	.63416	.56670	.50669	.40573	.32557	.26180
24	.62172	.55288	.49193	.39012	.31007	.24698
25	.60953	.53939	.47761	.37512	.29530	.23300
26	.59758	.52623	.46369	.36069	.28124	.21981
27	.58586	.51340	.45019	.34682	.26785	.20737
28	.57437	.50088	.43709	.33348	.25509	.19563
29	.56311	.48866	.42435	.32065	.24295	.18456
30	.55207	.47674	.41199	.30832	.23138	.17411
31	.54125	.46511	.39999	.29646	.22036	.16425
32	.53063	.45377	.38834	.28506	.20987	.15496
33	.52023	.44270	.37703	.27409	.19967	.14619
34	.51003	.43191	.36604	.26355	.19035	.13791
35	.50003	.42137	.35538	.25342	.18129	.13011
36	.49022	.41109	.34503	.24367	.17266	.12274
37	.48061	.40107	.33498	.23430	.16444	.11579
38	.47118	.39128	.32523	.22529	.15661	.10924
39	.46195	.38174	.31575	.21662	.14915	.10306
40	.45289	.37243	.30656	.20829	.14205	.09722

TABLE B-2   Present Value of 1

8%	9%	10%	11%	12%	15%	(n) Periods
.92593	.91743	.90909	.90090	.89286	.86957	1
.85734	.84168	.82645	.81162	.79719	.75614	2
.79383	.77218	.75132	.73119	.71178	.65752	3
.73503	.70843	.68301	.65873	.63552	.57175	4
.68058	.64993	.62092	.59345	.56743	.49718	5
.63017	.59627	.56447	.53464	.50663	.43233	6
.58349	.54703	.51316	.48166	.45235	.37594	7
.54027	.50187	.46651	.43393	.40388	.32690	8
.50025	.46043	.42410	.39092	.36061	.28426	9
.46319	.42241	.38554	.35218	.32197	.24719	10
.42888	.38753	.35049	.31728	.28748	.21494	11
.39711	.35554	.31863	.28584	.25668	.18691	12
.36770	.32618	.28966	.25751	22917	.16253	13
.34046	.29925	.26333	.23199	.20462	.14133	14
.31524	.27454	.23939	.20900	.18270	.12289	15
.29189	.25187	.21763	.18829	.16312	.10687	16
.27027	.23107	.19785	.16963	.14564	.09293	17
.25025	.21199	.17986	.15282	.13004	.08081	18
.23171	.19449	.16351	.13768	.11611	.07027	19
.21455	.17843	.14864	.12403	.10367	.06110	20
.19866	.16370	.13513	.11174	.09256	.05313	21
.18394	.15018	.12285	.10067	.08264	.04620	22
.17032	.13778	.11168	.09069	.07379	.04017	23
.15770	.12641	.10153	.08170	.06588	.03493	24
.14602	.11597	.09230	.07361	.05882	.03038	25
.13520	.10639	.08391	.06631	.05252	.02642	26
.12519	.09761	.07628	.05974	.04689	.02297	27
.11591	.08955	.06934	.05382	.04187	.01997	28
.10733	.08216	.06304	.04849	.03738	.01737	29
.09938	.07537	.05731	.04368	.03338	.01510	30
.09202	.06915	.05210	.03935	.02980	.01313	31
.08520	.06344	.04736	.03545	.02661	.01142	32
.07889	.05820	.04306	.03194	.02376	.00993	33
.07305	.05340	.03914	.02878	.02121	.00864	34
.06763	.04899	.03558	.02592	.01894	.00751	35
.06262	.04494	.03235	.02335	.01691	.00653	36
.05799	.04123	.02941	.02104	.01510	.00568	37
.05369	.03783	.02674	.01896	.01348	.00494	38
.04971	.03470	.02430	.01708	.01204	.00429	39
.04603	.03184	.02210	.01538	.01075	.00373	40

TABLE B-3 Future Value of an Ordinary Annuity of 1

$$\text{FVF-OA}_{n,i} = \frac{(1 + I)^n - 1}{i}$$

(n) Periods	2%	2$\frac{1}{2}$%	3%	4%	5%	6%
1	1.00000	1.00000	1.00000	1.00000	1.00000	1.00000
2	2.02000	2.02500	2.03000	2.04000	2.05000	2.06000
3	3.06040	3.07563	3.09090	3.12160	3.15250	3.18360
4	4.12161	4.15252	4.18363	4.24646	4.31013	4.37462
5	5.20404	5.25633	5.30914	5.41632	5.52563	5.63709
6	6.30812	6.38774	6.46841	6.63298	6.80191	6.97532
7	7.43428	7.54743	7.66246	7.89829	8.14201	8.39384
8	8.58297	8.73612	8.89234	9.21423	9.54911	9.89747
9	9.75463	9.95452	10.15911	10.58280	11.02656	11.49132
10	10.94972	11.20338	11.46338	12.00611	12.57789	13.18079
11	12.16872	12.48347	12.80780	13.48635	14.20679	14.97164
12	13.41209	13.79555	14.19203	15.02581	15.91713	16.86994
13	14.68033	15.14044	15.61779	16.62684	17.71298	18.88214
14	15.97394	16.51895	17.08632	18.29191	19.59863	21.01507
15	17.29342	17.93193	18.59891	20.02359	21.57856	23.27597
16	18.63929	19.38022	20.15688	21.82453	23.65749	25.67253
17	20.01207	20.86473	21.76159	23.69751	25.84037	28.21288
18	21.41231	22.38635	23.41444	25.64541	28.13238	30.90565
19	22.84056	23.94601	25.11687	27.67123	30.53900	33.75999
20	24.29737	25.54466	26.87037	29.77808	33.06595	36.78559
21	25.78332	27.18327	28.67649	31.96920	35.71925	39.99273
22	27.29898	28.86286	30.53678	34.24797	38.50521	43.39229
23	28.84496	30.58443	32.45288	36.61789	41.43048	46.99583
24	30.42186	32.34904	34.42647	39.08260	44.50200	50.81558
25	32.03030	34.15776	36.45926	41.64591	47.72710	54.86451
26	33.67091	36.01171	38.55304	44.31174	51.11345	59.15638
27	35.34432	37.91200	40.70963	47.08421	54.66913	63.70577
28	37.05121	39.85980	42.93092	49.96758	58.40258	68.52811
29	38.79223	41.85630	45.21885	52.96629	62.32271	73.63980
30	40.56808	43.90270	47.57542	56.08494	66.43885	79.05819
31	42.37944	46.00027	50.00268	59.32834	70.76079	84.80168
32	44.22703	48.15028	52.50276	62.70147	75.29883	90.88978
33	46.11157	50.35403	55.07784	66.20953	80.06377	97.34316
34	48.03380	52.61289	57.73018	69.85791	85.06696	104.18376
35	49.99448	54.92821	60.46208	73.65222	90.32031	111.43478
36	51.99437	57.30141	63.27594	77.59831	95.83632	119.12087
37	54.03425	59.73395	66.17422	81.70225	101.62814	127.26812
38	56.11494	62.22730	69.15945	85.97034	107.70955	135.90421
39	58.23724	64.78298	72.23423	90.40915	114.09502	145.05846
40	60.40198	67.40255	75.40126	95.02552	120.79977	154.76197

TABLE B-3   Future Value of an Ordinary Annuity of 1

8%	9%	10%	11%	12%	15%	(n) Periods
1.00000	1.00000	1.00000	1.00000	1.00000	1.00000	1
2.08000	2.09000	2.10000	2.11000	2.12000	2.15000	2
3.24640	3.27810	3.31000	3.34210	3.37440	3.47250	3
4.50611	4.57313	4.64100	4.70973	4.77933	4.99338	4
5.86660	5.98471	6.10510	6.22780	6.35285	6.74238	5
7.33592	7.52334	7.71561	7.91286	8.11519	8.75374	6
8.92280	9.20044	9.48717	9.78327	10.08901	11.06680	7
10.63663	11.02847	11.43569	11.85943	12.29969	13.72682	8
12.48756	13.02104	13.57948	14.16397	14.77566	16.78584	9
14.48656	15.19293	15.93743	16.72201	17.54874	20.30372	10
16.64549	17.56029	18.53117	19.56143	20.65458	24.34928	11
18.97713	20.14072	21.38428	22.71319	24.13313	29.00167	12
21.49530	22.95339	24.52271	26.21164	28.02911	34.35192	13
24.21492	26.01919	27.97498	30.09452	32.39260	40.50471	14
27.15211	29.36092	31.77248	34.40536	37.27972	47.58041	15
30.32428	33.00340	35.94973	39.18995	42.75328	55.71747	16
33.75023	36.97371	40.54470	44.50084	48.88367	65.07509	17
37.45024	41.30134	45.59917	50.39593	55.74972	75.83636	18
41.44626	46.01846	51.15909	56.93949	63.43968	88.21181	19
45.76196	51.16012	57.27500	64.20283	72.05244	102.44358	20
50.42292	56.76453	64.00250	72.26514	81.69874	118.81012	21
55.45676	62.87334	71.40275	81.21431	92.50258	137.63164	22
60.89330	69.53194	79.54302	91.14788	104.60289	159.27638	23
66.76476	76.78981	88.49733	102.17415	118.15524	184.16784	24
73.10594	84.70090	98.34706	114.41331	133.33387	212.79302	25
79.95442	93.32398	109.18177	127.99877	150.33393	245.71197	26
87.35077	102.72314	121.09994	143.07864	169.37401	283.56877	27
95.33883	112.96822	134.20994	159.81729	190.69889	327.10408	28
103.96594	124.13536	148.63093	178.39719	214.56275	377.16969	29
113.28321	136.30754	164.49402	199.02088	241.33268	434.74515	30
123.34587	149.57522	181.94343	221.91317	271.29261	500.95692	31
134.21354	164.03699	201.13777	247.32362	304.84772	577.10046	32
145.95062	179.80032	222.25154	275.52922	342.42945	644.66553	33
158.62667	196.98234	245.47670	306.83744	384.52098	765.36535	34
172.31680	215.71076	271.02437	341.58955	431.66350	881.17016	35
187.10215	236.12472	299.12681	380.16441	484.46312	1014.34568	36
203.07032	258.37595	330.03949	422.98249	543.59869	1167.49753	37
220.31595	282.62978	364.04343	470.51056	609.83053	1343.62216	38
238.94122	309.06646	401.44778	523.26673	684.01020	1546.16548	39
259.05652	337.88245	442.59256	581.82607	767.09142	1779.09031	40

TABLE B-4 Present Value of an Ordinary Annuity of 1

$$\text{PVF-OA}_{n,i} = \frac{1 - \frac{1}{(1+i)^n}}{i}$$

(n) Periods	2%	2½%	3%	4%	5%	6%
1	.98039	.97561	.97087	.96154	.95238	.94340
2	1.94156	1.92742	1.91347	1.88609	1.85941	1.83339
3	2.88388	2.85602	2.82861	2.77509	2.72325	2.67301
4	3.80773	3.76197	3.71710	3.62990	3.54595	3.46511
5	4.71346	4.64583	4.57971	4.45182	4.32948	4.21236
6	5.60143	5.50813	5.41719	5.24214	5.07569	4.91732
7	6.47199	6.34939	6.23028	6.00205	5.78637	5.58238
8	7.32548	7.17014	7.01969	6.73274	6.46321	6.20979
9	8.16224	7.97087	7.78611	7.43533	7.10782	6.80169
10	8.98259	8.75206	8.53020	8.11090	7.72173	7.36009
11	9.78685	9.51421	9.25262	8.76048	8.30641	7.88687
12	10.57534	10.25776	9.95400	9.38507	8.86325	8.38384
13	11.34837	10.98319	10.63496	9.98565	9.39357	8.85268
14	12.10625	11.69091	11.29607	10.56312	9.89864	9.29498
15	12.84926	12.38138	11.93794	11.11839	10.37966	9.71225
16	13.57771	13.05500	12.56110	11.65230	10.83777	10.10590
17	14.29187	13.71220	13.16612	12.16567	11.27407	10.47726
18	14.99203	14.35336	13.75351	12.65930	11.68959	10.82760
19	15.67346	14.97889	14.32380	13.13394	12.08532	11.15812
20	16.35143	15.58916	14.87747	13.59033	12.46221	11.46992
21	17.01121	16.18455	15.41502	14.02916	12.82115	11.76408
22	17.65805	16.76541	15.93692	14.45112	13.16300	12.04158
23	18.29220	17.33211	16.44361	14.85684	13.48857	12.30338
24	16.91393	17.88499	16.93554	15.24696	13.79864	12.55036
25	19.52346	18.42438	17.41315	15.62208	14.09394	12.78336
26	20.12104	18.95061	17.87684	15.98277	14.37519	13.00317
27	20.70690	19.46401	18.32703	16.32959	14.64303	13.21053
28	21.28127	19.96489	18.76411	16.66306	14.89813	13.40616
29	21.84438	20.45355	19.18845	16.98371	15.14107	13.59072
30	22.39646	20.93029	19.60044	17.29203	15.37245	13.76483
31	22.93770	21.39541	20.00043	17.58849	15.59281	13.92909
32	23.46833	21.84918	20.38877	17.87355	15.80268	14.08404
33	23.98856	22.29188	20.76573	18.14765	16.00255	14.23023
34	24.49859	22.72379	21.13184	18.41120	16.19290	14.36814
35	24.99862	23.14516	21.48722	18.66461	16.37419	14.49825
36	25.48884	23.55625	21.83225	18.90828	16.54685	14.62099
37	25.96945	23.95732	22.16724	19.14258	16.71129	14.73678
38	26.44064	24.34860	22.49246	19.36786	16.86789	14.84602
39	26.90259	24.73034	22.80822	19.58448	17.01704	14.94907
40	27.35548	25.10278	23.11477	19.79277	17.15909	15.04630

TABLE B-4 Present Value of an Ordinary Annuity of 1

8%	9%	10%	11%	12%	15%	(n) Periods
.92593	.91743	.90909	.90090	.89286	.86957	1
1.78326	1.75911	1.73554	1.71252	1.69005	1.62571	2
2.57710	2.53130	2.48685	2.44371	2.40183	2.28323	3
3.31213	3.23972	3.16986	3.10245	3.03735	2.85498	4
3.99271	3.88965	3.79079	3.69590	3.60478	3.35216	5
4.62288	4.48592	4.35526	4.23054	4.11141	3.78448	6
5.20637	5.03295	4.86842	4.71220	4.56376	4.16042	7
5.74664	5.53482	5.33493	5.14612	4.96764	4.48732	8
6.24689	5.99525	5.75902	5.53705	5.32825	4.77158	9
6.71008	5.41766	6.14457	5.88923	5.65022	5.01877	10
7.13896	6.80519	6.49506	6.20652	5.93770	5.23371	11
7.53608	7.16073	6.81369	6.49236	6.19437	5.42062	12
7.90378	7.48690	7.10336	6.74987	6.42355	5.58315	13
5.24424	7.78615	7.36669	6.98187	6.62817	5.72448	14
8.55948	8.06069	7.60608	7.19087	6.81086	5.84737	15
8.85137	9.31256	7.82371	7.37916	6.97399	5.95424	16
9.12164	8.54363	8.02155	7.54879	7.11963	6.04716	17
9.37189	8.75563	8.20141	7.70162	7.24967	6.12797	18
9.60360	8.95012	8.36492	7.83929	7.36578	6.19823	19
9.81815	9.12855	8.51356	7.96333	7.46944	6.25933	20
10.01680	9.29224	8.64869	8.07507	7.56200	6.31246	21
10.20074	9.44243	8.77154	8.17574	7.64465	6.35866	22
10.37106	9.58021	8.88322	8.26643	7.71843	6.39884	23
10.52876	9.70661	8.98474	8.34814	7.78432	6.43377	24
10.67478	9.82258	9.07704	8.42174	7.84314	6.46415	25
10.80998	9.92897	9.16095	8.48806	7.89566	6.49056	26
10.93516	10.02658	9.23722	8.54780	7.94255	6.51353	27
11.05108	10.11613	9.30657	8.60162	7.98442	6.53351	28
11.15841	10.19828	9.36961	8.65011	8.02181	6.55088	29
11.25778	10.27365	9.42691	8.69379	8.05518	6.56598	30
11.34980	10.34280	9.47901	8.73315	8.08499	6.57911	31
11.43500	10.40624	9.52638	8.76860	8.11159	6.59053	32
11.51389	10.46444	9.56943	8.80054	8.13535	6.60046	33
11.58693	10.51784	9.60858	8.82932	8.15656	6.60910	34
11.65457	10.56682	9.64416	8.85524	8.17550	6.61661	35
11.71719	10.61176	9.67651	8.87859	8.19241	6.62314	36
11.77518	10.65299	9.70592	8.89963	8.20751	6.62882	37
11.82887	10.69082	9.73265	8.91859	8.22099	6.63375	38
11.87858	10.72552	9.75697	8.93567	8.23303	6.63805	39
11.92461	10.75736	9.77905	8.95105	8.24378	6.64178	40

PRACTICE MULTIPLE CHOICE QUESTIONS

1. Which of these tables has the largest interest factors?

    a. Future value of a sum

    b. Present value of a sum

    c. Future value of an ordinary annuity

    d. Present value of an ordinary annuity

Solution: The correct answer is **c**. Future values are always greater than present values because the money earns interest over time. Since annuities represent a stream of payments, the future value of an annuity will be greater than the future value of a sum.

2. On January 1, 2006, Avex Corporation issues $700,000 in 8%, 10-year bonds. The bonds pay interest annually on December 31. The bonds were issued to yield 10%. Using the following interest factors, compute the issue price of the bonds:

Present value of a sum at 8% for 10 periods	.46319
Present value of an ordinary annuity at 8% for 10 periods	6.71008
Present value of a sum at 10% for 10 periods	.38554
Present value of an ordinary annuity at 10% for 10 periods	6.14457

    a. $700,000

    b. $613,974

    c. $645,616

    d. $378,876

Solution: The correct answer is **b**. The issue price of a bond is computed by adding the present value of the principal to the present value of the interest payments, all discounted at the market or yield rate of interest. Therefore, in this problem, the present value of the principal is $700,000 × .38554 = $269,878. The present value of the interest payments, which is an ordinary annuity, is $56,000 × 6.14457 = $344,096. The sum of the two present values is the issue price of the bonds: $269,878 + $344,096 = $613,974. The other answers are therefore wrong.

3. In determining present value, which of the following relationships is true?

    a. The lower the discount rate and the shorter the discount period, the lower the present value.

    b. The lower the future cash flow and the shorter the discount period, the lower the present value.

    c. The higher the discount rate and the longer the discount period, the lower the present value.

    d. The higher the future cash flow and the longer the discount period, the lower the present value.

Solution: The correct answer is **c**. An easy way to think this through is to ask yourself how much money would you have to put in the bank to have a specific dollar amount, say a million dollars, at a certain time. Now, how would changes in these variables affect your situation? Well, if the bank pays a higher rate of interest, you won't need to put as much money in the bank today, compared to what would have been necessary if the bank was paying a lower rate of interest. Thus, the higher the interest rate, the lower the present value. With regard to the time, obviously, the longer the time your money has to accumulate, the less money you have to deposit today. Thus, the longer the discount period, the lower the present value. Therefore, c is the correct answer and the other choices are wrong.

4. The table that would have the smallest value for five periods at 8% is the

    a. future-value-of-a-sum table.

    b. present-value-of-a-sum table.

    c. present-value-of-an-ordinary-annuity table.

    d. present-value-of-an-annuity-due table.

Solution: The correct answer is **b**. Present values are always less than future values, since future values have earned interest along the way. Also, since annuities consist of a stream of payments, the present value of a single sum must be less than the present value of an annuity.

5. The interest factor that will enable you to calculate the amount to which periodic payments of $1,000 per period will accumulate if the payments are received at the end of each period is contained in the

    a. future value of $1 table.

    b. future value of an ordinary annuity of $1 table.

    c. present value of an ordinary annuity of $1 table.

    d. future value of an annuity due of $1 table.

Solution: The correct answer is **b**. We want to know how much a stream of payments (an annuity) will be worth at some time in the future. The key word in the problem is "accumulate." Therefore, we want the future value of an ordinary annuity. It is an ordinary annuity because each payment comes at the end of the period. If the payments came at the beginning of the period, then choice **d** would be the correct answer.

GROSS PROFIT INVENTORY COMPUTATION

THE GROSS PROFIT METHOD

Sometimes you need to determine the ending inventory, and you don't want to go to the trouble of counting every single unit, or you are unable to count it. For example, let's say that there was a fire and the entire inventory in Warehouse No. 25 was destroyed. How can we determine the cost of goods sold if we cannot count the ending inventory? We simply use a technique called the **gross profit method**, which allows us to estimate both cost of goods sold and the ending inventory.

Remember this basic relationship:

Sales
Less cost of goods sold
Gross profit

Furthermore, for our company, the numbers look like this:

Sales	100%
Cost of goods sold	70%
Gross profit	30%

EXAM TIP

Even though this technique is called the gross profit method, it is easier to work with the cost of goods sold percentage. In the calculation above, the gross profit percentage is 30%, so the cost of goods sold percentage must be $1.00 - .30$, or 70%.

Assume that a fire destroyed the entire inventory on hand. Also, let us assume a beginning inventory of $75,000, purchases of $125,000, and sales of $150,000. Compute the amount of inventory destroyed by the fire and prepare the income statement. We can use to the gross profit method to solve this problem very easily.

First, determine the goods available for sale:

Beginning inventory	$ 75,000
+ Purchases	125,000
Goods available for sale	200,000

Now all you have to do is multiply the sales for the period times the cost of goods sold percentage to get an estimate of the cost of goods sold:

Sales	$150,000 (100%)
Cost of goods sold	$105,000 ($150,000 × 70%)
Gross profit	$45,000 (30%)

Now we can estimate the ending inventory that was destroyed:

Beginning inventory	$75,000
Purchases	125,000
Goods available for sale	200,000
Less Estimated cost of goods sold	<105,000> (150,000 × .7)
Estimated ending inventory	$95,000

Income statement:

Sales	$150,000
Less cost of goods sold	<105,000>
Gross profit	45,000

EXAM TIP

The cost of goods sold percentage must be based on the *selling price*. Sometimes you are given a problem and the gross profit or cost of goods sold percentage is stated based on a markup on cost. To use this technique (the gross profit method), you have to convert any markup on cost to a markup on selling price. To make this conversion, use the following:

$$\% \text{ markup on selling price} = \frac{\text{the mark-up on cost}}{100\% + \text{ the mark-up on cost}}$$

If markup on cost is 25%, then the markup on sales is 20%

$$\frac{25}{(100 + 25)} = 20$$

Here is a simple problem to illustrate the gross profit method:

Beginning inventory	$150,000
Purchases	$400,000
Sales	$500,000

Gross profit 25%, based on selling price
(Therefore, the cost of goods sold percentage is 75%.)
The entire inventory was destroyed by a fire.

(continued)

Required: Compute the amount of inventory destroyed by the fire.
Prepare the income statement.

Beginning Inventory	$150,000	
Purchases	400,000	
Goods available for sale	550,000	
Less Estimated Cost of Goods Sold	<375,000>	($500,000 × .75)
Estimated Ending Inventory	$175,000	
Partial Income Statement:		
Sales	$500,000	
Cost of Goods Sold	375,000	
Gross Profit	125,000	

DEMONSTRATION PROBLEM   *Inventory—Gross Profit Method*

Joseph Browdy Inc.'s beginning inventory was $150,000. Purchases of merchandise inventory were $300,000. Purchase returns and allowances were $10,000 and purchase discounts were $15,000. Sales during the period were $500,000; sales returns and allowances were $18,000; and sales discounts were $5,000. On December 31, 2007, a fire destroyed the company's only warehouse, which contained their entire inventory. Compute the estimated inventory on December 31, 2007 assuming

- Markup on cost 25%
- Markup on selling price 30%

Solution: The gross profit method is quite easy to apply. One thing to keep in mind when you compute the estimated cost of goods sold is that you need to use a markup percentage based on the selling price, not on the cost. If you are given a markup based on cost, you can convert it to a markup on selling price using this formula:

$$\text{Markup on selling price} = \frac{\text{Markup on cost}}{(100\% + \text{Markup on cost})}$$

For this problem, the computations are

Beginning inventory	$150,000
Purchases	300,000
Less purchase returns and allowances	<10,000>
Less purchase discounts	<15,000>
Goods Available for Sale	425,000

Sales	$500,000
Less sales returns and allowances	<18,000>
Sales discounts	<5,00>
Net sales	477,000
× Cost of goods sold percentage	.80
Estimated cost of goods sold	381,600
Estimated ending inventory	$43,400

(Markup on selling price) $= 25\%/(100\% + 25\%)$, or $25/125$, or 20%

If the markup on selling price is 30%, then

Goods available for sale =		$425,000 (same as above)
Net sales	$477,000	
× Cost of goods sold percentage	.70	333,900
Estimated ending inventory		$91,100

■

Problem-Solving Takeaway

Even though this is called the gross profit method, the problem is easier if you work with the cost of goods sold percentage, which is 100% less the gross profit percentage. Thus, if the markup on the selling price is 30%, the cost of goods sold percentage is simply $1 - .3$, or $.7$.

You can convert the markup on cost to the markup on the selling price using this formula:

$$\text{Markup on selling price} = \frac{\text{Markup on cost}}{100\% + \text{Markup on Cost}}.$$

ADVANCED TOPICS FOR CHAPTER FIVE: CAPITALIZATION OF INTEREST AND NONMONETARY EXCHANGES

CAPITALIZATION OF INTEREST ON SELF-CONSTRUCTED ASSETS

Instead of buying a building or a large piece of equipment, the company may simply build the building or equipment for its own use.

There are two issues related to self-constructed assets:

- Do we include overhead as part of the cost?
- Do we include interest during the construction period?

GAAP indicates that a portion of the company's overhead costs should be added to the cost of a self-constructed asset. This is based on the assumption that if another company had built it, that company would have included overhead as part of the cost of the asset.

Interest expense incurred during the construction period is addressed in FASB Standard 34 (FAS 34), which established a very specific procedure for computing the amount of *interest to be capitalized* (i.e., included as part of the cost of the asset).

There are five steps in this calculation:

1. Calculate the **weighted average accumulated expenditure** for the self-constructed asset. This is simply the weighted average of the money expended during the period on the asset being constructed. To make this calculation, take each payment and multiply it by a fraction, which represents the period of time over which the money was expended. For example, an expenditure made on January 1 would be multiplied by 12/12, an expenditure made on April 1 would be multiplied by 9/12, and so on. The total of all the expenditures made during the period, multiplied by the appropriate fraction, equals the average accumulated expenditure. (If the problem you are working on covers an entire

calendar year, when you calculate the weighted average accumulated expenditure, be sure to check that you have accumulated 12 months of expenditures.)

2. Calculate the average interest rate on the other debt. Calculating the avoidable interest (which is a component of this computation) requires the use of two interest rates: the interest rate on the construction loan and the average interest on the "other debt." The interest rate on the construction loan is simply the interest rate on the loan that was earmarked to finance the construction project, which is usually identified simply as the construction loan. The interest on the other debt is an average of the interest on all the other (nonconstruction loan) debts. Compute the average interest on the other debt by calculating the interest on all the loans or bonds, and divide that total by the total principal.

Let us say that the other debt consists of a $100,000 note payable at 6%, $500,000 of 8% bonds, and a 10% bank loan of $300,000. The average interest on the other debt is

$$\$100,000 \times .06 = \$6,000$$
$$\$500,000 \times .08 = \$40,000$$
$$\$300,000 \times .10 = \$30,000$$

$$\frac{\$6,000 + \$40,000 + \$30,000}{\$100,000 + \$500,000 + \$300,000} = \frac{\$76,000}{\$900,000} = 8.44\%$$

3. Calculate the avoidable interest by multiplying the average accumulated expenditure by the interest rate on the construction loan. If the construction loan is less than the average accumulated expenditure, the remaining amount of the average accumulated expenditure is assumed to be financed by the other debt.

EXAMPLE

Assume that the construction loan is $500,000 at 7%
Average accumulated expenditure: $750,000
Interest on other debt: 8%
The avoidable interest computation is

a. The first $500,000 of the average accumulated expenditure is assumed to be financed by the construction loan. Multiply $500,000 × .07 = $35,000.

b. The remaining average accumulated expenditure, $750,000 − $500,000, or $250,000, is assumed to be financed by the other debt.

Therefore, multiply $250,000 × .08 = $20,000.
The total of these two numbers ($35,000 + $20,000 = $55,000) is the avoidable interest. ∎

4. Calculate the actual interest. The actual interest reflects all the interest on all the company's debt. In our case, simply multiply the principal amount of each debt by the interest rate. Multiply the construction loan amount by the interest rate of 7% ($500,000 × .07 = $35,000).

For the other debt:

$100,000 × .06 =	$6,000
$500,000 × .08 =	40,000
$300,000 × .10	30,000
Total	$111,000

5. Capitalize **the lesser of the avoidable interest and the actual interest**. In our example, the avoidable interest is $55,000 and the actual interest is $111,000. GAAP requires the lesser of the avoidable and actual interest to be capitalized. In our example, since $55,000 is less than $111,000, this capitalize the $55,000. The journal entry to record the interest that is capitalized is

Self-Constructed Asset	$55,000	
Interest Expense		$55,000

NONMONETARY EXCHANGES

Sometimes a company trades in an old asset when it acquires a new asset. A question arises about the transaction: Should the company recognize a gain or a loss on this particular transaction? There has been a recent change in the accounting for this type of transaction. The new rule requires the accountant to distinguish between a transaction that has commercial substance versus a transaction that does not have commercial substance. The rule is very simple. Compare the book value and the fair value of the old asset. If the fair value is greater than the book value, a gain has occurred; if the book value is greater than the fair value, there is a loss. If there is a loss, the loss is always recognized. If there is a gain, then it depends on whether the transaction has commercial substance. If the transaction has commercial substance, then the gain is recognized. If the transaction lacks commercial substance, than there are three possibilities:

1. No cash involved, no gain is recognized
2. Cash given, no gain is recognized
3. Cash received, then a portion of the gain is recognized on the basis of this formula:

$$\frac{\text{Cash received}}{\text{Cash received plus the fair market value (FMV) of any asset received}} \times \text{Actual gain}$$

EXAM TIP

When doing problems related to this topic, there are three possible questions that you could be required to answer:

1. How much gain or loss should be recognized?
2. What is the cost of the new asset?
3. What is the journal entry to record this transaction?

Note that if you can make the appropriate journal entry, you will be able to answer all three questions.

Therefore, the way to solve these problems is to follow these three steps:

1. Calculate the actual gain or loss on the transaction. This is done by comparing the fair market value of the old asset with the book value of the old asset as previously indicated. If the fair market value of the old asset is greater than the book value of the old asset, a gain has occurred. If the fair market value of the old asset is less than the book value of the old asset, a loss has occurred.

2. Apply the rule to determine whether a gain or a loss should be recognized.

3. Make the journal entry; the first account to be debited is the new asset. Begin the journal entry as indicated below; be sure to draw the box.

New Asset   [_____]
Accumulated depreciation – Old Asset
*Cash
*Loss
           Old asset − Cost
           *Cash
           *Gain

Note: The elements with an asterisk may or may not be involved in the transaction.

Enter all the numbers; leave the box blank. After all the numbers have been entered, plug in the final debit necessary to balance the journal entry in the box adjacent to the account New Asset. This is the cost of the new asset.

EXAM TIP

Remember to bring the accumulated depreciation up to date before you record the journal entry. Most companies only record depreciation expense at year-end. That means that if you sell an asset on any day other than December 31, you will need to bring the accumulated depreciation up to date (i.e., recored depreciation expense from January 1 until the date that the asset was sold).

DEMONSTRATION PROBLEM   *Nonmonetary Exchange*

Ian Inc. traded in an old machine and purchased a new one on July 1, 2008. The old machine was purchased on January 1, 2005, for $250,000. It was being depreciated over a 5-year estimated life using the sum of the year's digits depreciation method. Depreciation is recorded once a year on December 31. The new machine has a list price of $400,000. Ian Inc. traded in the old machine and paid an additional $300,000 in cash. The fair market value of the old machine on July 1, 2008, was $100,000.

Required: Prepare the journal entry for Ian Inc. (1) assuming that the transaction has commercial substance, and (2) assuming that the transaction lacks commercial substance.

Solution: There are two things that must be done in this problem at the beginning. The first thing is to recognize that depreciation was last recorded on December 31, 2007. Therefore, we must bring the depreciation up to date by recording depreciation for the first 6 months of 2008.

Remember that with the sum of the year's digits method, you can compute the depreciation for several years by adding the numerators for each year. In this problem, we need to calculate the accumulated depreciation for the first 3 years. That's easy if you know this trick. Instead of computing each year separately, we can compute the 3-year total by doing this: $5 + 4 + 3 / 15 = 12/15$. Now just multiply 12/15 by the depreciation base, which in this problem is $250,000, and you get $200,000. That's the accumulated depreciation at January 1, 2008. Now you need the depreciation expense for the first 6 months of 2008. That's not hard; it's just $250,000 \times 2/15 \times 1/2$, or $16,667. Now you need to bring the accumulated depreciation up to date. Calculate the actual gain or loss on this transaction by comparing the book value and the fair market value of the old asset. The book value is $250,000 − $216,667 (the accumulated depreciation is the beginning balance of $200,000 plus the depreciation for the first 6 months of 2006, which was $16,667). The book value is $33,334, and the fair market value is $100,000. The gain is $66,667. ($100,000 − $33,334). ∎

EXAM TIP

Sometimes it is not spelled out on the exam what the fair market value of the old asset is, but you can figure it out by seeing what kind of trade-in allowance you are getting for the old machine. For example, if you go into a BMW showroom and ask the price of that shiny new 325i convertible, the salesperson will ask, "What you are trading in?" So, you show the salesperson your car and he or she tells you, "The price is $65,000, but if you buy it and give us your old car, you can have it for $50,000 cash." What the salesperson is telling you is that your old car is worth $15,000. You can use that same logic to determine the fair market value of the old asset in these accounting problems.

Getting back to our problem, we have a book value of $33,334 and a fair market value of $100,000, so the actual gain is $66,667. The new rule for nonmonetary exchanges is this: If the transaction has commercial significance, any gain or loss is to be recognized; if there is no commercial significance, then losses are always recognized and a gain may be recognized if some cash is received. Applying that rule to our problem, make the following entries. Entry 1 assumes some commercial significance, entry 2 assumes that the transaction lacks commercial significance.

EXAM TIP

When making these journal entries, put a box next to the debit to the New Asset. Fill in all the other numbers and plug in the cost of the new asset. It works every time!
Entry 1:

New Asset	400,000	
Accumulated depreciation	216,667	
Old asset		250,000
Gain		66,667
Cash		250,000

Entry 2:

New Asset	333,333	
Accumulated depreciation	216,667	
Old asset		250,000
Cash		300,000

Note: For entry 2, there was a gain, but the gain is not recognized in this case because cash was given. (Since cash was given, no cash was received and thus no gain is recognized.) Thus, the New asset is debited for $333,333.

THE CPA AND THE AUDITOR'S REPORT

INTRODUCTION

A CPA is a certified public accountant. Typical CPA firms perform three basic types of services: audit, tax, and consulting.

Audit services include two elements: (1) performing an investigation of a set of financial statements and (2) issuing an audit report containing an opinion, based on the audit, regarding whether or not the financial statements are fairly presented.

Tax services also involve two major activities: (1) assisting clients in planning their business transactions to minimize income taxes and (2) preparing tax returns.

Consulting services include installing computer-based data processing systems; establishing health care and retirement plans; and providing litigation support, which involves assisting the client during a trial with financial information.

It is interesting to note that with one major exception, all the activities that CPAs do can be done by other financial or accounting practitioners. The one service that only a CPA can provide is auditing a set of financial statements and issuing an audit report.

The letter *P* in CPA stands for public. This is very significant as it relates to the audit function. Individual business entities hire a CPA firm to perform an audit of their financial statements. These entities, which are the CPA's clients, are responsible for paying audit fees to their CPAs, which can run into the millions of dollars. Yet, in reality, the CPA is really working for the public. Banks, mutual funds, and individual investors—large and small—all rely on the information contained in audited financial statements to do their work. These institutions and individuals need to know that the financial statements with which they work are fairly presented. They rely on the auditor's opinion, which is contained in the audit report, to tell them that these statements, in fact, are fairly presented. Thus, in the final analysis, the CPA's ultimate client is the public.

Related to the audit function is the issue of auditor independence. The auditor must be completely independent and objective as he or she performs audit engagements. Even though the CPA may be paid millions of dollars by a specific audit client, the CPA's ultimate responsibility is to tell the public whether or not the financial statements are fairly presented and whether the information contained in the statements can be relied upon. As you might imagine, auditor independence is a very sensitive issue.

The Financial Statement Audit

The purpose of an audit is to examine the financial statements and to determine whether they are fairly presented in accordance with generally accepted accounting principles (GAAP).

To make this examination of the financial statements, the auditor follows a set of standards referred to as generally accepted auditing standards (GAAS). These 10 standards were established by the American Institute of Certified Public Accountants (AICPA).

GENERALLY ACCEPTED AUDITING STANDARDS

There are ten individual standards divided into three categories:

1. General standards
2. Standards of field work
3. Reporting standards

The general standards[1] relate to who may perform audit work, and how it is done. Auditors must have the appropriate *technical training*, they must maintain an *independent mental attitude*, and they must exercise *due professional care*.

The field work standards deal with planning the audit, evaluating the system of internal controls, as well as the *nature of the audit evidence* that must be obtained. The audit must be *properly planned*, and junior auditors must be *adequately supervised*. The auditors must *study and evaluate the internal control system* for two reasons:

1. To assess the *risk of material misstatement*
2. To design the *type and the timing of the auditing procedures* to be used.

The reporting standards require the auditor to state whether the financial statements have been *fairly presented* in accordance with *generally accepted accounting principles*. This involves ascertaining that the appropriate financial principles have been consistently applied. The auditor must indicate the *degree of responsibility* that he or she is taking regarding the financial statements.

Types of Opinions

There are essentially four types of opinions that can be expressed by the auditor:

1. Unqualified
2. Qualified
3. Adverse
4. Disclaimer

---

[1] http://en.wikipedia.org/wiki/Generally_Accepted_Auditing_Standards.

An **unqualified opinion** means that the financial statements are fairly presented. Members of the public can rely on these statements in making decisions about the entity, such as buying the common stock of the entity or lending it money. (Remember that the *P* in CPA stands for "Public.")

A **qualified opinion** indicates that, except for one matter or one issue, the financial statements, when taken as a whole, are fairly presented.

An **adverse opinion** means that the financial statements are not fairly presented according to generally accepted accounting principles.

A **disclaimer** indicates that the auditor was unable to express an opinion. This is usually due to one of two circumstances:

1. There is a major uncertainty about the entity's ability to continue as a going concern.

2. Accounting records are unavailable, thus the auditor is unable to gather the appropriate audit evidence needed to arrive at an opinion regarding the financial statements.

The Standard Unqualified Auditor's Report

Here is what the standard unqualified auditor's opinion looks like:

To the Board of Directors and Stockholders of XYZ Company:

We have audited the accompanying balance sheet of XYZ Company as of December 31, 2008, and the related statements of income, retained earnings, and cash flows for the year then ended. These financial statements are the responsibility of the Company's management. Our responsibility is to express an opinion on these financial statements, based on our audit.

We conducted our audit is accordance with auditing standards generally accepted in the United States of America. These standards require that we plan and perform the audit to obtain reasonable assurance about whether the financial statements are free of material misstatement. An audit includes examining, on a test basis, evidence supporting the amounts and disclosures in its financial statements. An audit also includes assessing the accounting principles used and the significant estimates made by management, as well as evaluating the overall financial statement presentation. We believe that our audit provides a reasonable basis for our opinion.

In our opinion, the financial statements referred to above present fairly, in all material respects, the financial position of XYZ Company as of December 31, 2008, and the results of its operations and its cash flows for the year then ended in conformity with accounting principles generally accepted in the United States of America.

San Francisco, California   Eugene D. Kline & Company
                                   Certified Public Accountants
                                   March 1, 2009[2]

[2] Ray Whittington and Kurt Pany, *Principles of Auditing and Other Assurance Services* (New York: McGraw–Hill/Irwin, 2008), 47.

The three paragraphs of the standard unqualified opinion are referred to as the introductory, scope, and opinion paragraphs. Note that in the introductory paragraph, the auditor spells out exactly what management's responsibilities and the auditor's responsibilities are regarding the financial statements. Management is responsible for preparing the statements and the auditor is responsible for expressing an opinion regarding the fairness of the presentation, based on their audit.

In the second, or scope paragraph, the auditor briefly describes how the audit was performed. In short, the auditor says that he or she followed generally accepted auditing standards. In the final paragraph, the opinion paragraph, the auditor presents his or her opinion.

Although the 10 generally accepted auditing standards were developed by the AICPA, since the passage of Sarbanes–Oxley the rules governing how an audit is to be conducted are determined by the PCAOB (Public Companies Accounting Oversight Board).

In some cases, where an unqualified report is issued, the wording of the standard unqualified audit report must be modified in some way. For example, let us assume that in the year under audit the company changed from calculating depreciation expense using the straight-line method to the sum of the year's digits method, or they changed accounting for inventory from using LIFO to using FIFO. Such changes are referred to as changes in accounting principles and these changes must be disclosed in a separate (fourth) paragraph of the unqualified opinion. The reason for this required disclosure is very important. Changing accounting principles may have a significant impact on the company's net income in the year of the change.

Consider these figures:

	2007	2008
Old principle (LIFO)	$100,000	$125,000
New principle (FIFO)	$120,000	$225,000

If the company changed from LIFO to FIFO in 2008, its net income would go up by $110,000. Without the change in accounting for inventory, the net income would have increased by only $25,000. As a reader of the financial statements, you need to know whether GAAP has been consistently applied from period to period; otherwise you could certainly be misled. In this example, without the change in accounting principle, net income went from $100,000 to $125,000. With the change in accounting principle, the net income went from $100,000 to $225,000; that's a difference of $100,000.

When a company changes the application of an accounting principle, this is referred to as a lack of consistency in reporting. Consistency, in this context, refers to the application of the same accounting principles from year to year. The reader of the financial statements must be alerted to this matter, and it would be discussed in an additional (or fourth) paragraph in the auditor's report.

GLOSSARY

Account All accounting data is maintained in accounts. The account is the storage device for financial information. Every account has two sides; a debit (or left hand side) and a credit (or right hand side). There are seven types of accounts: asset, liability, owners' equity, revenue, expense, gain, and loss. Assets, expenses and losses all increase on the debit side. The other four types of accounts increase on the credit side.

Accounting The process of accumulating, measuring, interpreting, and communicating financial information to be used to make business decisions. Accounting is often referred to as the language of business.

Accounting Periods Accountants make the assumption that a business is a going concern, that it has an unlimited life. Accountants also assume that this unlimited life can be divided into meaningful shorter periods of time, such as months and years.

Accounts Payable The amount of money one company owes to another company for purchases made on account.

Accounts Receivable Money owed to the business by its customers who have purchased goods or services and agreed to pay for these purchases in the future. These transactions are referred to as credit sales. A typical credit term for these transactions is 2/10, n/30, which means that the customer gets a 2% discount if payment is made within 10 days; the total is due within 30 days. Accounts receivable are shown on the balance sheet at net realizable value, which is the gross receivables less an allowance for doubtful accounts. The net realizable value is what the company's management realistically expects to collect from its customers.

Accrual The recognition of an increase in an account. If personnel perform work for a week, but are not paid, we would have to recognize this event by recording both salary expense and salary payable. This would be the accrual of salary expense and salary payable. Interest that has been earned, but not received, must be accrued—by increasing interest receivable and interest income. Accrual is the formal recognition in the accounts that an expense on revenue recount (and the related asset or liability) has increased.

Accrual Basis A method of accounting where revenue is recognized when it is earned (regardless of when cash is received), and expenses are recognized when they are incurred (regardless of when cash is paid). Net income is determined by matching revenues and expenses.

Accumulated Depreciation The total amount of depreciation recorded on a particular asset from the date of acquisition to the current date. Depreciable assets are listed on the balance sheet at book value, which reflects the cost of the asset less the accumulated depreciation.

Adjusting Entries Journal entries that are necessary to recognize revenue and expenses in the correct period and to bring the related balance sheet accounts up-to-date. For example, a typical adjusting entry involves recognizing that salaries have been earned but not yet paid. The adjusting entry includes a debit to salary expense (which records an expense in the current period when the salaries were earned) and a credit to salaries payable (which records a liability to pay these salaries in the future). Virtually all adjusting entries involve either a debit to an expense account, or a credit to a revenue account, with a corresponding credit or debit to a related balance sheet account.

Advances from Customers A liability account that is created when a company's customers pay for a product or service before they receive it. For example, when a baseball team sells season tickets, this type of liability arises. If you purchase a two year subscription to *Time* magazine, a liability called advances from customers or unearned revenue is created.

Adverse Opinion After a CPA conducts an audit, an auditor's report is prepared which includes an opinion regarding the fairness of the presentation of the financial statements. An adverse opinion means that the financial statements are not fairly presented in accordance with generally accepted accounting principles.

Aging A listing of all accounts receivable in categories based on their ages (the amount of time that has elapsed since the receivable was recorded). A typical aging will have the following categories: current, 30–60 days, 60–90 days, >90 days. The required balance in the allowance for uncollectible account is determined by multiplying the total in each age category by a percentage which reflects how much of these receivables the company expects not to be able to collect.

Average Accumulated Expenditure When calculating interest to be capitalized on a self-constructed asset, one of the required calculations involves determining how much money was expended on the project, on a weighted average basis. This amount is called the average accumulated expenditure. To compute this number, take each expenditure and multiply it by the period of time the money was expended and the end of the period. For example, if $10,000 was spent on May 31, multiply $10,000 × 7/12 (May 31–December 31 = 7 months). If $10,000 was spent on October 31, multiply $10,000 × 2/12 (October 31–December 31 = 2 months). Then simply add all of these time-weighted expenditures to get the average accumulated expenditure.

Allowance for Doubtful Accounts A contra-asset account that is subtracted from total accounts receivable to measure the net realizable receivables—the amount the company realistically expects to collect from its customers.

Amortization The gradual writing off of an amount. Deprecation and depletion are forms of amortization. Bond discount and premium are amortized over the term of the bond using either straight-line amortization or effective interest method amortization. The cost of intangible assets are amortized over the economic life of the asset.

APB (Accounting Principles Board) The direct predecessor to the Financial Accounting Standards Board, the APB was made up of 18 members, most of whom were CPAs in public practice. This board was a committee of the AICPA. During its existence (from 1939 to 1973), the APB issued 31 opinions.

Assets Resources that are owned or controlled by the entity that will provide future benefits. Examples of assets include cash, marketable securities, inventory, land, buildings, equipment, and goodwill. Assets are generally recorded at their acquisition (historical) cost, and disclosed on that basis on the balance sheet. One notable exception to this rule is that certain marketable securities are shown on the balance sheet as current market value ("trading" and "available for sale") securities.

Available for Sale Securities Investments in other corporation's stock, where the intent of the company is to hold these securities for the long run, rather than actively trade them. They are listed on the balance sheet under long-term investments and are shown at their current market value. Any unrealized gains and losses are included under "other comprehensive income," which is a part of owner's equity and appears on the balance sheet. Realized gains and losses, are included in net income.

Bad Debt Expense The expense related to the firm's inability to collect all of their receivables. Reasons for this cost include extending credit to individuals or businesses that are not creditworthy, customers becoming bankrupt, customers leaving the country without paying their bills, and so forth.

Balance Sheet A financial statement that shows the financial position of a firm at a point in time. The balance sheet shows the assets, liabilities, and owner's equity of the firm. The assets are divided into four categories: correct assets; long-term investments; property, plant, and equipment; and intangible assets. The liabilities are divided into current and noncurrent liabilities. Owner's equity is shown in two parts: contributed capital and retained earnings.

Bank Overdraft Money paid out of a checking account in excess of the balance in the account. Under certain circumstances, a bank will pay (or cover) a check written for a dollar amount that exceeds the balance in the account. A $500 check that is written when the balance is only $100 will produce a $400 overdraft (assuming that the bank covers the check).

Bank Reconciliation A way to verify that the accounting for cash on the books agrees with the cash balance per the bank. A standard bank reconciliation begins with the unadjusted balance per the books and the unadjusted balance per the bank. Each of these numbers is adjusted by adding or subtracting reconciling items such as deposits in transit and outstanding checks. When the reconciliation is complete, the adjusted balance per the books will equal the adjusted balance per the bank.

Basic Earnings per Share The actual earnings of the company, less any preferred dividends, divided by the number of shares of common stock outstanding. (*See also* Earnings per Share)

Basket (Lump Sum) Purchase When several different items are purchased together for a single lump sum, the transaction is referred to as a basket purchase. The total lump sum amount is allocated to the individual assets acquired in proportion to their relative market or appraised value. For example, if a parcel of land, a building and several pieces of equipment were purchased for $2,000,000, the appraisal values for these three assets are as follows: land: $800,000, building $1,000,000; and equipment $900,000. The $2,000,000 cost of all three items would be allocated as follows:

$$\$800,000 + \$1,000,000 + \$900,000 = \$2,700,000$$
$$800,000/2,700,000 \times \$2,000,000 = \$592,592 \text{ to the land}$$
$$\$1,000,000/\$2,700,000 \times \$2,000,000 = \$740,740 \text{ to the building, and}$$
$$\$900,000/\$2,700,000 \times \$2,000,000 = \$666,666$$

Bond Discount The buyer of a bond is purchasing two cash flows; the principal or face amount of the bond which is paid back on the maturity date and interest on the principal amount which is paid every period. If the present value of the two cash flows is less than

$1,000, the bond will sell at a discount. The discount is the difference between the $1,000 face amount and the present value of the two cash flows.

Bond A promise to pay a principal amount and interest on the principal on a specified date, which is referred to as the maturity date. Most individual bonds have a principal of $1,000. If the stated rate of interest on the bond is less than the market rate of interest, the bond will sell for a discount. If the stated rate of interest on the bond is greater than the market rate of interest, the bond will sell for a premium.

Bond Indenture The agreement that covers all the rights and obligations of the issuing company and the bondholders.

Book Value The value of an asset or liability reported on the balance sheet, net of the related contra or adjunct account. For example, the book value of a building would be the cost of the building less the accumulated depreciation. The book value of a bond would be the face value of the bond plus any premium or minus any discount.

Capitalization of Interest When a company builds an asset for its own use (and not for resale), a component of the cost of the project is the interest on borrowed money during the construction process. FASB #34 covers this topic and prescribes a way to measure the interest cost that will be capitalized. The amount of interest capitalized becomes part of the cost of the asset being built, rather than an expense of the period.

Capitalize When a company has an expenditure it can typically be accounted for in one of two ways. If an asset is acquired, we would say that we are going to capitalize the expenditure and debit an asset account. If an expense is incurred, we say that we are going to expense the expenditure and debit an expense account.

Capital Lease A lease that transfers most of the rights and obligations of ownership to the lessee. *Generally accepted accounting principles* require the lessee to record an asset and a liability equal to the present value of the minimum lease payments for a capital lease.

Cash Currency and money available to the company in a bank account.

Cash and Cash Equivalents A balance sheet classification that includes currency, cash in bank checking accounts, as well as other investments that are the equivalent of cash (such as treasury bills).

Cash Basis A method of accounting where revenue and expenses are recognized as cash is paid or received.

Cash Flow from Financing Activities This is the cash flow from issuing stock and bonds and from borrowing. It also includes paying cash dividends and buying back shares of the company's stock, which we call treasury stock. It is the third section of the statement of cash flows. For young, growing companies, cash flow from financing activities is usually a positive number because these companies are still in the process of accumulating capital. For mature companies, this number is usually negative because these companies are in the position of being able to retire stock or redeem bonds. Mature companies generate enough cash from their operating activities that they do not need any additional external financing.

Cash Flow from Investing Activities This is the amount of cash that was generated by buying and selling assets. It is the second section of the statement of cash flows. Young, growing companies tend to have a net cash outflow for this category because they are typically at a point where they are buying more assets. Mature companies usually have a positive cash flow from investing activities because they are in a position to be selling assets instead of buying them.

Cash Flow from Operating Activities This is the cash flow that is generated by the core business operations. It is the first section reported on the statement of cash flows. There are two ways to calculate this number: the direct approach and the indirect approach. Using the direct approach, we add all the cash receipts from operating activities and subtract all the cash disbursements from operating activities. This seems simple; however, because most companies keep their books on an accrual basis instead of a cash basis, this would mean converting all the numbers from an accrual basis to a cash basis. The indirect approach starts with net income and simply eliminates from net income all of the items that are included in net income but did not involve cash. What you are left with after subtracting all these noncash items is cash from operating activities.

Chart of Accounts A list of all the accounts being used by a specific business entity. All the accounts are numbered in sequence, so all asset accounts could be numbered from 0001 to 0099, liability accounts from 0100 to 0200, and so forth. Creating the chart of accounts is an important task because the accounting system can only accumulate information within the framework of its existing accounts. For example, if the company wants to show revenue by product line on its financial statements, their chart of accounts must have a sales revenue account for each product line. Simply having a single sales revenue account would not work.

Closing Entries After all transactions for the period have been recorded in the journal and posted to the ledger, the income statement accounts are "closed" and the balance sheet accounts are balanced. This is done for two reasons. First, the income statement accounts are all closed by transferring their balances to an income summary account, which will then contain all the numbers that will appear on the income statement. The balance in the income summary account will be equal to the net income for the period. This number is then transferred to the retained earnings account. Second, when the next period begins, the income statement accounts should all have zero balances. After closing the income statement accounts to income summary, all these accounts will have zero balances. The closing process consists of four separate entries, usually referred to as A, B, C, and D.

Entry A closes all the revenue and gain accounts to income summary. Entry B closes all the expense and loss accounts to income summary. Entry C closes the income summary account to retained earnings; the C entry is equal in amount to the net income. Entry D closes the dividends to retained earnings.

Committee on Accounting Procedure The first official accounting standard-setting body in the United States. The committee was made up of some of the finest accounting minds of its time. Established in 1939, it issued 51 Research Bulletins, which immediately became generally accepted accounting principles. In 1959, the Committee on Accounting Procedure was replaced by the Accounting Principles Board.

Common Size Financial Statements In an effort to analyze a company's performance and financial position, accountants sometimes convert the income statement and the balance sheet from dollars to percentages. We call these common size statements. A common size income statement has total revenue as 100%, and every other number on the statement is stated as a percentage of total revenue. On a common size balance sheet, every number is stated as a percentage of total assets. These common size statements make it easier to compare a company with itself over time, as well as to compare the company with other companies, which may be of very different sizes.

Common Stock The residual equity interest in a corporation. Individuals (and other corporations) invest in a corporation by purchasing shares of common stock. The rights associated with common stock ownership include the right to elect members of the board of directors, the right to receive dividends, the right to receive assets (if any) after a liquidation, and the preemptive right—a right that allows stockholders to maintain their percent interest in the corporation.

Comprehensive Income All changes in the net assets of a business from non-owner sources. Ninety-nine percent of comprehensive income is made up of net income. There are three items that are often included in comprehensive income; these are usually referred to as "other comprehensive income." They are unrealized gains and losses on available-for-sale securities, foreign currency translation gains and losses, and gains and losses arising from the recognition of the minimum liability related to a pension plan. "Other comprehensive income" is part of owner's equity and is reported on the balance sheet.

Conservatism This concept tells the accountant that whenever there are two ways of accounting for a given transaction, and each approach is equally acceptable, we should select the approach that is least likely to overstate income or overstate assets.

Contingent Liability A situation where a loss may have occurred and an obligation has been created, but there is still uncertainty about how much is owed to whom. Contingent liabilities must be accrued—received in the accounts—if two criteria are met: (1) It is probable that a loss has been incurred, and (2) the amount can be reasonably estimated. A typical example of a contingent liability occurs when a customer in a Safeway store slips on a wet floor, breaks an arm and a leg while falling, and files a lawsuit. In this case, it is clear that Safeway is at fault and that a loss has occurred. Their attorneys probably have a very good idea of how much money it will take to settle this lawsuit. But at this point, we can only make an estimate.

Contributed Capital The amount paid to the entity in exchange for an ownership interest. In the case of a corporation, the contributed capital consists of cash or other assets given to the business in exchange for shares of stock. The amount listed on the balance sheet for contributed capital is found in two accounts. The common stock account contains an amount equal to the number of shares issued multiplied by the par or stated value. The additional paid-in capital account (also called the paid-in capital in excess of par account) contains just that—the amount paid in excess of the par amount.

Convertible Bond A bond that may be converted, at the option of the bondholder, into a predetermined number of shares of stock. By making the bond convertible, the issuing company may be able to issue the bonds at a slightly lower interest rate.

Copyright Granted by the US Patent and Trademark office, a copyright gives an artist the exclusive right to produce and sell their creation. The legal life of a copyright is the life of the creator plus 70 years.

Cost of Goods Sold This is the first expense listed on the income statement of a merchandising company. It reflects the cost to the business of all merchandise sold during the period. Sales less cost of goods sold is referred to as gross profit.

Counterbalancing Error Errors in accounting for inventory often involve more than one accounting period. For example, if the ending inventory in year 1 is overstated; cost of goods sold in year 1 will be understated. Gross profit and net income will be overstated in year 1. Because the ending inventory in year 1 is the same as the beginning inventory in year 2, beginning inventory in year 2 is also overstated. This will result in cost of goods sold in year 2 to be overstated, and the gross profit and net income in year 2 will be understated. Thus, the overstatement of net income in year 1 is counterbalanced by the understatement of net income in year 2. The balance in retained earnings at the end of year 2 will be absolutely correct.

Credit In accounting, this term simply means the right-hand side. There are four accounts that increase the credit, or right-hand, side: liabilities, owners' equity, revenue, and gains. There are three accounts that increase the debit side: assets, expenses, and losses. Credits to these three accounts cause those accounts to decrease.

Current Portion of Long-Term Debt A long-term debt is an obligation that is due in more than 1 year. An example is a 10-year note payable, or a 10-year serial bond, where one-tenth of the bond's face value is due each year. The part of a long-term liability that is due within 1 year is shown on the balance sheet as a current liability, labeled "current portion of long-term debt."

Debenture A fancy word to indicate an unsecured bond. Some bonds, such as mortgage bonds, are backed by collateral. If the company cannot make the payments on the bond, the bondholders may be satisfied by converting the collateral (which may be a piece of real estate) into cash and paying the bondholders.

Debit In accounting, the term debit simply means the left-hand side. There are three accounts that increase the debit, or left-hand, side: assets, expenses, and losses. Every journal entry involves an equal dollar amount of debits and credits. There are four accounts that increase on the credit side: liabilities, owners' equity, revenue, and gains. Entering a debit to one of these accounts causes the account to decrease.

Deferred Annuity An annuity (a series of equal payments) where the first payment comes one or more periods into the future. For example, if today is 1/1/08, and you are evaluating an investment that will pay $1,000 every year on the last day of the year, beginning in 2012, you would be looking at a deferred annuity.

Depletion The process of allocating the cost of a wasting asset such as a coal mine or an oil field, over its useful life. Depletion is a form of amortization, similar to depreciation.

Deposits in Transit A bank deposit that was made by the customer but which has not yet been received or recorded by the bank.

Depreciation Conventions Since depreciation calculations are essentially an estimate, there is no need to be precise about a guess. Therefore, many companies adopt simplifying assumptions regarding the depreciation calculations, which are referred to as depreciation conventions. A simple example is the half-year convention. Using this convention, a company takes a half year's worth of depreciation in the year of acquisition, and a half year in the final year, regardless of the actual date of acquisition. Another convention would be to take a full year's depreciation in the year of acquisition, and no depreciation in the year of disposal.

Depreciation Expense Depreciation is the allocation of the cost of an asset over its useful life. Depreciation expense is a function of the asset's cost, its estimated service life, its estimated salvage value, and the depreciation method used. The depreciation methods used include straight-line, sum of the year's digits, and double declining balance.

Diluted Earnings per Share A hypothetical computation of what Earnings per Share would be if all potentially dilutive securities were assumed to have been exercised. (*See also* Earnings per Share)

Direct Approach (Statement of Cash Flows) The cash from operating activities with this approach is calculated by taking the cash receipts and cash disbursements from operations. Items included here would be cash receipts from customers, cash receipts from interest and dividends, cash paid to suppliers, cash paid to employees, and cash paid for taxes.

Disclaimer After a CPA conducts an audit, an auditor's report is prepared that includes an opinion regarding the fairness of the presentation of the financial statements. A disclaimer indicates that the CPA was not able to gather enough evidence to reach an opinion regarding the fairness of the presentation of the financial statement. This does not happen very often. One situation that could give rise to a disclaimer would be if the company's financial records were lost or destroyed; this would prevent the auditor from gathering the necessary evidence to reach an opinion.

Discontinued Operations Income, gains, and losses associated with closing a major segment of the business must be reported in a separate category on a multiple step income statement. These items must also be shown on a per share basis.

Dividend An amount of money paid to the stockholders of a corporation which represents a distribution of the earnings of the entity. In most states the corporation must have a positive (credit) balance in retained earnings to be able to distribute dividends. Dividends are almost always paid in cash, although dividends may also be paid with the corporation's own stock; this is called a stock dividend. A third type of dividend is called a property dividend. It consists of some type of property; the most common type of property dividend consists of shares of stock of another corporation which are currently owned by the company.

Double Declining Balance Depreciation A method for allocating the cost of an asset over its useful life. The computation using this method involves multiplying a fixed percentage (which is equal to twice the straight line rate. The straight line rate is 1/life.) times an ever decreasing balance (hence the name double declining balance). Salvage value is ignored initially. The balance begins with the cost of the asset and is reduced each year by the amount of depreciation taken in that year. For example, consider an asset that cost $12,000, an estimated service life of five years, and an estimated salvage value of $2,000. Depreciation for the first three years using DDB (Double Declining Balance) depreciation would be as follows:

$$\$12,000 \times 1/5 \times 2 = \$4,800$$
$$\$12,000 - \$4,800 = \$8,200 \times 1/5 \times 2 = \$3,280$$
$$\$12,000 - \$3,280 = \$4,920 \times 1/5 \times 2 = \$1,968$$

DuPont Analysis A method for evaluating a firm's ROI (return on investment) by dividing ROI into two components—margin and turnover. The analysis is completed using the following equation: ROI (Net income/Average total assets) = Margin (Net income/Sales) × Turnover (Sales/All total assets). To improve the ROI would require improving the margin, which most firms approach by cutting operating expenses, and/or improving turnover, which most firms approach by streamlining the business by selling assets.

Earnings Per Share This is a measure of the income of the business per one share of common stock. It is calculated by dividing net income less preferred dividends by the number of shares of common stock outstanding. If the firm has a simple capital structure—only common stock—then a single presentation of earnings per share is made. If the firm has a complex capital structure—common stock plus other potentially dilutive securities that could become common stock (such as convertible bonds or convertible preferred stock)—then a dual presentation of earnings per share must be made. A dual presentation would present the actual earnings per share (called basic EPS) and the diluted EPS, which is the result of a "what if" calculation. It shows what the earnings per share would be IF all the owners of the potentially dilutive securities actually converted their securities into shares of common stock.

Entity In accounting for a business, we account for the transactions of the business separate and apart from the owners of the business. It does not matter if the business is organized as a sole proprietorship, a partnership, or a corporation.

Estimated Liability for Warranties When a company sells a product covered by a warranty, the accounting problem is to determine how much of the cost of the warranty is associated with the time period of the warranty. Companies that sell products covered by warranties generally know how much it will cost, in total, to make repairs to fix items covered by the warranty. Let us say that the total cost to make warranty repairs over the three year warranty period is $150. This amount is then recorded as an expense of the current period. Since all the revenue was recorded in the year of the sale, all the expenses related to that sale must also be recorded in the same period.

Expenses The costs of operating a business. When total expenses are subtracted from total revenue, the resulting figure is called the profit or net income.

Extraordinary Items Unusual and infrequent items that are reported in a separate category on a multiple step income statement. Examples of extraordinary items include natural disasters and acts of foreign governments. These items must also be shown on a per share basis on the income statement.

FASB (Financial Accounting Standards Board) Established in 1973, this seven-member board has responsibility for establishing generally accepted accounting principles (GAAP) through the issuance of statements of financial accounting concepts and standards, interpretations, technical bulletins, and Emerging Issues Task Force statements. To date, the board has issued more than 150 statements. The board is made up of full-time board members who are paid very well; they have no clients and they are completely independent. In comparison, members of the two predecessor boards (the Committee on Accounting Procedure and the Accounting Principles Board) were CPAs in public practice.

The board has a large research staff and it goes through a very elaborate set of due process procedures before a statement is issued. Three different documents are prepared for a given topic: (1) a discussion memorandum sets forth the issues and a potential approach; (2) an exposure draft reflects the board's views after public hearings and written comments have been evaluated; and (3) a statement of accounting standards is released, which becomes GAAP.

The Securities Exchange Act of 1934 created the SEC (Securities and Exchange Commission) and gave it the ultimate authority to establish accounting principles. The SEC has chosen to delegate this function to the accounting profession—this responsibility is currently carried out by the FASB. More recently, Congress passed the Sarbanes–Oxley Act, which created, among other things, the PCAOB (Public Companies Accounting

Oversight Board). This board was given the authority to establish accounting standards. Currently, the PCAOB has permitted the FASB to continue to establish GAAP.

FIFO (First In, First Out) Inventory flow is based on the assumption that the oldest goods on hand—the first ones in—are the first units sold. When prices are going up, FIFO produces the lowest cost of goods sold and thus the highest net income.

FOB Shipping Point and FOB Destination These are terms used in conjunction with freight or shipping costs. FOB shipping point means that the buyer is paying for the freight costs and the title to the goods passes from the seller to the buyer when the goods are placed on the truck or the plane. FOB destination means that the seller is paying for the freight costs and the title to the goods passes when the goods are taken off the truck and delivered to the buyer.

Free Cash Flow This is the cash that is generated by operating activities less payments for capital expenditures and dividends. Free cash flow is an indicator of how much cash the business produces from its core business operations, after subtracting capital expenditures and dividends.

Full Disclosure This principle states that if there is information about a business that would "make a difference" to the reader of the financial statements, then that information should be disclosed either in the body of the financial statements or in the notes to the statements.

Future Value of a Sum If a sum of money is deposited in a bank today, the total value of that bank account on any day in the future (original deposit plus all interest earned) is referred to as the future value of a sum. All of this assumes that the bank is paying interest at a stated rate.

Future Value of an Ordinary Annuity An ordinary annuity is a series of equal payments received over a period of time, where the first payment comes at the end of the first period. (When the first payment comes at the beginning of the first period, it is called an annuity due.) The future value of an ordinary annuity reflects how much money you would have (payments plus interest) at the end of a specified time, assuming that the bank pays interest at a specific rate.

GAAP (Generally Accepted Accounting Principles) Collectively, these are the official rules of accounting that are developed over time through actual business practices and by virtue of the pronouncements of the Committee on Accounting Procedure, the Accounting Principles Board, and the Financial Accounting Standards Board. After completing a financial statement audit, the CPA will generally conclude that the financial statements are fairly presented in accordance with GAAP.

GAAS (General Accredited Auditing Standards) These are the standards or the rules that govern how a CPA should conduct the audit. These standards were originally created by the Auditing Standards Committee—a committee of the American Institute of Certified Public Accountants. More recently, the passage of the Sarbanes–Oxley Act gave the Public Company Accounting Oversight Board (PCAOB) the authority to establish GAAS. The PCAOB was established in 2002, and it has already issued several auditing standards.

When a CPA audits a client financial statement, the second paragraph of the audit report (the "scope" paragraph) includes the following reference: "Our audit was conducted in accordance with standards established by the PCAOB" (the previous wording was "in accordance with GAAS").

Gains When a business entity sells something that it is not in the business of selling for more than it paid for the item, a gain arises.

Generally Accepted Auditing Standards (GAAS) The standards that govern how a CPA conducts an audit. GAAS was originally established by the AICPA (American Institute of Certified Public Accountants). However, since the passage of Sarbanes–Oxley, GAAS is now established by the PCAOB (Public Companies Accounting Oversight Board).

Goods in Transit Merchandise that has been purchased or sold and is currently on a truck, plane, or freight car somewhere between the buyer and the seller. Ownership of the merchandise is determined by reference to the shipping terms. If the merchandise was shipped FOB destination, then title passes to the buyer when the goods are delivered to the buyer's location. If the goods are shipped FOB shipping point, title passes to the buyer when the goods are put on the truck, plane, or freight car.

Going Concern When accounting for an entity, we make the assumption that the business is going to continue for the long run, as opposed to liquidating in the short run.

Goodwill This word has several different meanings. In accounting, goodwill only emerges as part of a transaction where one company purchases another company and pays more than the fair market value of the net assets acquired. Historically, goodwill was recorded and amortized (written off) over a period of time not to exceed 40 years. Under current generally accepted accounting principles, goodwill is not amortized, but is subject to impairment. An asset becomes impaired if its market value falls below its book value. Impaired assets are written down to their current market value and a loss is recognized. Subsequent increases in market value are ignored. Once an asset is written down, it is never written back up.

Gross Profit Gross profit is the difference between sales and the cost of goods sold. For a merchandising company, gross profit is typically the third line on the income statement, following sales and cost of goods sold.

Gross Profit Method A technique that permits a company to determine inventory on hand on a specific date, without taking a physical count of the merchandise. This method is often used when preparing an interim financial statement and the company wants to avoid the expense of taking a physical inventory. It is also used when there is a fire loss, and the insurance company needs to know how much inventory was on hand just prior to the fire (obviously it cannot be counted). The computation is very straightforward. The company needs to know its gross profit percentage, which is simply Gross Profit/Sales. When making this calculation, it is much easier to work with the cost of goods sold percentage, which is 1 − the gross profit percentage. To compute the cost of the inventory on hand, begin by adding the beginning inventory and the purchases for the period. This amount is called the goods available for sale. Then estimate the cost of goods sold by multiplying the sales for the period by the cost of goods sold percentage. Subtract the estimated cost of goods sold from the goods available for sale, and the resulting figure is the cost of the ending inventory.

Held-to-Maturity Securities Corporate bonds, which a firm buys as an investment, that are relatively liquid and earn a higher rate of return than money in a checking account. Held-to-maturity securities are carried on the books, and are listed on the balance sheet at the amortized cost. This means that the carrying value is continuously adjusted by reducing (amortizing) any discount or premium that was paid.

Historical Cost We account for most things at historical cost—the actual purchase price. Historical cost has two features that accountants like. First, it is an objective and verifiable measure. Second, on the day of the transaction, historical cost is the best estimate of the current value of the item in question. Unfortunately, as time passes, the current value changes, and hence the historical cost ceases to bear any relationship to the current value.

Horizontal and Vertical Analysis Horizontal analysis involves looking at a company's performance over time. A typical horizontal analysis would consist of looking at a company's income statement for the past 5 years. In doing this analysis, we would be looking horizontally on the page, from left to right. A vertical analysis would involve looking up and down. A typical vertical analysis would consist of an income statement where all the numbers were expressed as a percentage of total revenue. Total revenue becomes 100%, and every other number is a percentage of total revenue. This type of statement is sometimes referred to as a common size income statement.

Impairment The recognition of the loss in value of an asset. Impairment loss is recorded when the value of an asset falls below its carrying value (book value). In some instances, impairment involves two steps. First, a recovery test is made. An asset has become impaired if the expected future net cash flows are less than the carrying amount. If the recovery test indicates that an asset has become impaired, the amount of the impairment is the amount by which the carrying amount of the asset exceeds the current market value, or fair market value, of the asset.

Income from Continuing Operations A subtotal of net income reported on a multiple step income statement. Not included in this number, but reported below on the income statement, are the results of discontinued operations and extraordinary items.

Income from Operations When a multiple step income statement is prepared, one of the main subtotals is income from operations. This number reflects the income from the normal, day-to-day operations. Not included in this number, but reported below the caption income from operations on the income statement, are the results of discontinued operations and extraordinary items.

Income Statement A financial statement that shows the results of operations of an entity for a specific period of time. The two basic styles of income statements are single step and multiple step.

Indirect Approach (Statement of Cash Flows) In this approach, the cash from operating activities begins with net income and then eliminates the items that are included in net income, but did not involve cash. The typical adjustments are the depreciation and amortization expense (added), the loss on sale of the asset (added), the income from the investment using the equity method (subtracted), and the gain on sale of the asset (subtracted). Net income plus/minus these adjustments equals the cash flow from operating activities.

Intangible Assets A category of assets listed on a firm's balance sheet. Included in this category are assets created by an individual's intellect—often referred to as intellectual property. Examples of intangible assets are patents, copyrights, trademarks, and goodwill. Intangible assets are shown on the balance sheet at cost less accumulated amortization. Intangibles with a limited life are amortized. Assets with an unlimited life are not amortized but are subject to impairment.

Intellectual Property Assets developed by an individual's intellect, also referred to as intangible assets. Examples would include patents, copyrights, and trademarks.

Interest The payment made for the use of another entity's money. Laborers are paid a salary or wage for their services, landlords are paid rent for the use of their property, and banks and other financial institutions are paid interest for the use of their money. Simple interest is calculated using the following equation: Interest = Principal × Rate × Time, where the rate of interest and the time must be stated in the same context (e.g., if the rate of interest is per year, then the time must be stated in a fraction of a year; 3 months would not be 3, but 3/12, or 25%).

Interest Bearing Note Payable A note payable is a formal written promise to pay a certain amount of money on a specified date. An interest bearing note includes as stated rate of interest.

Interest Payable A liability that indicates how much interest expense has been incurred but not yet paid. Simple interest is generally used to calculate interest payable. The formula for simple interest is: Principle × Rate × Time.

Internal Control All of the policies and procedures put in place by a company to safeguard its assets, ensure accurate financial reporting, encourage employees to follow accurate financial reporting, encourage employees to follow company procedures, and promote efficient operations. Internal controls are a way to try to get everyone in the company to do what should be done. The Sarbanes–Oxley Act requires the CEO and CFO of the company to certify that internal controls are in place and are working effectively. Furthermore, the law requires that the company's CPA evaluate management's certification of the internal controls, which have always been an important element of a company's overall management. However, today, in the post-Enron environment, internal controls have become even more critical and important.

Inventory The merchandise that the company is in the business of selling. General Motors' inventory consists of cars and trucks. Dell's inventory consists of computers and printers. General Motors' computers and printers, as well as Dell's cars and trucks would be considered property, plant, and equipment.

Journal One of the two "books of accounting," the other being the ledger. The journal is referred to as the book of original entry. Every transaction is entered or recorded in the journal on a chronological basis, similar to entries in a diary. Periodically, all the entries in the journal are transferred or "posted" to the ledger, where a single "page" is maintained for each account. The journal is useful if you want to know which transactions took place on a particular date. The ledger, on the other hand, would be the place to go if you wanted to know the balance in a particular account.

Journal Entry All business transactions are entered in the journal on a chronological basis. Each journal entry involves one or more accounts to be debited, and one or more accounts to be credited, where the total debits equal the total credits.

Lease A contract whereby the owner (lessor) of an asset conveys some of the rights of ownership of the asset to the user (lessee) in return for a series of payments. There are two types of leases: an operating lease and a capital lease. Only a capital lease requires the lessee to show an asset and a liability on the balance sheet for property acquired under the lease.

Ledger The ledger (or general ledger) is one of the two "books of accounting," the other being the journal. After all the transactions are recorded in the journal, they are transferred or "posted" to the ledger on a periodic basis. The ledger contains a separate page for each account after posting the current balance in each account.

Leverage Financial leverage involves borrowing money at a fixed rate of interest and investing that money in the business, where it earns a higher rate of return than the cost of borrowing. The excess return goes to the owners or stockholders. What the business has accomplished is to lift or increase the rate of return on owner's equity. (Leverage is the process of lifting.)

Liabilities Amounts owed to other entities as the result of a past transaction or event. Examples of liabilities include accounts payable, salaries payable, interest payable, taxes payable, and bonds payable. Liabilities are shown on the balance sheet as either current (due within 1 year) or noncurrent (due after 1 year).

LIFO (Last In, First Out) An inventory flow based on the assumption that the last units purchased are the first units sold. This method matches against current sales the most current or recent costs of purchases. When prices are increasing, LIFO produces the highest cost of goods sold and thus the lowest net income. Companies like to report to the IRS on a LIFO basis because it minimizes income taxes. If you use LIFO on your tax return, you must report to the stockholders using LIFO as well.

LIFO Liquidation If a business has been using LIFO and it has a problem receiving new merchandise (due perhaps to a strike by the freight company), and the company winds up selling all its "old inventory," which is carried on the books at very low cost, this liquidation of old LIFO costs produces a large reported net income and thus causes the company to pay a very large income tax bill.

LIFO Reserve This is the difference between the value of the inventory using LIFO and the value of the inventory if the company had been using FIFO or average cost.

Liquidity This is a measure of the firm's ability to pay their current obligations. Indicators of liquidity are the current ratio (current assets divided by current liabilities), the quick ratio (cash, marketable securities, and accounts receivable divided by current liabilities), and net working capital (current assets less current liabilities).

Long Term Investments Assets that the company plans to hold for several accounting periods. Examples of long term investments would include shares of stock of another corporation, and money set aside to retire a bond.

Losses When a business sells something that it is not in the business of selling for less than it paid for the item, a loss arises. In addition, a loss may arise when there is a natural disaster, such as an earthquake or fire.

Lower of Cost or Market This is a conservative method of inventory valuation that requires companies to write down inventory that has lost value and have the loss recorded in the period when the value declined, instead of recording a loss when the merchandise is ultimately sold or disposed. It sounds like a simple calculation. You look at the cost of the inventory and the market value, and pick the one that's lower. However, it is a bit more complicated. Market is defined as replacement cost; however, there is an upper and a lower limit. The upper limit (or ceiling) is not realizable value (selling price less the costs to complete and disperse) and the lower limit (or floor) is net realizable value less a normal profit.

The first thing to do is to calculate the designated market value, which is the replacement cost, if it is within the upper and lower limits. If the replacement cost is above the upper limit, the upper limit is the designated market value. The same goes for the lower limit. Then compare the designated market value with the cost and take the lower number. If the total value of the inventory is lower than the cost, a journal entry is made debiting a loss and crediting the inventory account. If you are doing this calculation in Excel, you can have the computer select the designated market value by finding the median of the three market figures (replacement cost, ceiling value, and floor values).

Marketable Securities Stocks and bonds issued by other corporations that a business buys as an investment. In 1993, the Financial Accounting Standards Board (FASB) issued Accounting Statement 115 for certain marketable securities; this represented a completely new and innovative approach for accounting for these investments. The FASB created three categories: held to maturity, trading, and available for sale. Held-to-maturity securities are bonds (shares of stock do not have a maturity date); trading and available-for-sale securities are shares of stock. The most interesting (and controversial) element of SFAS 115 is the requirement to show these assets on the balance sheet at current market value instead of historical cost. Furthermore, for trading securities, any unrealized gains and losses are included in need income. These requirements represent a significant departure from previous generally accepted accounting principles. (See the references to each of the three categories in this glossary for more details.)

Matching This is the principle underlying the income statement. First, we determine the revenue to be recognized, applying the revenue recognition principle. Then, we match that revenue with the expenses that were incurred to generate that revenue. The difference between the revenue and the expenses is the net income.

Materiality A concept that accountants apply when it doesn't make sense to follow a rule to the letter. For example, if a company purchases a hammer for $20 that it thinks will last for 5 years, a strict application of generally accepted accounting principles would tell you to capitalize the $20 expenditure and depreciate the hammer over 5 years. The amount in this case is so small that it seems silly to record $4 of depreciation expense each year for 5 years. As a prudent matter, the simple approach is to expense the entire $20 in the year of the purchase. The reason for this is that the amount is simply not material.

Maturity Date (of a bond) The day that the bond matures. This is the day when the bond holder will receive repayment of the principal amount plus any accrued interest.

Monetary Unit We do accounting in the United States using the US dollar as the measuring unit. We assume that this is a stable measuring unit, even though, in fact, the purchasing power of the dollar does fluctuate slightly from year to year.

Mortgage Bond A bond is a long-term liability. With a mortgage bond, there is some form of collateral that can be sold and the proceeds can be used to pay off the bond if the issuing company does not have enough cash to retire the bond at maturity.

Net Realizable Value Accounts receivable are shown on the balance sheet at net realizable value. That is the gross or total value of the receivables less an allowance for uncollectibles, which represents the total receivables that the company estimates it will be unable to collect. The gross receivables less the allowance for uncollectibles is the net realizable value, the amount the company expects to collect.

Net Worth The accounting equation states that Assets = Liabilities + Owners' Equity; therefore, owners' equity, or the net worth of the business, is simply assets less liabilities. The terms owners' equity and net worth mean the same thing.

Non-Interest Bearing Note Payable A note payable is a formal written promise to pay a certain amount of money on a specified date. Non-interest bearing notes do not include a stated rate of interest.

Non-Monetary Exchange When a company purchases a new asset and pays for it by giving the seller an old asset as part of the payment, we refer to this as a non-monetary exchange. (Two non-monetary assets are being exchanged; there may or may not be any cash involved.) As it turns out, most non-monetary exchanges involve some cash.

Notes Payable An obligation to repay principal and interest in return for receiving a sum of money. The obligation is documented in the form of a note indicating the principal amount, the interest rate, and the term or maturity date.

Notes Receivable A promise by another party to repay, to a company, the principal plus interest in return for receiving a sum of money from the company. The details of this transaction are documented in the note itself (principal amount, interest rate, and maturity date).

Operating Lease A lease that conveys the minimal rights of ownership in a property. It is more like a short-term rental (e.g., renting a car to drive to Lake Tahoe to go skiing for the weekend). Neither an asset or a liability is recorded by the lessee. This transaction is sometimes referred to as "off balance sheet financing."

Outstanding Checks Checks which were written by a customer, but which have not yet been presented to the bank for payment.

Owners' Equity The owners' claims to the assets of a business. In a corporation, the term used is stockholder's equity. Owner's or stockholder's equity is sometimes referred to as the net worth of the business, since it reflects total assets less total liabilities. The basic accounting equation is Assets = Liabilities + Owners' equity; therefore, owners' equity is simply assets less liabilities.

Paid-In Capital The amount of money contributed to a business in return for an ownership interest. When money is invested in a corporation, the investors are referred to as stockholders and shares of stock in the corporation are issued as evidence of their ownership interest.

Partial-Year Depreciation When using an accelerated depreciation method, such as sum of the year's digits or double declining balance, a computation problem arises when an asset is acquired on a date other than the first day of the year. The first year of the accelerated depreciation will span 2 calendar years. For example, assume that the asset was acquired on April 1; therefore, the first year's accelerated depreciation covers 9 months of the first calendar year and 3 months of the second calendar year. The depreciation expense for calendar year 2 would be the first year's accelerated depreciation, calculated using the appropriate equation multiplied by 3/12, plus the second year's accelerated depreciation multiplied by 9/12. Drawing a time diagram and superimposing each year's accelerated depreciation over each calendar year will help you get the right answer.

Patent Granted by the US Patent and Trademark Office, a patent gives the holder of the patent the exclusive right to sell a specific product or service covered by the patent. The legal life of a patent is 20 years.

PCAOB (Public Companies Accounting Oversight Board) This board was created by the Sarbanes–Oxley Act, which was the congressional reaction to the fraudulent financial reporting of the past 4 years, which culminated in the demise of Enron and the CPA firm of Arthur Andersen.

The board has the authority to regulate the accounting profession, which they accomplish through inspections. This replaced the peer review process where one CPA firm audited another CPA firm. In addition, the PCAOB has the authority to establish generally accepted accounting principles; however, they have delegated this responsibility to the Financial Accounting Standards Board.

Periodic Inventory An inventory method that requires a physical count of the inventory for the firm to calculate the cost of goods sold. The calculation is simple: Beginning inventory + Purchases = Goods available for sale. These goods can end up in only one of two places: either we sold them or we still have them. We count what we have and subtract that amount from the goods available for sale. The difference is cost of goods sold. A sale is recorded by making a simple journal entry debiting cash or AIR and crediting sales. No effort is made to record the cost of the inventory that was sold. The cost of goods sold using this method is determined at the end of the period (hence the name periodic) when the ending inventory is counted.

Perpetual Inventory A method for keeping track of all inventory coming into the company and going out. Instead of maintaining a purchases account, when merchandise is acquired, the inventory account is debited (increased). When inventory is sold, two entries are made—one entry is to record the sale (debit, cash, or AIR and credit sales), and at the same time, the cost of goods sold is debited (increased) and inventory is credited (decreased). Now we know the cost of goods sold, and we didn't have to disrupt the business while we counted all the inventory. The bar code scanner and the computer are the two pieces of technology that enable firms to implement the perpetual inventory system (when you buy a box of corn flakes at Safeway and the clerk scans your purchase, the computer system simultaneously records a sale at the selling price, and reduces the inventory by the cost of one box of cereal which is added to the cost of goods sold).

Petty Cash An amount of currency kept on hand to pay for incidental expenses. When an individual uses some of the petty cash, a "petty cash voucher" is prepared that indicates how much money was spent and for what purpose. At any time, the currency and petty cash vouchers should equal the size of the petty cash fund. When the currency in the petty cash fund gets low, the custodian of the fund requests a reimbursement. All the vouchers are summarized, and an amount of money equal to the total of all the vouchers is withdrawn from the company's bank account and given to the petty cash custodian. The reimbursement journal entry consists of debits to the various expense accounts and a single entry to cash.

Physical Inventory The process of counting all the merchandise on hand at a certain point in time. Once the number of items has been determined, that amount is multiplied by the cost of the item in order to determine the total inventory cost. In most cases, the cost of the inventory is determined by using one of the following flow assumptions: LIFO, FIFO, or average cost.

Posting Transferring all the transaction data from the journal to the ledger is referred to as posting. Periodically, all the entries in the journal are posted to the ledger, which has a page for each account. Thus, the journal entry to record a sale on account would involve a debit to accounts receivable and a credit to sales. In posting this entry to the ledger, the debit to accounts receivable would be posted to the debit side of the accounts receivable account in the ledger and the credit to sales would be posted to the credit side of the sales account in the ledger.

Potentially Dilutive Securities A security that is not common stock presently, but that could become common stock if the owner of the security decided to exercise his or her option to convert their existing securities into shares of common stock. Examples of potentially dilutive securities are convertible bonds, convertible preferred stock, and stock options.

Preemptive Right A right of common stockholders (granted either by the corporation in its charter or bylaws or by the state's corporation laws) that permits the shareholders to maintain their existing ownership percentage. If a stockholder owns 22% of the outstanding stock and the corporation is about to issue another 1 million shares, that stockholder (by virtue of the preemptive right) has the opportunity to purchase up to 22% of any new shares before they are offered to the general public.

Preferred Stock Some companies have two types of stock. The basic stock is referred to as common stock. In addition to common stock, some corporations have another type of security called preferred stock, which has certain preferences associated with it. These preferences include receiving a fixed dividend each year (e.g., a 5% $100 par value preferred stock will pay a $5 dividend every year, regardless of the income earned by the company), being paid first before common stockholders in the event of a liquidation, and a conversion feature that allows the owner to convert their shares into shares of common stock. Some preferred stock is cumulative, which means that if the company does not have the cash to pay the preferred dividends in a given year, these dividends accumulate and no dividends can be paid to the common shareholders until all the accumulated dividends are paid to the preferred shareholders.

Prepaid Expenses When a company pays an expense in advance, it is recorded as a prepaid expense, which represents a current asset. For example, if someone paid your rent for the next 6 months—You would like that!—it would be an asset for you. It would provide a future benefit—you could live in your apartment for "free" for the next 6 months. When prepaid expenses expire, usually due to the passage of time, an expense is debited and the prepaid expense account is credited. This reflects the fact that an asset has expired and has been recognized as an expense.

Present Value of a Sum How much money you would have to put in the bank today to be able to withdraw a specified amount of money on a specified date, assuming that the bank is paying a specified rate of interest.

Present Value of an Ordinary Annuity How much money you would have to put into the bank today, assuming that the bank pays interest at a specified rate, to be able to withdraw a series of equal payments, where each payment comes at the end of the period.

Property, Plant, and Equipment A category of assets listed on a firm's balance sheet. Included in this category are land, buildings, equipment, vehicles, computers, and so forth. Assets in this category, with the exception of land, are shown on the balance sheet at historical cost less accumulated depreciation.

Purchase and Sales Returns and Allowances Returns and allowances are contra accounts to purchases and sales; they reduce total purchases or total sales. A return occurs when the buyer returns merchandise to the seller. An allowance occurs when the merchandise is defective and the seller gives the buyer a discount off the purchase price to encourage the buyer to keep the merchandise and not to return it.

Qualified Opinion After a CPA conducts an audit, an auditor's report is prepared which includes an opinion regarding the fairness of the presentation of the financial statements. A qualified opinion means that except for one material item, the financial statements taken as a whole are fairly presented in accordance with generally accepted accounting principles.

Reconciling Items When preparing a bank reconciliation, there are transactions which have been recorded by the bank but not by the customer, or recorded by the customer but not by the bank. These transactions are referred to as reconciling items. These items are either added to or subtracted from the balance per bank or the balance per books, when preparing the actual bank reconciliation. When the reconciliation is complete, the adjusted balance per bank will equal the adjusted balance per books.

Relevance Information is relevant if it will have an impact on a decision. If your sailboat just capsized, and you are looking for something to hang on to, the relevant piece of information is: does it float? The color of the item is completely irrelevant.

Reliability Information is reliable if you can count on it. A thermometer that always gives the correct temperature is reliable. A copy machine that always produces clean copies is reliable. A television that plays some of the time but not always and for no apparent reason is an example of an unreliable appliance.

Research and Development Research is usually described as the search for new knowledge, and development is described as a search for the application of research to a specific product or service. Under current GAAP, all expenditures for research and development must be expensed as incurred.

Restricted Cash A balance in a bank account that is required to be maintained at all times. Thus, this amount of money is not available to pay current obligations, and it is listed on the balance sheet as a long term investment, rather than a current asset.

Retained Earnings The total of all of the income of the entity from the day that the firm began business, less all distributions to the stockholders in the form of dividends. In most states, the amount of dividends that a corporation may legally distribute as dividends is limited to the balance in the retained earnings account.

Revenue Recognition The rule that tells accountants when to recognize that a sale has taken place and that revenue should be recorded. The rule has two parts. Revenue is recognized when it is earned (when the product or service is delivered) and when it is realized or realizable.

ROI (Return on Investment) This is one of the key measures of an entity's financial performance. ROI is calculated by dividing net income by average total assets.

Rules for Debit and Credit Every account has two sides; a debit (or left hand side) and a credit (or right hand side). There are seven types of accounts: asset, liability, owners' equity, revenue, expense, gain, and loss. Assets, expenses and losses all increase on the debit side. The other four types of accounts increase on the credit side.

Salaries Payable Salaries that have been earned by employees but which have not yet been paid are called salaries payable.

Sales Taxes Payable The amount of money that a business has collected from its customers on sales transactions that is owed to various government entities. The company simply collects the money from its customers, and then sends it to the appropriate government agency.

Serial Bond A bond is a long-term liability. With a serial bond, part of the bond becomes due each year.

Short Term Debt Expected to be Refinanced A balance sheet category for liabilities that are short term in nature, which the company plans to refinance on a long term basis. If these two criteria are met: an intention to refinance, and a commitment from a lender to consummate the refinancing, then this liability may be shown on the balance sheet as long term debt. Reclassifying short term debt into long term debt makes the company look better, so the accountant must make sure that all the requirements have been met before the debt may be reclassified.

Statement of Cash Flows A financial statement that explains the change in cash from the beginning to the end of the period. The cash flows are categorized as being derived from operating, investing, or financing activities. There are two basic approaches to preparing a statement of cash flows: the direct approach and the indirect approach.

Statement of Owners' Equity A financial statement that shows all the changes in each component of owner's equity. The statement is prepared in the form of a spreadsheet or grid: Across the top (the column headings) are all the various owners' equity accounts (common stock, additional paid-in capital, retained earnings, treasury stock, accumulated other comprehensive income, and so forth), and along the left side of the statement are all the transactions that caused an increase or a decrease in one or more of the owner's equity accounts (the first row is usually the beginning balance, followed by transactions such as issue common stock, declare cash dividend, purchase treasury stock, and so forth; the last item is typically the ending balance).

Stock Dividend A distribution of company earnings to the stockholders in the form of shares of the company's stock. This occurs when a firm has earnings, but does not have enough cash to pay a cash dividend. This transaction causes retained earnings to be decreased and contributed capital to be increased. Stockholders who do not wish to own more shares can simply sell the shares that they received as a dividend. Stock dividends are accounted for as a function of the percentage of shares issued. A small stock dividend—less than 20%–25% of the outstanding shares—is accounted for by using the market value of the stock. Large stock dividends—more than 20%–25% of the outstanding shares—are accounted for by using the par value of the stock. Companies can issue a 100% stock dividend (stockholders receive one share of stock for each share they own). A 100% stock dividend has the same impact on the market price of the stock (the market price drops in half) as a stock split. The difference between a 100% stock dividend and a 2:1 stock split is the fact that a journal entry is made to record the stock dividend, while there is no journal entry for a stock split.

Stock Split The typical stock split is two for one, although it could be 3:1 or more. In a 2:1 split, the shareholders receive two new shares for every old share that they own. The par value is cut in half, and the market value will also drop by half. Stockholders are in exactly the same position after the split as they were before. A stockholder who owned 10% of the stock before the split still owns 10% of the stock; he just has twice as many shares worth half as much per share. Stockholders like to receive stock splits because the market price of their shares often goes back up to a higher level.

Straight-Line Depreciation A method for allocating the cost of an asset over its useful life. The formula used to calculate straight line depreciation is:

$$\frac{\text{Cost} - \text{Salvage Value}}{\text{Life}}$$

Sum of the Years Digits Depreciation A method for allocating the cost of an asset over its useful life. In making this calculation, the cost minus the salvage value (the depreciation base) is multiplied by a fraction where the numerator begins with the useful life of the asset and is then reduced by one each year. The denominator is given by the following formula: $n(n - 1)/2$.

For example, consider an asset that cost $12,000, with an estimated useful life of 5 years and an estimated salvage value of $2,000. Depreciation for the first three years using sum of the year's digits depreciation would be as follows:

$$\$12,000 - \$2,000 = \$10,000 \times 5/15 = \$3,333$$
$$\$12,000 - \$2,000 = \$10,000 \times 4/15 = \$2,666$$
$$\$12,000 - \$2,000 = \$10,000 \times 3/15 = \$2,000$$

Supplies Items that the firm uses in the normal course of business. Examples of supplies would differ by industry. For a bank, supplies would include paper, pens and pencils, toner cartridges, and so forth. For a light manufacturer, supplies might include sandpaper, glue, lubricating oil, and so forth.

Term Bond A bond is a long-term liability. With a term bond, the entire amount of the bond becomes due at the end of the term of the bond, hence the name term bond.

Trademark and Trade Name Words or symbols that distinguish the products of a specific company. Trademarks can be renewed indefinitely every 10 years.

Transaction Analysis The process of evaluating a business transaction, determining which accounts are affected and whether these accounts will increase or decrease as a result of the transaction. Transaction analysis is usually done using a horizontal model, where all the accounts are listed horizontally across the page. Once you have mastered transaction analysis it is easy to move to the next step which is the preparation of journal entries.

Trading Securities Investments in other corporation's stock, where the intent of the company is to actively trade these securities and make a profit. They are listed on the balance sheet as a current asset (right below cash) at their current market value, which represents a major departure from previous generally accepted accounting principles. Furthermore, any unrealized gains and losses are included in net income. Realized gains and losses, as in the past, are also included in net income.

Treasury Stock Treasury stock consists of the company's own shares of stock that the company has repurchased on the open market. The main reason that a company would repurchase shares of its own common stock would be to fund various company stock purchase and stock option plans. Of course, the company could simply print a bunch of new shares of stock, but these shares would have to be registered with the SEC, and that is an expensive process. Thus, many firms simply find it cost effective to call a local stockbroker and buy some of the company's stock.

Trial Balance A tool that the accountant uses to ensure that debits equal credits. A list is prepared of each account and its debit or credit balance; hopefully, the total debits equal the total credits. If we begin the period in balance, and we make an equal number of debits and credits during the period, then the trial balance should balance. Note that even if the trial balance balances, that does not guarantee that there are no errors. For example, if the company purchased land and debited "building" instead of "land," there would be an error, although the trial balance would balance.

Units of Activity Depreciation Depreciation calculated using the units of activity method is very similar to the straight line method, except that the life of the asset is expressed in units of activity rather than in years. For example, assume a vehicle was acquired for $32,000, an estimated salvage value of $2,000, with an estimated service life of 500,000 miles. Assume that in year one the vehicle was driven 25,000 miles. The depreciation for the first year would be computed as follows:

$32,000 − 2,000 = $30,000 $30,000/500,000 = $.06   25,000 miles × $.06 = $1,500

Unqualified Opinion After a CPA conducts an audit, an auditor's report is prepared that includes an opinion regarding the fairness of the presentation of the financial statements. An unqualified opinion means that the financial statements have been fairly presented in accordance with generally accepted accounting principles.

INDEX